Ideas of Greatness

Ideas and Forms
in English Literature

Edited by John Lawlor
Professor of English, University of Keele

The English Georgic
John Chalker

Number Symbolism
Christopher Butler

Voices of Melancholy
Bridget Gellert Lyons

Ideas of Greatness
Heroic drama in England

Eugene M. Waith
Department of English,
Yale University

London
Routledge & Kegan Paul

First published in 1971
by Routledge & Kegan Paul Ltd
Broadway House 68–74 Carter Lane
London EC4V 5EL
Printed in Great Britain
by The Camelot Press Ltd, London and Southampton
© Eugene M. Waith 1971

ISBN 0 7100 7034 9

for M D W

General Editor's Introduction

This series aims to explore two main aspects of literary tradition in English. First, the role of particular literary forms, with due emphasis on the distinctive sorts of application they receive at English hands; second, the nature and function of influential ideas, varying from large general conceptions evident over long periods to those concepts which are peculiar to a given age.

Each book attempts an account of the form or idea, and treats in detail particular authors and works rather than offering a general survey. The aim throughout is evaluative and critical rather than descriptive and merely historical.

J. L.

Contents

Illustrations

1 St George's Portico   *facing page* 84
An Inigo Jones design for Prince Henry's Barriers in the Devon-
shire Collection, Chatsworth. Reproduced by permission of the
Trustees of the Chatsworth Settlement. This drawing, formerly
associated with another masque, was correctly identified by Roy
Strong, Director of the National Portrait Gallery.

2 Horace and Curiace   *facing page* 85
Frontispiece of the original edition of Corneille's *Horace*, 1641.
Reproduced by courtesy of the Harvard College Library. Though
the action depicted is only reported in the play, and though the
representation of the stage is somewhat fanciful, the costumes and
gestures may give some notion of contemporary performances.

3 'The Indian Queen'   *facing page* 100
Mezzotint by W. Vincent, published by J. Smith; reproduced by
courtesy of the Harvard Theatre Collection. It is probable that
the feathers are those presented by Aphra Behn to the King's
Men for the heroine's costume in Dryden and Howard's play,
though the engraving was done many years later, and is thought to
represent Anne Bracegirdle, who took the part of another 'Indian
Queen' in Aphra Behn's play, *The Widow Ranter* (1689).

4 Muly Labas and Morena in Prison   *facing page* 101
Act I of Settle's *The Empress of Morocco* at the Duke's Theatre in
Dorset Garden. Engraving by W. Dolle in the first edition (1673),
reproduced by courtesy of the Beinecke Rare Book and Manuscript Library, Yale University. Though the proscenium of the
theatre is presumably an accurate representation, the prison,
with its ceiling and suspended lamp, must be merely the artist's
impression of the scenery.

Preface

Few literary forms seem more remote than heroic drama in the age of the anti-hero and the common man, yet no age is truly against heroes, however distrustful it may be of heroic rhetoric. What is admired today, however, differs considerably from what was admired in the years when heroic drama flourished; hence any account of this form must be based on an understanding of the characteristics considered heroic at that time. The chapter on chivalric ideals, which I believe to be at the centre of heroic drama, is essentially a chapter of definition, and the distinctions drawn in later chapters continue the process of marking off the area of the heroic. Yet my concern is not primarily theoretical. All but a small fraction of the book is devoted to discussions of English plays affected to varying degrees and in various ways by the concept of the heroic. Since this concept alters in the course of the 150 years covered, and since successive artists, in any case, feel obliged to work out new solutions to the problems they inherit from their predecessors, the discussions are intended to demonstrate both the nature of individual works of dramatic art and the evolution of a form. While most space is given to plays that matter because of some mark of artistic excellence, a considerable number of less good plays have been included, especially in Chapters 2 and 3, because of the light they throw on better plays, or because of what they show about the evolving form. For somewhat similar reasons an interchapter deals with the work of a great foreign playwright which both illumines and influences the English drama. It needs to be stressed that only a few of the playwrights represented here set out to write what they would have called 'heroic plays'. Hence, both the generic and the temporal boundaries are misty, and I have had to make arbitrary decisions about what to include and where to stop. I hope the bases of my decisions have been made clear at the appropriate places.

For guidance in my research I am indebted not only to the authors mentioned in notes (and doubtless to many unmentioned), but also to several colleagues at Yale: Mrs Harry Miskimin, Thomas M. Greene and A. Bartlett Giamatti of the English Department helped to direct my reading and advised me in other ways in the preparation of my first chapter; Jacques Guicharnaud of the French Department not only gave me advice on Corneille but read and commented on what I wrote. To Roy Strong, the Director of the National Portrait Gallery, I am particularly obliged for his detailed answers to my queries about the Inigo Jones designs for Prince Henry's Barriers. The greatest burden of editorial assistance fell on my wife, whose maddening refusal to understand what was not clear led, as always, to innumerable improvements. John Lawlor, the General Editor of the series, has shown an ideal combination of sympathy and care for detail in making numerous suggestions from which I have profited. I am grateful to Yale University for a Senior Faculty Fellowship in 1967–8, which gave me the time to do a large share of the work on this project, and to the institutions named in the list of illustrations for permission to reproduce the prints in their collections.

One

The Ideals of Chivalry

When Sir William Davenant dedicated *The Siege of Rhodes* to the Earl of Clarendon in 1663 he referred to the continuing Puritan opposition to drama as a reason for seeking protection for his play. 'Those vertuous enemies deny *heroique plays* to the gentry', he wrote, and presumably *The Siege of Rhodes* was such a play. As proof that it was worthy of protection he spoke of his efforts to cleanse the stage 'from the corruption of manners; nor have I wanted care to render the *ideas* of greatness and vertue pleasing and familiar.'[1] In these last words he gave an important indication of what he meant by the term 'heroic play', which soon became common. Davenant may not have invented the term (he seemed to expect it to be understood), but he may have been the first to use it in print. It was a logical companion to terms like 'heroic poem', a familiar designation of epic, or 'heroic virtue', the extraordinary strength and integrity of a Hercules—of the proper subject of a heroic poem. Davenant clearly assumes that a heroic play would dramatize the '*ideas* of greatness and vertue' associated with the heroic.

At about the time when Davenant was writing his dedication heroic plays became a vogue in England, and playwrights supplied the theatre with great quantities of them. Consequently, when 'heroic play' or 'heroic drama' are mentioned, we think first of the period 1660–1700. The terms are sometimes further restricted to plays in rhymed pentameter couplets—what had come to be called 'heroic verse'[2] because of its association with heroic poems—and it is true that Dryden, the greatest writer of heroic plays in this period, maintained for several years that rhyme was most proper for this kind of drama. Yet when he turned to Shakespeare's blank verse for a model, he did not entirely abandon the heroic concepts which informed his rhymed

I

plays. To insist that only plays in rhyming couplets are heroic is to reduce the usefulness of the term and to put too much emphasis on form. Even *The Siege of Rhodes* would not qualify if this criterion were strictly applied, for it is written in a variety of rhyming verse forms. Nor should the years following the Restoration constitute a strict limit. Restoration writers themselves thought of the earlier plays of Corneille as heroic, and there are even English plays of earlier years to which the term can fairly be applied.

In this book I shall use 'heroic play' and 'heroic drama' in a considerably broader sense, but one which is closely related to Davenant's description of his intentions. Many of his contemporaries, including Dryden, did not agree that 'ideas of greatness and virtue' should be rendered 'familiar', for there is no disguising the fact that these qualities are awesome and rare; nor did Dryden believe it necessary to make the protagonists of heroic plays what he called 'patterns of exact virtues'. Yet Davenant's generally positive emphasis, similar to that of others who wrote about the heroic drama, helps to distinguish this genre from conventional tragedy.

Literary men for centuries had assumed that all serious drama was intended to point the way to virtue, and serious drama for critics in the classical tradition meant tragedy, which presented the stories of 'great' (or illustrious) men. For example, Minturno, in *L'Arte Poetica* (1564), not only says that the tragic poet teaches, delights and moves spectators so as to purge the passions from their minds, but also explains that this Aristotelian function is to be performed by bringing before our eyes 'the example of the life and the manners of those who surpass others in greatness and in dignity and the favors of Fortune . . .'. Sir Philip Sidney, in *An Apology for Poetry* (1595, but written some twelve years earlier), defends tragedy from enemies of poetry by saying, 'For it were too absurd to cast out so excellent a representation of whatsoeuer is most worthy to be learned.'[3]

Though tragedy, as seen in these comments, was certainly concerned with ideas of greatness and virtue, the commonest pattern of tragic action, bringing the protagonist to misfortune or death, supported a different emphasis from Davenant's. The hero, great and virtuous as he might be, was usually in part responsible for his downfall through some error of judgment or weakness of character. Minturno, in the passage already cited, continues his descrip-

2

tion of the superior personages of tragedy, who 'yet are through human error thrown into extreme unhappiness', thus illustrating the mutability of fortune and the frailty of man. That is, instead of focusing on ideas of greatness and virtue, tragedies more often pointed to some fatal limitation. The kind of drama Davenant was designating was therefore distinguished from the usual tragedy by its emphasis upon ideals and upon the greatness of which man is capable.[4] In a considerable number of cases, to be sure, the virtue treated in these plays was closer to *virtù* than to moral goodness. In a few cases a clearly immoral greatness distinguished the hero from ordinary men; yet even here the emphasis was on potentiality rather than upon limitation.

The distinction is far from absolute. Most tragedy is touched by the heroic,[5] and in the case of a sub-genre recognized in the Renaissance, the tragedy with a happy ending, virtue finally surmounts all obstacles. To make matters still more puzzling for classifiers, not all heroic plays end happily. But, as Davenant's wording suggests, the heroic play in its purest form is a kind of celebration of greatness, where the conflicts of tragedy are replaced by ritual exaltation. In a far greater number of examples some recognition of limitation modifies and complicates the assertion of greatness.

I shall consider the concern with potentiality rather than limitation—with greatness rather than error—as a fundamental distinguishing characteristic of heroic drama, more important than the date of composition or the verse form adopted by the dramatist. Certain other characteristics of the genre will emerge from the discussion of particular plays. However, the object of this study is not to sort plays into neat piles of 'heroic', 'almost heroic' and 'non-heroic', but to examine the various manifestations of the heroic in English drama.

Basic to an understanding of the ideals which informed heroic drama is some consideration of the literature in which these ideals were first clearly formulated. Dryden discussed the antecedents of heroic drama in 1672 in his essay 'Of Heroic Plays', prefixed to *The Conquest of Granada*. 'For Heroic Plays . . ., the first light we had of them, on the English theatre, was from the late Sir William D'Avenant.' After doing justice to *The Siege of Rhodes*, Dryden quoted the opening lines of Ariosto's *Orlando Furioso*, which 'gave me light to all I could desire:

Le donne, i cavalier, l'arme, gli amori,
Le cortesie, l'audaci imprese io canto, etc.

For the very next reflexion which I made was this, that an heroic
play ought to be an imitation, in little, of a heroic poem; and,
consequently, that Love and Valour ought to be the subject of
it.'[6] A few pages later, in discussing the ancestry of his hero,
Almanzor, he said: 'The first image I had of him, was from the
Achilles of Homer; the next from Tasso's *Rinaldo* (who was a copy
of the former), and the third from the *Artaban* of Monsieur Calprenède, who has imitated both' (Ker. I, 155).

Obviously, the epic is the major source of inspiration for the
heroic play, and if we glance again at Sidney, we find in his
comments on the epic the same emphasis upon greatness and
virtue as in Davenant's remarks on heroic plays. The 'heroicall',
according to Sidney, 'maketh magnanimity and iustice shine
throughout all misty fearefulnes and foggy desires' (Smith, I,
179). But if epic is the model for heroic drama, it is also obvious
from both Dryden quotations that he was thinking not only of
classical epic, but also—and mainly—of more recent epics like
Ariosto's and Tasso's, which were influenced by the tradition of
medieval romance. How basically influenced is clear from
Ariosto's first words, 'Le donne', for we know what slight importance women have in Homer (except for those superwomen, Hera,
Athena and their fellow goddesses), and even in Virgil, Dido and
Lavinia are not to be thought of as the subjects of his song.
Ariosto's ladies, loves and courtesies belong without doubt to the
world of chivalric romance. Anyone familiar with *The Conquest
of Granada* and with any other heroic plays by Dryden and his
contemporaries knows that there, too, the chivalric world is more
often recalled than the Homeric. The heroes behave towards
each other and towards their ladies in a style suggestive of knights
in armour, jousts and fair ladies in distress. In the essay just
referred to, Dryden acknowledged his debt to a seventeenth-
century French romance, La Calprenède's *Cléopâtre*, a representative of a variety which developed after five hundred years of the
popularity of this form of narrative literature. In fact, the ideas
of greatness and virtue celebrated in heroic drama derive largely
from ideals formulated in the heyday of chivalry and expressed
partially in the *chansons de geste*, then fully in that runaway literary

success, the chivalric romance. Here they were given artistic life. That these ideals, however changed, however adapted to new conditions, retained their grip on men's minds for so long a time, gives the romance a special importance in literary history. Its direct bearing on heroic drama is illustrated by the fact that the first plays that might be put in this category were crude dramatizations of romance, such as *Clyomon and Clamydes* and *Common Conditions*. The heroic entered English drama through the door of chivalric romance.

The *chansons de geste* were heroic poems composed in French in the eleventh century or even earlier, and first sung by *jongleurs*. According to tradition, the *jongleur*, Taillefer, rode ahead of William the Conqueror into the Battle of Hastings (1066) singing some version of the most famous of them, the *Chanson de Roland*.[7] The earliest written version of it which has survived (in a manuscript of about a hundred years later) is a poem of impressive artistic power about Roland's fight against hopeless odds to save the rear-guard of Charlemagne's army from the Saracens at the pass of Roncevalles. Other *chansons* dealt with other stories of Charlemagne and his twelve peers, and gradually more adventures were invented, filling in the childhood of the famous knights and adding new heroes to the roster until there was a formidable accumulation of Charlemagne stories. Occasional *chansons de geste*, such as *Raoul de Cambrai*, dealt with French pseudo-history unrelated to Charlemagne.

Alongside these 'epics' the romance developed in the late-eleventh and the twelfth centuries. The word 'romance' (*roman* in French) originally designated the vernacular romance language as opposed to Latin, but soon came to mean narratives in verse (and later in prose) which were not always totally different from the *chansons de geste*. Many of them dealt with pseudo-history, such as the Trojan war, the story of Oedipus or the court of King Arthur, which we might regard as one step further removed from actual history than the stories of the court of Charlemagne. But the medieval authors and their audience did not make such distinctions. When Jean Bodel wrote in the late twelfth or early thirteenth century that there were only three 'matières' for any poet: 'De France, et de Bretaigne, et de Rome la grant'[8] he lumped *chansons de geste* and romances together. The material of 'Rome la grant' included all of classical legend and history. In this category belonged the earliest French romance, the *Roman d'Alexandre*, one version of which, written in twelve-syllable couplets, gave its name to the alexandrine, the verse of later French heroic poetry and drama. The *Roman de Troie*, from which the story of Troilus and Cressida derived, was another of the not very historical narratives based on classical material. The 'matière de Bretaigne' comprised the 'history' of Britain (including that of Brittany) from the time of its legendary founding by Brutus, a Trojan escaped from the Greeks. Geoffrey of Monmouth told the story in his Latin *Historia regum Britanniae* (*c.* 1135), where for the first time Arthur appears as a great king surrounded by loyal knights. Twenty years later, Wace retold and elaborated the story in his vernacular *Roman de Brut*, and the great romances of Chrétien de Troyes, Gottfried von Strassburg and Wolfram von Eschenbach exploited this Arthurian material. These treatments of the 'matter of Britain' show how closely related 'historia' and 'romance' might be, and when, in the thirteenth century, the 'historical' *chansons de geste* began to be reworked in prose, they too became romances.

To make absolute distinctions between medieval epic and romance, both presented as historical, is clearly impossible, but as romances proliferated and influenced one another, certain generic characteristics began to appear, a few of which are relevant to this sketch of the background of heroic drama. The most distinguished authors of romances were chiefly interested in the mind and feelings of individuals, and therefore developed a technique of extended psychological analysis which is rarely seen in the *chansons de geste*. Also, the marvellous assumed a greater importance in romances—not only enchantments but mysterious adventures imposed by the lord of a castle or by a damsel in distress. Seeking adventure for the sake of adventure became a hall-mark of these stories, and, finally, they assigned much larger roles to ladies, whether as suppliants, as cruel mistresses or as the embodiments of an ideal.

In twelfth-century France the *chansons de geste* and the romance existed side by side, each telling in its own way of the deeds of great heroes, and together comprising a large proportion of the literature of the day. Soon the romance began to displace the *chanson de geste*, and, as translated and reworked by poets of other nationalities, swept over all of Western Europe, carrying with it

6

the accumulated values that we call chivalric. Many of the ideals which informed these two closely related forms of literature came directly from the aristocracy of the twelfth century—the nobles, whose power resided largely in their effectiveness as warriors on horseback, or *chevaliers*. Some of the chivalric ideals, such as those having to do with love, and found only in the romances, had sources far removed from the daily life of feudal knights, yet eventually began to alter their attitudes and affect their behaviour. More surprising, the entire code of conduct—the pattern for the complete knight—continued to exert its influence for centuries after chivalry as a practical way of life was dead.

In his study of *French Chivalry* Sidney Painter writes: 'The ideal knight of feudal chivalry was the lineal descendant of the heroes of Germanic legend and the ancestor of the modern gentleman. . . . The cultural tradition and the environment of the eleventh-century noble combined to instill in him an admiration for martial qualities. The Teutonic barbarian and the Frankish aristocrat had prized personal bravery, physical strength, and skill in the use of arms. As warfare was the chief occupation of the nobleman, he was bound to value the traits which made a man an effective soldier. Summed up under the term prowess, the ability to beat the other man in battle, these qualities became the fundamental chivalric virtues.'[9] In the *Chanson de Roland* prowess is lauded above all other virtues, as can be seen in the key episode of the poem, where Roland refuses to summon aid by sounding his horn, though his friend, Olivier, urges him to do so: 'May it never please the Lord God or his angels that because of me France should lose her honour. I would rather die than suffer shame. The better we fight, the more the emperor loves us.'[10] Roland's honour and the honour of France can be sustained in the eyes of God only by prowess—'prouesse'. Both Olivier and Roland are 'preux', and Olivier has two other qualities, a practical wisdom and a sense of proportion ('mesure') which the poet values highly. At the crucial point of Olivier's wise urging, the distinction between the two heroes is made in one simple sentence which haunts every reader of the poem: 'Roland est preux et Olivier est sage'—or in the Old French, 'Rollant est proz et Oliver est sage' (l. 1093). The simplicity masks a complex judgment based on a perfect understanding that in one sense Olivier is right, and that Roland's lack of wisdom and 'mesure' brings about the tragic defeat. Yet this perception is almost obliterated by admiration for Roland's extraordinary spirit. Though the syntax of the sentence seems to deny any relative evaluation of 'proz' and 'sage', there is no doubt that the poem is a song of praise for Roland and his prowess.

Another appreciation of valour within a framework of sophisticated moral awareness is found in *Raoul de Cambrai*, a somewhat later *chanson de geste* which differs greatly from the *Chanson de Roland* in its outlook. A foolish king of France deprives Raoul of his inheritance while he is a fatherless child, and later attempts to right this wrong by giving Raoul the fief which the sons of Hubert of Vermandois rightly expect to inherit. Raoul is determined to take possession of these lands despite the dissuasions of his mother and of his vassal Bernier, who is related to the dispossessed brothers. The situation created by the king's irresponsible acts is one in which no one is absolutely right. Raoul, as the poet reminds us several times, is entitled to compensation from the king. On the other hand, he is not only obstinate but heartless in the war he wages against the sons of Hubert, in one engagement burning a convent where Bernier's mother is a nun. On balance, the poet seems to recognize that Raoul is more wrong than right, showing none of Roland's respect for God or concern for France. Raoul's pride and his lack of moderation lead to a break with his faithful vassal Bernier, who finally kills him, and to a bloody feud which continues after Raoul's death. All this is made clear; yet the poet reiterates that 'Raoul the count was no coward', and at his death says, 'Then the soul of the gentle knight ['gentil chevalier'] took its flight; may God receive it—if we dare pray on his behalf!'[11] While the view of the entire situation is remarkably fair and even dispassionate, the response to Raoul is finally a warm admiration for his prowess and sheer energy.

Prowess in these poems is not very different from the *areté* of Homeric epic, which Werner Jaeger defines as 'a combination of proud and courtly morality with warlike valour'.[12] Considered as the supreme manly virtue, it is also analogous to the Latin *virtus*, meaning first of all 'strength', and related to both *vir* ('man') and *vis* ('energy'). The heroes of the *chansons de geste*, like their classical predecessors, may or may not exercise this virtue in the service of God and country. Raoul, in his fierce concern with his rights, is more like Achilles; Roland, fighting for both

8

his honour and the honour of 'douce France', is more like Aeneas, who must found Rome.

In the romances knights often cultivate prowess, not in order to protect their country nor as a means to self-advancement, but as the basic virtue every knight should possess—the *sine qua non* for what we might call self-fulfilment. In *Le Chevalier au Lion (Yvain)* by Chrétien de Troyes a wandering knight who has been asked what he is seeking replies, 'Adventures to test my prowess and my courage' (II, 362–3).[13] The hero of this romance is a warrior whose great bravery brings him what might be called a premature success, after which he commits such a grievous error that he feels himself disgraced and goes into a self-imposed exile. His rehabilitation, the subject of the entire second half of the story, begins with a fight in which the onlookers marvel at his 'proesce' and say that he surpasses the achievements of Roland 'against the Turks at Roncevalles' (l. 3233). Shortly afterward he rescues a lion from a serpent in the forest, instantly choosing in favour of the nobler beast (l. 3371), who then accompanies Yvain on his adventures, giving him his sobriquet of 'the knight with the lion'. It would be hard to miss the symbolic value of this obliging creature who helps his master to repossess his lost honour and, in effect, to re-acquire his identity.

The feudal system, founded upon the mutual obligations of vassal to suzerain, gave loyalty an unusually high place in the scale of values. In his biography of William Marshall, Painter shows how both William and his father were rewarded for their outstanding fidelity to the sovereigns they served.[14] Bernier's loyalty to Raoul de Cambrai keeps him in check when his overlord attacks his family, and he is very moderate in his reproaches when Raoul is responsible for his mother's death (pp. 45–51). Happily, loyalty is not always put to such a cruel test in these poems, but the forms it takes may startle a modern reader. When the knights whom Perceval defeats in Chrétien's romance promise him one after another to go to King Arthur's court and report their defeat, even a reader who is not totally cynical may wonder whether they will be true to their word; but all of them are. Painter cites evidence that this kind of loyalty was commonly practised by the feudal nobility.[15]

Because loyalty was so basic a virtue, conflicting loyalties provided chivalric literature with unusually interesting situations.

Bernier's dilemma is essentially a conflict between loyalty to his liege lord and to his family, and many other dilemmas arise in *Raoul de Cambrai* as obligations to friends, to the king and to God become hopelessly entangled. In the romances loyalty to a lady makes for one more possible complication. The sorrows of young Yvain, for instance, are caused by his breaking his promise to his wife, Laudine. In two of the best-known stories of romance literature, loyalty to a lady causes disloyalty to a king. Gottfried von Strassburg exalts the perfect love of Tristan and Isolde, but also shows sympathy for King Mark. In a passage of analysis love is shown winning over honour and loyalty in the mind of Tristan and thus preparing his tragic situation. In Sir Thomas Malory's *Morte Darthur* the conflict is made even more explicit in his treatment of Lancelot, the loyal lover whose disloyalty to his king brings about the dissolution of the Arthurian court. Lancelot never directly admits the treachery of his affair with Queen Guenever, even when accused of it by the king, but before her death the queen says, 'Through this man and me hath all this war been wrought, and the death of the most noblest knights of the world; for through our love that we have loved together is my most noble lord slain.'[16] At the end Lancelot remembers 'how by my default, mine orgulity and my pride, that they were both [Arthur and Guenever] laid full low' (p. 398). Because chivalric loyalty was a highly personal bond, the poem seems to present the disaster for Britain as hardly more important than the betrayal of the man, Arthur.

Loyalty, as an obligation to another person, was a curb on the proper exercise of prowess, as was courtesy, another major ideal of chivalry. Even in the midst of the bloodiest battle the knight was expected to be courteous—not to take advantage of an unarmed opponent and to release on parole one who had surrendered. The extraordinary lengths to which knightly courtesy might go in fiction can be seen in *Raoul de Cambrai* in the account of the duel between Bernier, the slayer of Raoul, and Gautier, the hero's nephew. After they have seriously wounded each other and have agreed to stop fighting until they have recovered their strength, Gautier's fierce kinsman, Guerri the Red, starts to attack Bernier. Bernier appeals to his enemy to protect him, and Gautier replies, 'I would rather be torn limb from limb than that you should suffer hurt before the truce is over. . . . It is better that you mount your horse as best you can, and I myself will help you to depart', whereupon Gautier holds Bernier's stirrup for him (pp. 148–9). Much as the poet admires prowess, he is keenly aware of the tragedy that courtesy such as this does not prevail over the fierceness of Guerri.

The institution of the tournament provided fighting with a maximum of courtesy and also made it a spectator sport which ladies might attend. Just how or why or when tournaments arose is uncertain, but by the twelfth century they were common, not only in fiction but in fact.[17] We find that William Marshall became a professional participant in tournaments in his younger days, and not merely out of love for the sport, but to win prizes and to collect ransom from captured knights.[18] It is not surprising that this practical aspect of tourneys hardly appears in romances, where they are tests of prowess and courtesy.

Courtesy often means not only the proper way of fighting but a kind of behaviour which anticipates the recommendations of Castiglione in *The Courtier*. A beautiful scene in Chrétien's *Conte du Graal*, analysed with great finesse by Reto R. Bezzola,[19] shows how Gawain's courtesy touches Perceval when force has failed to move him. And at the beginning of *Yvain* Chrétien describes a festive occasion at the court of King Arthur, 'whose prowess teaches us that we should be brave and courteous [preu et cortois]' (ll. 2–3). Knights and ladies feast together, tell stories and discuss the joys and sorrows of love. The scene is a perfect illustration of the courtly atmosphere that pervades Chrétien's writing and justifies the term 'courtly romance' for this subdivision of the genre. To succeed in these circumstances the knight must be able to speak well and dress well and perhaps to dance and sing or play a musical instrument. In short, he must be like Chaucer's Squire. Though he must, of course, know how to manage a horse and a lance, these skills will not suffice if he is to please the ladies.

The insistence on courtesy in its fullest meaning is one of the memorable features of chivalric romances, and one which makes an important part of the difference between them and the epics of either classical or medieval times. If courtesy seems at times to be a set of do's and don't's for the well-bred, it is always much more than this in the romances and also in the 'courtesy books' to which they point the way. Underlying the concern with courtesy is the conviction that it is the proper expression of man's social nature and hence a step toward the achievement of the ideal humanity to which the knight must aspire.

Liberality, or 'largesse', is another virtue which may at first seem to receive an exaggerated emphasis in the world of chivalry. The practical value to a feudal lord of giving generously to his vassals and retainers is obvious, and no doubt many feudal bonds were cemented in this way. That it was natural, as Painter suggests, for indigent minstrels to extol largesse is also true, but are these practical considerations sufficient to explain why it is called 'the dame and queen who illuminates all virtues' at the opening of *Cligès*?[20] There the young Alexander, son of the King of Greece, has requested his father's permission to go to the court of King Arthur, 'whose fame is so great for courtesy and prowess' (ll. 150–1), to be made a knight, and to this end has asked for 'a great plenty of your gold and your silver' (l. 107). His father not only grants the boon without hesitation but also explains that this queenly virtue of largesse is what makes a 'prodome' (l. 197), the chivalric equivalent of a gentleman. Praise of liberality occurs in every sort of medieval literature from lyric to allegory and from romance to biography. We may start with examples from two thirteenth-century poems. In a brief dream allegory by Rutebeuf, 'De la mort larguece', the personification of this quality claims seigniory over all loyal and courteous men,[21] and in that very long dream allegory, the *Roman de la Rose*, we are told that there is no worse sin for a great man than avarice, the enemy of largesse.[22] Of John Marshall, the biographer of his son William says that though he was not a count or a very rich lord, everyone marvelled at his abundant largesse.[23] Another historical figure, the husband of Chrétien's patroness, Marie of Champagne, was known as Henri le Larges, and Chrétien compares Philip, Count of Flanders, who asked him to write the *Conte du Graal*, to Alexander the Great, the model of largesse for the Middle Ages. Philip's generosity even surpasses Alexander's, says Chrétien, since it partakes of Christian charity, of which the great pagan knew nothing. Although the poet's motives in praising his patron might be impugned, like those of the indigent minstrels, Philip seems, in fact to have played the part of a Maecenas.

The extraordinarily high place assigned to liberality, in life and in literature, can best be understood by examining some of the contexts in which 'largesse' is used and the words with which it is closely associated. In ethical discussions such as those in the *Roman de la Rose*, largesse is often distinguished from 'folle largesse' which is giving with no sense of proportion or propriety. The distinction corresponds exactly to that which Aristotle makes between liberality and prodigality.[24] Cicero in *De officiis* (I, xiv, 42), which was well known in the Middle Ages, makes similar stipulations for the proper exercise of 'liberalitas', which he relates closely to one of the four cardinal virtues, justice. To give properly one must consider carefully one's means and also the worthiness of the recipient. Largesse is sometimes an almost exact equivalent of this Aristotelian and Ciceronian kind of reasonable and controlled beneficence. Abelard used the term 'largitas' for it.[25]

The largesse planned by Alexander and his father in *Cligès*, however, seems to be a far more splendid thing. It resembles what Aristotle calls 'megaloprepeia',[26] the generosity befitting a great man—a virtue usually translated as 'magnificence'. As examples of what he means Aristotle refers to a public-spirited citizen who fits out a trireme or defrays the cost of a state embassy. These are gestures which only a wealthy man can make, and if they are in good taste, they will not appear vulgarly excessive. Though the outfitting of the fleet in which Alexander is to sail to Britain will not benefit the state except in so far as it enhances King Arthur's opinion of the prince, it is presented as an appropriate gesture for a wealthy monarch and obviously impossible for anyone who had to count the cost. Thus, despite the use in both English and French of the two words, 'largesse' and 'magnificence', it is clear that their meanings overlapped, and that either one might on occasion be used to designate the spectacular degree of generosity characteristic of a great man.[27]

Largesse overlapped with magnificence in another context. In the widely disseminated *Book of the Order of Chivalry*, the thirteenth-century Catalan philosopher, Ramón Lull, discusses the seven virtues which every knight should have—the three theological virtues: faith, hope and charity, and the four cardinal virtues: justice, prudence, fortitude and temperance. Fortitude, which we have seen to be the virtue *sine qua non* in less philosophical treatments of chivalry, is also accorded a full treatment here, where it appears as the knight's bulwark against the seven deadly sins. To combat avarice, here as elsewhere a corrupter of 'noble courage', the knight must use largesse, following the example of Alexander the Great, the pattern of the generous warrior.[28] In presenting largesse as an aspect of fortitude or as its natural accompaniment Lull follows Cicero's arrangement in *De inventione* (II, liv, 163), where 'magnificentia' is one of the parts of 'fortitudo', and in *De officiis* (I, xx, 68), where Cicero, in discussing fortitude, warns against ambition for wealth, characteristic of littleness of soul, and says there is nothing more honourable and magnificent ('honestius magnificentiusque') than indifference to money if one does not possess it, or generosity with it if one does.

Both Cicero and Lull treat avarice as a demeaning vice and its opposite—call it 'magnificentia' or 'largesse'—as the virtue of one who scorns material rewards. In fact, 'magnificentia', literally 'doing great things', means not only magnificent generosity but also what Aristotle calls 'megalopsychia', greatness of soul or mind. Cicero often uses it as a synonym for 'magnanimitas', as in the passage of *De inventione* already cited, where H. M. Hubbell translates it as 'high-mindedness'.[29]

A very similar constellation of ideas appears in *Cligès* in a speech of young Alexander (whose name is no accident). Having asked for large supplies of gold and silver for his voyage, he explains that repose and glory are incompatible—that the wealthy man must not be idle, and that he who spends his time guarding and increasing his wealth is its slave. The prowess Alexander seeks is associated with a high-minded disdain for such miserly behaviour. Thus in Aristotle's useful terms, the connotations of largesse in this passage extend from liberality to magnificence and magnanimity. With this range of suggestion, no wonder that Alexander's father calls largesse 'the dame and queen who illuminates all virtues'!

Another meaning of this very flexible word (not present in the opening of *Cligès*) is charity or pity. Chrétien makes use of it in proving the superiority of his patron Philip to Alexander the Great, and in that amazing compendium of household hints and moral instruction, *Le Ménagier de Paris* (*c.* 1393), largesse, again opposed to avarice, is equated with 'miséricorde', and said to be manifested in the corporal works of mercy.[30] Though the context here is thoroughly bourgeois, largesse is also associated with pity in certain chivalric works. In the thirteenth-century prose redaction of the Arthurian romances known as the Vulgate Cycle, the Damsel of the Lake tells Lancelot about the history of chivalry.

14

When envy and avarice brought about a decline from man's ideal state, and might began to take over from right, the noblest men were chosen to restore order—in effect to bring back the Golden Age.[31] In this highly ethical, even pious, account of the calling of the knight, his first duty is to uphold justice by defending the weak, and hence he must be 'compassionate towards sufferers, and generous' ('piteux envers les souffra[i]tex & larges'), in addition to being brave, strong, loyal and honourable.

This long excursus has shown that largesse was one of the most widely connotative of the chivalric virtues. Whether the context relates it directly to the giving of gifts or to the exercise of pity, it always suggests an opening up of mind and heart—a breadth of vision as well as a loosening of purse-strings.

Since the ideal knight was, in effect, the ideal man, every virtue of the good pagan and of the good Christian is somewhere required of him. Certain ones receive more persistent emphasis than others, however, and give a distinctive character to the chivalric ideal. To prowess, loyalty, courtesy and largesse, one more must be added, which is not so much a virtue in itself as an indication of virtue—namely, the desire for glory, fame and honour. To enjoy the reputation that these words indicate, the knight must behave in a way approved by his fellows. In other words, he must display some or all of the virtues already discussed. Yet the insistence upon this motive for behaviour in works of chivalry entitles it to separate consideration. Some of its diverse manifestations have already been seen. Determination not to lose honour keeps Roland from sounding his horn; a raging thirst for honour launches Raoul on his bloody career. So concerned with honour are the heroes of chivalric romance that it often transforms their lives into a quest. Prince Alexander, inspired by the international fame of King Arthur, seeks 'to acquire honour and win glory and fame' ('por enor aprandre/Et por conquerre pris et los'),[32] and sails away to Britain. Yvain wins Laudine by his valour and then leaves her for fear of losing his reputation as a fighter. Pursuit of one kind of honour, however, involves him in the loss of another, when he breaks his promise to return to his wife. The rest of the story is his gradual emergence from disgrace by demonstrating once more his chivalric virtues. Having won new fame as the Knight with the Lion, he is finally pardoned by Laudine.

In practice, among twelfth-century knights the love of fame and glory was no doubt, as Painter says, 'an ethical rationalization which seemed to endow their endless turbulence and violence with an elevated motive,'[33] but in literature, and especially in the romance, it is the 'elevated motive' that counts. The same concern is ever present in the classical epic, and if in either place we sometimes see its disadvantages, it remains 'that last infirmity of noble mind'.

A final aspect of chivalry, conspicuously absent from classical epic and even from the *chansons de geste*, is the warrior's obligations to ladies. In Lull's *Order of Chivalry* these obligations are bracketed with the knight's function of protecting the weak and sick: 'Thoffyce of a knight is to mayntene and deffende wymmen/ wydowes and orphanes/and men dyseased and not puyssaunt ne stronge.'[34] Perceval's mother in Chrétien's romance gives the enterprise a slightly more inspiring character when she advises her boy, 'Serve ladies and maidens; that way you will be honoured everywhere' (ll. 541–2). But in many romances, as everyone knows, this sort of service is complemented by the knight's devotion to the lady he loves. Here we encounter the idealized love characteristic of troubadour poetry, where it is often called 'fine amor', and in those stories in which ladies are loved with a 'fine amor', the lives of their knights are much complicated. Love enters into the 'matter of Rome' and above all into the 'matter of Britain' as Chrétien presented it. At first it was not present in the romances based on the 'matter of France', as Boiardo was to note with disappointment: Charlemagne was less estimable than King Arthur because he closed the door to love and gave himself only to holy battles.[35] Boiardo remedied the deficiency in his romance of Roland in love, *Orlando Innamorato* (1486–94), and from this time Charlemagne's paladins could compete with the Arthurian knights as lovers. Ariosto politely put 'le donne' before 'i cavalier' as the subject of his song in *Orlando Furioso*, and when Tasso turned to the subject of the liberation of Jerusalem, he too gave great importance to the topic of love.

The nature and proper designation of the love which figures so largely in Chrétien de Troyes and other romancers have been the subjects of much speculation and controversy. For over sixty years scholars have referred to 'courtly love', following the example of Gaston Paris, who found the term 'amour courtois' used in one troubadour poem.[36] After the publication of C. S. Lewis's influential book, *The Allegory of Love*, in 1936, a considerable accumulation of guesses about 'courtly love' seemed to have congealed into a block of solid fact, which only recently has begun to defrost. 'Courtly love' was assumed to be a relationship between a married woman and a lover whom she might or might not reward after a long period of arduous servitude. It was further assumed that such relationships were accepted in society as in literature, and that a treatise by Andreas Capellanus *De amore* (*c.* 1185) was to be taken seriously as describing ideal extra-marital love and actual courts of love held in Poitiers when Queen Eleanor of Aquitaine was there. (According to some, she was in fact the mistress of the troubadour Bernart de Ventadour, thus setting the pace for courtly lovers.) Only three more suppositions were needed to anchor the romances of Chrétien de Troyes firmly in the institution of courtly love. One was that Chaplain Andrew was at the court of Marie de Champagne, Eleanor's daughter. The second was that Marie, like her mother, was eager to spread the gospel of this adulterous love, which she did in part by commissioning her chaplain's disquisition. The third supposition was that she had the same end in mind when she gave Chrétien, as he says she did, the 'matter and meaning' ('matiere et san') of his *Chevalier de la Charrette* (or *Lancelot*).[37]

Every single one of the assumptions mentioned in the last paragraph has been shown to be very questionable or false.[38] It is patently not true that all the 'fine amor' of medieval lyric poetry or romance is adulterous, though some of it is. As for Chaplain Andrew's *De amore*, much of it seems to be written tongue in cheek,[39] and the praise of illicit love is slyly framed between a prefatory statement that no prudent man should indulge in this kind of thing and a final lengthy plea to refrain and thus win special favour from God, who 'is more pleased with a man who is able to sin and does not than with a man who has no opportunity to sin' (p. 187). Thus, if the chaplain does not advocate 'a fugitive and cloistered virtue', it is far from clear that he advocates adultery. It is unlikely that he was a chaplain at the court of Champagne, and still less likely that Marie de Champagne was an apologist for adulterous love. It is certain that in Chrétien's five surviving romances[40] three protagonists, Erec, Cligès and Yvain, marry the girls they love, and only Lancelot is an adulterous lover. In the lost *Tristan* Chrétien gave his version of one other famous story of adultery, but Fénice, the heroine of *Cligès*, expresses an almost Victorian distaste for this story: 'I could never bring myself to lead the life that Iseut led. Her love was too base, for her body belonged to two and her heart entirely to one' (ll. 3110–14). The record does little to establish Chrétien as a spokesman for courtly love as it has been understood in recent years.

Once the mass of misconceptions surrounding this term has been dissipated, it is possible to see the true nature and importance of 'fine amor'. There is no doubt that medieval lyric poets wrote about a love which differed from the disastrous, absurd or merely inconvenient passion of much classical literature, though Peter Dronke has shown how closely it resembled the sentiments expressed in Ovid's love poetry, notably the *Amores* and the *Heroïdes*.[41] He has also pointed to poems from other periods and in other languages where love has many of the characteristics assigned to it in medieval love lyrics (pp. 1–46). Following the lead of Joseph Bédier, he lists these characteristics as the lover's worship of the beloved, the educative and ennobling effect it has upon him, and the price he has to pay for it in suffering and in difficulties to be overcome (pp. 4–7). Dronke suggests that what distinguished the medieval poet's presentation of love from earlier love poetry was his use of a language borrowed from the mystical descriptions of divine love and from philosophical speculations on knowledge of the divine and the relation between wisdom and love (pp. 57–97).

Love in the chivalric romances is often strikingly similar to love in the lyrics. Chrétien, who translated and adapted Ovid, excels in psychological analysis, often ornamented with wit, as when he describes the onset of love between Alexander and Soredamors in *Cligès*, as they sail to Brittany. Soredamors carries on a long debate with herself, revealing her conflicting emotions, while the queen, observing both lovers pale and sighing, wonders whether they are in love or seasick (ll. 435–566). Later in this romance, à propos of the love of Cligès for Fénice, Chrétien discourses on the tyrannical power of love over his trembling subjects.

If these passages deal with the pathology of love, the opening of *Yvain* dwells more on the benefits it confers. In the days of King Arthur, Chrétien writes, when the cult of love flourished as it no longer does, lovers made themselves known as courteous, brave, generous and honourable ('cortois . . . preu . . . large . . . enorable', ll. 21–3). Love, that is, reinforced the qualities demanded of a good knight. Though Chrétien does not go so far as some of the troubadours, who seem to suggest that love is the chief cause of valour and the other virtues, he leaves no doubt about its ennobling effect.

Gottfried von Strassburg in his *Tristan* praises above all the loyalty of the ideal lover, though observing, like Chrétien, that today such lovers are not to be found (pp. 202–3). At times his treatment of love borders on the mystical, as his translator, A. T. Hatto, remarks (pp. 14–18), calling attention especially to the echoes of St Bernard in Gottfried's Prologue. Both Chrétien and Gottfried speak of the ideal love as a thing of the past, part of a Golden Age, as Malory and Caxton were to speak of the entire institution of chivalry. This nostalgia for a lost perfection expressed by so many writers of chivalric romances is one of the clearest indications of their concern with ideal modes of behaviour.

Happily for the reader of romances, flat statements about the power of love and its beneficent effects are infrequent. It is characteristic of this form of literature that the various adventures which comprise the action are themselves charged with the meaning.[42] *Yvain*, for instance, begins with the general remarks already quoted, but most of what the story has to say about love is implied in the relationship of the hero to the beautiful and mysterious Laudine. In the initial adventure Yvain kills her husband in combat and falls in love with her when he sees her in the funeral procession. Worshipping her from afar and overwhelmed by the extraordinary awkwardness of his position as her husband's slayer, he is the very type of the romantic lover and she of the seemingly unattainable beloved. Eventually, through the machinations of a clever girl (often the counterpart in romance of the tricky slave in Roman comedy), he is brought face to face with Laudine, pledges his total devotion to her, begs forgiveness, is pardoned and marries her, but this brings the reader only to the end of the first part of the story. The second part is a much longer and more arduous trial of love brought on when Yvain breaks his promise to return to Laudine on a certain day, after making the rounds of the available tournaments. The rehabilitation of Yvain as the Knight with the Lion has been discussed in relation to prowess, symbolized by the lion, and to the new reputation won by the hero when his first one is blotted with dishonour. Yvain's hardships in the second part of the romance are also expiation of his sin against love, beginning with an ascetic retreat from the world with a hermit who cures him of the madness brought on by his disgrace. His further adventures can be seen as a kind of education or re-education of the lover. Several of them are undertaken at the request of ladies in distress, and he becomes known as their helper (ll. 4811–12). One of the strangest of his adventures and one of the richest in symbolic suggestion is at the castle of Pesme Avanture (Evil Adventure), where he arrives by chance and is received with a mixture of politeness and ominous hints. Outside the gate a woman advises him to turn around, but he replies: 'My foolish heart draws me on; I shall do what my heart wants' (ll. 5170–1), rejecting the counsel of prudence like Roland, but for a different reason. Inside he finds to his amazement (though possibly not to ours, for we have come to expect no less) three hundred damsels, victims of the as yet unexplained custom of the castle. Though his intention was to spend the night in the castle and go on his way the next day, he is now told that, regardless of his wishes, he must overcome two fiends if he is to leave the castle. Before this fierce encounter he sees a surprisingly peaceful family scene in the garden of the castle, where the lord and his wife are reclining while their daughter reads a romance to them. The family treat Yvain with the utmost courtesy, and give him a comfortable lodging for the night, but the next morning the hospitable 'preudome' tells him that whether it is right or wrong, he must follow custom and fight the two fiends. No rational explanation of this evil practice is offered, and the contrasting, seemingly incoherent, episodes leading up to the combat make it all the more mysterious. It is a trial of strength which Yvain cannot avoid once he has followed the dictates of his heart. When, with the lion's help, he wins, the three hundred maidens are released and he again sets forth. To see the appropriateness of this adventure in Yvain's painful struggle to atone for his broken promise and win the pardon of his lady it is not essential to seek the precise meaning of each detail. The power of love to exact service and punish transgression is the more impressive for being left a mystery.

Important as love is in Chrétien's romances, it is not the whole duty of the knight, as the emphasis on prowess constantly reminds us. In fact, both in *Yvain* and *Erec et Enide*, love and prowess confront each other as what appear to be alternate courses of action. The reason Yvain leaves Laudine is that Gawain tells him he will lose his renown as a warrior if he pays attention only to his wife. Whereupon Yvain, against his instincts, goes with Gawain, promising to return after a year of knight-errantry. Though it is clear that he is wrong to overstay his time, the implied conflict between the values of warrior and lover is more puzzling. By the standards of chivalry his year of tourneying with Gawain is good in itself. The puzzle is increased by a turn of the plot which leads Yvain to a fight against Gawain as the culminating episode of his rehabilitation. Neither one knows the other, and Chrétien dwells on the irony that these companions should engage in mortal combat—that hate should co-exist with a friendship which he calls 'perfect and noble love' ('Amors antiere et fine', l. 6007). Thus for a moment the 'fine amor' for Laudine seems to be rivalled by another love, Yvain's devotion to his friendly-enemy, Gawain, the apologist for the warrior's life. Since the two knights are evenly matched, the fight ends in a draw. There is no suggestion that friendship or prowess suffers a symbolic defeat in this episode. Both, in fact, are reasserted, for though the fighting is fierce, the end is a contest of courtesy, once the friends have recognized each other. However, Yvain, having proved himself his friend's equal on the field of battle, is free to return to Laudine, who at last grants him his pardon. The re-acquisition of the manly virtues leads to the restoration of love.

If the final emphasis in *Yvain* is upon an adjustment of the warrior's values to a scheme of things dominated by love in the person of Laudine, in the earlier *Erec et Enide* the *égoïsme à deux* of the happily married couple is obliged to adjust to the demands of a chivalric society which will not allow one of its best knights to be removed from circulation.[43] After Erec has won and married Enide, his friends begin to complain that although he is still very generous with his knights, he spends too much time in bed and no longer goes to tournaments.[44] Enide hears the criticism, and blaming herself, passes it on to Erec, who is alarmed by her report and annoyed with her for giving it. The second part of the romance is largely concerned with the consequences of Erec's decision to regain his reputation by seeking adventures accompanied by his wife, whom he forbids to warn him of approaching danger. That she breaks this rule is one part of a lengthy demonstration of her love for him in circumstances almost as trying as Griselda's. The main thrust of the adventures they encounter together is suggested most clearly in 'The Joy of the Court', the adventure in which Erec defeats a knight in an enchanted garden where he has promised to stay with his lady-love until a knight comes who can defeat him. Since he is an excellent warrior, she has hoped by this means to keep him for herself. His release through defeat by Erec puts an end to her possessiveness and restores him to the court. The analogy with the main story is obvious, even though Enide had no deliberate intention of possessing Erec wholly.

In the various treatments of love in the romances the basis was laid for several of the *topoi* of later literature and drama—love as an educative, ennobling, even mystic experience, and the conflicts between love and friendship, love and honour, or love and duty (the latter especially in Gottfried's *Tristan* and in Malory's version of the Lancelot–Guenever story, discussed above as examples of conflicting loyalties). When Dryden says that love and valour should be the subject of the heroic play he testifies to the established place that love had been accorded in the constellation of chivalric values.

Some of the ideals of conduct found in the romances originated, as we have seen, in the customs of feudal society. In time literature seems to have repaid part of its debt to life by influencing conduct, though the evidence of this effect is not easy to evaluate. We are told that Richard Beauchamp, Earl of Worcester in the fifteenth century, fought in a three-day tournament near Calais, appearing each day in armour of a different colour.[45] Was this in imitation of episodes like the tournament in *Cligès* (ll. 4581–894), where the hero appears as the Black Knight, the Green Knight, the Vermilion Knight and the White Knight on successive days? Or was Chrétien making use of an actual custom in his romance? A more clear-cut case of acting out a situation from romance is that of Ulrich von Liechtenstein, riding about Europe in quest of adventures to satisfy the whim of a cruel lady with whom he was in love.[46] The persistence of tournaments long after this way of fighting had been abandoned testifies to what Arthur Ferguson calls a romantic attitude towards chivalry, which begins to be apparent at the end of the fifteenth century. [47] By this he means the clinging to customs and ideals which had little relevance to the social and political structure of the day. A glaring example is the 'Field of the Cloth of Gold', not far from Calais, where Henry VIII met Francis I in 1520 amidst a most extravagant chivalric display complete with tournaments and specially constructed palaces. The past as embodied in tradition, and tradition as embodied in literature, are responsible for the bizarre splendour of this historic occasion.

Another manifestation of romanticizing concerns us more nearly—the influence that the chivalric ideals exerted upon the writing of history. History, as has already been remarked, was not clearly distinguished from what we should call legend, or epic or romance, and it also, more logically to our minds, included biography. Moreover, the historian's objective when he dealt with the life of a famous man, was very similar to that of the author of a romance or a *chanson de geste*—to exalt the extraordinary virtue of his subject. The historian was often more explicitly didactic in asserting the benefits to be derived from reading about the exemplary conduct of great men.

Two examples will suffice to show why history was one of the main sources of heroic drama. A striking case of chivalric history is the fifteenth-century life of the French Charles V by Christine de Pisan. The title shows what the author has in store: *Le livre des fais et bonnes meurs du sage roy Charles V.*[48] After explaining how she came to write of 'the deeds and virtuous manners' of this 'wise king', Christine begins her biography by making 'noblece de courage' the theme of the first part, since it leads the human mind to 'salutary perfections' (I, 10). Noble courage is based on three things: striving for nobility, loving virtuous manners and managing one's affairs with prudence, all of which are closely related to the desire for a good name ('bonne renommée'), and are embodied in the person of Charles V. At times this biography seems like a *summa* of the standard virtues recommended in the Middle Ages—love of justice and wisdom, fear of God, mercy, good will, humility—but the special chivalric flavour is detectable in the comprehensive importance given to 'noblece de courage' and 'bonne renommée' and in the emphasis on 'libéralité et sage largèce', without which 'noblece de courage' is impossible (I, 79 ff.). Here is an exemplary life, then, of a man who is presented as a hero, similar in an extraordinary number of traits to the heroes of chivalric romance.

Of more immediate interest to the student of English drama is an English equivalent of Christine's biography, the anonymous *Life of Henry V* written in 1513. The author's concept of the king's character is at times very reminiscent of Christine: 'the virtuous manners, the victorious conquests, and the excellent sages and wisdomes of the most renowned Prince . . .'[49] immediately recalls 'bonnes meurs', 'noblece de courage', and 'sage roy'. And the exemplary function of these heroic traits is made explicit by the author's frank avowal that he undertook this enterprise so that Henry VIII might be inspired by the life and manners of his ancestor, and particularly so that he 'shoulde partlie be prouoked in his saide warr [against France] to ensue the noble and chivalrous acts of this so noble, so vertuous, and so excellent a Prince...' (p. 4). One of the main sources of this life is a mid-fifteenth-century life in Latin by the Italian, Tito Livio da Forli, who addressed his work to Henry VI in the hope of encouraging that unheroic king to emulate his father. As the English author translates his predecessor: 'I haue therefore written the life and shyninge Acts of this most victorious Kinge, thie father, to thee, the most Christian Kinge. . . . Not that I preferr and laude warr and discention, rather then tranquillitie and peace; but if thou maiest haue none honest peace, that then thou shalt seeke peace and rest wth victorie . . . by thy vertue and battaile, and by those feates by w[ch] thie father attamed both his aduersaries and thine' (p. 7).

The distinction between 'victorious Kinge' and 'Christian Kinge' is clear yet delicate, for both Tito Livio and the English author emphasize the Christian virtues of Henry V. In his Proem the English author picks out for special comment justice, continence and humility (p. 5), and repeatedly, in sections he has added to the translation of his sources, speaks of the divine inspiration and the piety of Henry V, who is also a 'most Christian Kinge'.[50] Nevertheless, the life, as presented by both authors, is mainly a story of victories, aimed at moving another king to glorious action.

Chivalry of a markedly religious cast appears in some of the romances. Chrétien's unfinished *Conte du Graal* with the mysterious rites at the castle of the Fisher King, never explained in the part

24

of the story he completed, was followed by romances in which a hero, such as Galahad, must demonstrate purity and spiritual zeal as well as prowess in order to achieve the quest of the grail. The pursuit of holiness by Spenser's Redcross Knight is a later version of religious chivalry. Hence, the combination of piety and prowess in the *Life of Henry V*, though not entirely typical of the chivalric tradition, is by no means outside its bounds.[51]

What at first seems to differentiate the treatment of Henry V more clearly from the usual hero of romance, though not from some of the heroes of the *chansons de geste*, is the stress on 'the constant loue of the publique weale in the Prince that desired rather to dye then to be unproffitable to the realme' (p. 18). Roland's devotion to Charlemagne and 'douce France' is exemplary, but 'love of the publique weale' is not an issue for Erec or Yvain. Loyal as they are to King Arthur, they are much more concerned with their personal honour and with the vexing problems posed by their ladies. The romance tends to make more of individual achievement than of contribution to society, and thus to be oriented more towards private than public virtue. As A. B. Ferguson says, 'The mounted and armed knight moves through the romances as through a political vacuum, a limbo symbolized by the ever present and boundaryless forest . . .'.[52] However, the idea that the knight has obligations to the community is a commonplace in manuals on chivalry, such as Ramón Lull's *Order of Chivalry*, and in discussions of the subject in romances, as in the speech of the Damsel of the Lake to Lancelot, describing the knight's function of protecting the weak and assuring justice.[53] A later work, *The Book of Noblesse* (1475), emphasizes the 'comon profite' of the region or country in discussing the duties of the knight, and cites examples of self-sacrifice from Roman history.[54] The presentation of Henry V's heroic devotion to the 'publique weale' is a logical development of one side of the chivalric ideal.

Though the *Life of Henry V* is neither outside the tradition of chivalric thought nor far removed from the treatment of heroic character in the romances, the chivalric ideal in the early sixteenth century began to be somewhat altered by the intellectual and political developments of the time. In its pure form chivalry lost its immediate relevance to life, as Ferguson points out (p. 104), once the concept of society protected by the knight was replaced by Renaissance ideas of the state and of the responsibility of the governing class. But the chivalric ideal survived by accommodating itself to these concepts, and the shift of emphasis was probably far less apparent in the sixteenth century than it is today. The same point might be made about education; for though the Renaissance ideal of humane studies to prepare the courtier for service to the state differed in important ways from the training of the knight, the new concept of education could still be put in chivalric terms in the fictional world of romance.[55] A knight learning how to overcome monsters and wicked men in the forest of Brocéliande can become the symbol of a courtier preparing himself to serve his prince.

Chivalric romance presented a compelling pattern of heroism, susceptible of many alterations and diverse interpretations. The protagonist was similar to the epic hero in all times, and especially to the hero of the *chansons de geste*, in that he was first of all a warrior, a 'preudome'. His loyalty to his liege lord or to his lady was more medieval than Greek or Roman, and he went beyond both the classical and the medieval epic hero in his cultivation of courtesy and largesse, ideals which acquired a vast significance in the romance tradition. He differed still more from his epic confrères in the importance he attached to the experience of love and in his idealization of the object of his affections. He was once more like epic heroes, however, in his ardent concern for a reputation based on his achievements.

The plot of romance was essentially a series of adventures. Episodic and ranging far in both time and space, it did not necessarily differ in essence from that of the epic, though it became, especially in later romances, more complex, and usually presented the interwoven stories of a number of characters of almost equal importance. For Italian critics of the sixteenth century this became the most significant difference between epic and romance.[56] The happenings in romance, however, were characteristically more fantastic than those in epic—less predictable and more often due to spells and enchantments.

Partly because of its removal from everyday reality the plot of romance often called for symbolic interpretation. The perils of enchanted castles and the combats with giants or fiends could easily be seen as tests of the hero or even as means of revealing a character not otherwise analysed in depth. The larger pattern of the quest, one of the most characteristic forms of plot, suggested a gradual development or maturing, and a striving for some ideal.[57]

The paradigm of romance has basic analogies with that of comedy[58] in that both typically end with a new order which provides what the protagonist has striven for. Though there are notable romances which end unhappily, such as *Tristan* or the *Morte Darthur*, it remains true that the form, closely related, as Northrop Frye says, 'to the wish-fulfilment dream' (p. 186), is logically completed by the successful end of the adventure or quest and the 'exaltation of the hero' (p. 187). Even those romances which end unhappily (and are therefore analogous to the normal pattern of tragedy) retain the 'exaltation of the hero', which may imply some sort of triumph even in death. Since the happy ending, in which a new world seems to be opening up to the hero, is most typical of romance, it is not surprising that the first dramatized romances were comedies, and that romance profoundly influenced a kind of comedy which became very popular on the English stage. When more serious drama was affected by the pattern of romance it often took the form of tragi-comedy or of that special form of tragedy which ends happily.

With its astonishing adventures and its heroes who triumph over seemingly insuperable opposition, romance was well suited to do what many Renaissance critics thought all serious poetry, but especially heroic poetry, should do—that is, to arouse 'admiration'. Antonio Minturno, who considered 'admiration' the distinctive effect of poetry, meant by this a kind of excited wonder aroused both by the poet's superlative mastery of his craft and by his subject-matter—in both cases by his appeal to the reader's imagination. Since the deeds of the greatest heroes were especially well suited to arouse wonder, he elevated epic, in defiance of Aristotle, to a higher rank than tragedy.[59] In a similar vein Tasso, speaking of actions suitable for heroic poetry in his *Discourse on the Heroic Poem* (1594), said, 'These actions in themselves win over the souls of the readers and produce expectation and marvelous pleasure, and when the art of an able poet is added there is nothing they cannot accomplish in our souls.'[60]

With such theories of poetry in the air, it was inevitable that some critics should see romance as the natural successor to epic, though others considered it a degenerate form. Minturno, who opposed it because of its structural complexity and looseness, admitted that it was 'an imitation of great and illustrious actions that are worthy of epic poetry', and Giraldi Cinthio, a proponent of romance, cited the essentially poetic nature of its marvellous happenings.[61] Sir Philip Sidney commented on the inspiring effect of even the *Amadis de Gaule*, a late and popular romance of obscure origins, the earliest surviving version being a Spanish one published in 1508. Speaking of the moving power of poetry, he wrote:

> Truely, I haue knowen men, that euen with reading *Amadis de Gaule* (which God knoweth wanteth much of a perfect Poesie) haue found their harts mooued to the exercise of courtesie, liberalitie, and especially courage. Who readeth *Aeneas* carrying olde *Anchises* on his back, that wisheth not it were his fortune to perfourme so excellent an acte?[62]

That he put Amadis (despite some reservations) in the company of Aeneas suggests that a reader of that time saw no need of distinguishing clearly between romance and epic, and in the preceding paragraph Sidney had spoken of the pleasure men find in 'tales of *Hercules, Achilles, Cyrus*, and *Aeneas*', hearing which, they 'must needs heare the right description of wisdom, valure, and iustice' (p. 172). Here epic heroes are associated with the legendary Hercules, epitome of heroism, and the historical Persian Emperor Cyrus I, about whom Xenophon wrote an exemplary (and partly fictitious) life, the *Cyropedia*, somewhat similar in nature and purpose to the lives of Charles V and Henry V discussed earlier. For Sidney the effect of romance, epic, heroic legend and a kind of historical writing was essentially the same.

His remarks on heroic poetry, already quoted in part, include a similar grouping of heroes, and testify again to the effect he expected their stories to have:

> There rests the Heroicall, whose very name (I thinke) should daunt all back-biters; for by what conceit can a tongue be directed to speake euill of that which draweth with it no lesse Champions then *Achilles, Cyrus, Aeneas, Turnus, Tideus*, and *Rinaldo*? who doth not onely teach and moue to a truth, but teacheth and mooueth to the

most high and excellent truth; who maketh magnanimity
iustice shine throughout all misty fearefulnes and foggy
desires; . . .

(Smith I, 179).[63]

In this list Tideus, a hero in Statius' *Thebaid*, is added to the
Homeric and Virgilian champions, Cyrus appears once more,
and finally Rinaldo from Tasso's *Gerusalemme Liberata*, an epic
much influenced by romance. The stories of such heroes, Sidney
believed, must surely accomplish the aim of all poetry, to move
the reader to a perception of truth and a relinquishing of all less
worthy attitudes in the immediate presence of great-mindedness
and justice.

Other English men of letters shared the opinion of romance
held by the author of the *Arcadia*. Spenser gave several of the
major characters in *The Faerie Queene* (Artegall, the champion of
justice, is a good example) attributes which relate them to both
the knights of chivalric romance and the heroes of classical
antiquity. And even Ben Jonson, great apologist for the classics
that he was, told William Drummond that 'for a Heroik poeme . . .
ther was no such Ground as King Arthurs fiction . . .'.[64]

There could be no better illustration of the comprehensive unity
of the heroic tradition than the entertainment devised by Jonson
and Inigo Jones as a prelude to the investiture of King James's son
Henry as Prince of Wales. Fond of jousting, the prince, as Sir
Charles Cornwallis wrote, 'not onely for his owne Recreation, but
also that the World might know, what a brave Prince they were
likely to enjoy',[65] issued a challenge under the name of Meliadus,
Lord of the Isles, to knights of Great Britain to meet him in a
joust on foot to be held on Twelfth Night, 1610, a little over a
month before his sixteenth birthday. Having already persuaded
his father to invest him as Prince of Wales the following June, he
had also obtained permission for the 'barriers', as this kind of
joust was called, and James had granted him the services of the
two men most in demand for court entertainments. Not only did
the prince have a taste for chivalric pageantry and sport, but he
also seems to have inspired in his contemporaries a properly
chivalric response, exemplified by the title of Sir Charles Cornwallis's biography: *The Life and Death of our late most incomparable
and Heroique Prince Henry, Prince of Wales. A Prince (for Valour and*

29

Virtue) fit to be imitated in succeeding Times (1641). Thus Jonson and Jones were being asked to apply their arts of poetry and scenic design to the celebration of princely heroism.

The Speeches at Prince Henries Barriers provided a dramatic context for the joust and a vastly extended symbolic perspective. First the Lady of the Lake appears to praise the king for having revived the glories of King Arthur's court, and at the same time to lament the seeming ruin of 'the house of *Chiualrie* . . . her buildings layd/Flat with the earth . . .'.[66] In their time, she says, they surpassed the pyramids, and she points to broken 'obelisks' and 'columns' which 'raisd the *British* crowne/To be a constellation' (ll. 38–9), though we would hardly have expected to find them in an Arthurian scene. She tells us that 'when this Ædifice stood great and high' (l. 45), there were porticos, seats for knights in search of adventure and niches for heroic statues which inspired young valour. Roy Strong has identified what he believes to be Inigo Jones's drawing for this 'Fallen House of Chivalry',[67] where a deserted open space is surrounded by broken columns and triumphal arches in a mass of classical ruins, overgrown with grass. When the Lady of the Lake has finished, Arthur appears as a star and urges her to release Merlin and bring forth a knight, who will 'restore/These ruin'd seates of vertue, and build more' (ll. 84–5). Merlin then rises from his tomb (apparently a splendid sarcophagus of classical design), and soon Meliadus is 'discovered' (perhaps by the drawing aside of a shutter at the back of the previous scene), together with six other knights, seated in a building which Merlin identifies as 'St George's portico'. In the drawing for this scene (again identified by Roy Strong—No. 20 in the catalogue) the portico appears as a Gothic fantasy in the exact centre of the classical ruins, which it clearly outshines. The Lady of the Lake now compares Meliadus (Prince Henry) and his assistants to Mars and 'the old *Graecian Heroes*' (l. 145) and summons them forth to make their virtue known, but they are not allowed to begin the combat until Merlin has interpreted for them a shield painted with the glories of British history, including representations of those great warrior princes, Richard the Lion-hearted, Edward I, Edward the Black Prince and Henry V.[68] Mythological and historical figures, warriors of Greece and Britain, appear in an undifferentiated continuum which is made visible in the Gothic portico and classical columns of the scenery.

As Prince Henry and his assistants move towards the 'barriers' to joust, the figure of Chivalry awakens, comes out of a cave where she has been sleeping, and opens the doors to a 'flood' of knighthood—the fifty-six 'defendants' who have answered the prince's challenge. The fighting then begins and lasts until after midnight, the prince acquitting himself 'with wonderous skill, and courage', according to one account.[69] When Henry was made Prince of Wales with great ceremony at Westminster Palace six months later, the symbolic incorporation of chivalry within the body politic was completed, and chivalry, as Jonson and Jones made plain, was nothing less than heroism as it had manifested itself at every high point of civilization.

Notes

1 Sir William D'Avenant, *Love and Honour and The Siege of Rhodes*, ed. James W. Tupper (Boston and London, 1910), 187–8. See W. S. Clark, 'The Definition of the Heroic Play in the Restoration Period', *Review of English Studies*, VIII (1932), 437–44.

2 See *The Works of John Dryden* (Berkeley and Los Angeles, 1956–), VIII, 264. This edition is hereafter referred to as 'California Dryden'.

3 For Minturno, *Literary Criticism: Plato to Dryden*, ed. Allan H. Gilbert (New York, 1940), 289; hereafter referred to as 'Gilbert'. For Sidney, *Elizabethan Critical Essays*, ed. G. Gregory Smith, 2 vols. (Oxford, 1904), I, 178; hereafter referred to as 'Smith'.

4 See B. J. Pendlebury's account of the heroic tradition in *Dryden's Heroic Plays* (New York, 1967; orig. 1923), esp. 68; also John M. Steadman, *Milton and the Renaissance Hero* (Oxford, 1967), 137–8.

5 See Cedric Whitman, *Sophocles* (Cambridge, Mass., 1951), 64.

6 *Essays of John Dryden*, ed. W. P. Ker, 2 vols. (Oxford, 1926), I, 149, 150; hereafter referred to as 'Ker'.

7 See Wace, *Roman de Rou*, ll. 8035 ff.

8 *Chanson des Saxons*, ed. F. Michel (Paris, 1839), I, 1.

9 (Ithaca, N.Y., 1965; orig. 1940), 28–9.

10 Ed. Joseph Bédier (Paris, 1931), ll. 1089–92, translated rather freely.

11 *Raoul de Cambrai*, tr. Jessie Crosland (London, 1926), tirades 133, 155.

12 *Paideia: the Ideals of Greek Culture*, 3 vols., I, 4th ed. (Oxford, 1954), 5. Like the *chansons de geste*, Homeric epic seems to have been sung before it was written down.

13 For Old French text see the edition of Mario Roques, *Les Romans de Chrétien de Troyes* (in *Les Classiques français du Moyen Age*), IV (Paris, 1967), from which all line-numbers in *Yvain* are taken. These editions are hereafter referred to as '*Romans*'. For English translations of Chrétien's romances,

with the exception of the *Conte du Graal*, see *Arthurian Romances by Chrétien de Troyes*, tr. W. W. Comfort, Everyman's Library (London and New York, 1914).

14 Sidney Painter, *William Marshall* (Baltimore, 1967; orig. 1933), 11–12, 73.

15 *French Chivalry*, 41–2.

16 *Tristan*, tr. A. T. Hatto (Baltimore, 1960), 195–6; *Le Morte D'Arthur*, 2 vols., Everyman's Library (London and New York, 1906), II, 357, 394.

17 Painter, *French Chivalry*, 46.

18 Painter, *William Marshall*, 30–60.

19 *Le sens de l'aventure et de l'amour* (Paris, 1947), 19–32. For Old French text see *Der Percevalroman* (*Li Contes del Graal*), ed. A. Hilka (Halle, 1932), ll. 4418–509; for an English translation see *The Story of the Grail*, tr. Robert W. Linker (Chapel Hill, N.C., 1952), 93–5.

20 'largesce est dame et reine/Qui totes vertuz anlumine, . . .', *Cligès*, ed. Alexandre Micha, *Romans*, II (Paris, 1968), ll. 189–90. All line-numbers in *Cligès* are taken from this edition. See Painter, *French Chivalry*, 31 and Marian P. Whitney, 'Queen of Medieval Virtues: Largesse', *Vassar Medieval Studies*, ed. Christabel F. Fiske (New Haven, 1923), 183–215.

21 Rutebeuf, *Œuvres complètes*, ed. Jubinal (Paris, 1839), II, 471.

22 *Roman de la Rose*, ed. F. Michel (Paris, 1864), ll. 1133 ff. See *The Romance of the Rose*, tr. H. W. Robbins (New York, 1962), 23–4.

23 *L'histoire de Guillaume le Maréchal*, ed. Paul Meyer (Paris, 1891), ll. 32–5.

24 *Nichomachean Ethics*, IV, i. Though the *Ethics* were not directly known in the west until the thirteenth century, many of the Aristotelian ideas were already familiar·through the works of others, such as Cicero. Jean de Meun, author of the second part of the *Roman de la Rose*, in which 'folle largesse' is mentioned (II, 7885 ff.), probably knew the *Ethics*, but Aristotle is cited here, not as a source, but as a point of reference. His terms are useful because they distinguish between qualities which fall together in other classifications.

25 Dom Odon Lottin, *Psychologie et morale aux XIIe et XIIIe siècles*, III, *Problèmes de morale, seconde partie*, 2 vols., continuous pagination (Louvain, 1949), 300.

26 *Nichomachean Ethics*, IV, ii.

27 See the long and illuminating discussion of magnificence in Rosemond Tuve, *Allegorical Imagery* (Princeton, 1966), 57–143.

28 *The Book of the Ordre of Chyvalry*, tr. William Caxton, ed. A. T. P. Byles, Early English Text Society, Original Series, 168 (London, 1926), 99–101.

29 *De inventione*, tr. H. M. Hubbell, Loeb Library (London and Cambridge, Mass., 1949), 330–1. On magnanimity see D. Douglas Waters, 'Prince Arthur as Christian Magnanimity in Book One of *The Faerie Queene*', *Studies in English Literature*, IX (1969), 53–62; Waters includes an extensive bibliography in his notes.

30 Société de Bibliophiles, 2 vols. (Paris, 1846), I, 28, 58.

31 *The Vulgate Version of the Arthurian Romances*, ed. H. O. Sommer, III, *Le Livre de Lancelot del Lac*, Part I (Washington, D.C., 1910), 112 ff.

32 *Cligès*, ll. 84–5.

33 *French Chivalry*, 34.

34 P. 38. Lull's formulation of the primary function of the knight is very similar to that of the Damsel of the Lake in the Vulgate Lancelot cited above.

35 *Orlando Innamorato*, ed. A. Panizzi (London, 1830–31), II, xviii, 1–2.

36 'Le conte de la Charette', *Romania*, XII (1883), 519–34.

37 *Le Chevalier de la Charette*, ed. Mario Roques, *Romans*, III (Paris, 1967), l. 26.

38 See Peter Dronke, *Medieval Latin and the Rise of the European Love-Lyric*, 2 vols. (Oxford, 1965), I, esp. 46–56, 82–5; John F. Benton, 'The Court of Champagne as a Literary Center', *Speculum*, XXXVI (1961), 551–91; E. Talbot Donaldson reviews the subject wittily, sanely, and briefly in *Ventures: Magazine of the Yale Graduate School*, Fall, 1965, 16–23. See also *The Meaning of Courtly Love*, ed. F. X. Newman (Albany, N.Y., 1968).

39 Andreas Capellanus, *The Art of Courtly Love*, tr. John J. Parry (New York, 1959; orig. 1941), especially the sections on 'The Love of the Clergy', and 'The love of Nuns', I, vii and viii, 141–4.

40 *Erec et Enide, Cligès, Le Chevalier de la Charrette, Yvain, Le Conte du Graal. Guillaume d'Angleterre* is of doubtful authorship.

41 Dronke, I, 163–8.

42 See Bezzola, *Le Sens de l'aventure*, esp. 64. ff.

43 See the discussions of both romances in Gustave Cohen, *Un Grand Romancier d'amour et d'aventure au XIIe siècle: Chrétien de Troyes et son ouvre* (Paris, 1948; orig. 1931), 115–68, 303–77; Jean Frappier, *Chrétien de Troyes* (Paris, 1957), 85–105, 147–69: and the lengthy analysis of *Erec et Enide* in Bezzola, *Le sens de l'aventure*, 73–247.

44 *Erec et Enide*, ed. Mario Roques, *Romans*, I (Paris, 1966), ll. 2430–64. All line-numbers in *Erec et Enide* are taken from this edition.

45 See William Matthews, *The Ill-Famed Knight* (Berkeley and Los Angeles, 1966), 40.

46 See Morton M. Hunt, *The Natural History of Love* (New York, 1959), 132 ff.

47 *The Indian Summer of English Chivalry* (Durham, N.C., 1960), 72, 104 and *passim*.

48 Ed. S. Solente, 2 vols. (Paris, 1936). On the subject of exemplary biography see O. B. Hardison, *The Enduring Moment* (Chapel Hill, N.C., 1962).

49 *The First English Life of King Henry the Fifth*, ed. C. L. Kingsford (Oxford, 1911), 4.

50 See, for example, 23, 29, 34, 45.

51 See Painter, 'Religious Chivalry', in *French Chivalry*, 65–94.

52 *Indian Summer*, 111.

53 *Vulgate Romances*, III, i, 112 ff. Cf. Ferguson, *Indian Summer*, 118.

54 *The Boke of Noblesse*, intro. J. E. Nichols (London, 1860), 56–62.

55 See Ferguson, *Indian Summer*, 162, 182 ff.

56 See Bernard Weinberg, *A History of Literary Criticism in the Italian Renaissance*, 2 vols. (Chicago, 1961), II, 954–1073.

57 See Tuve, *Allegorical Imagery*, 365, and Northrop Frye, *Anatomy of Criticism* (Princeton, 1957), 186–203

58 Frye discusses these in his *Anatomy of Criticism*, 177, 181 ff. His placing of comedy between irony-and-satire and romance is richly suggestive.

59 *De poeta* (Venice, 1559), 105–6. On the preference for epic see J. E.

Spingarn, *A History of Literary Criticism in the Renaissance*, 2nd. ed. (New York, 1908), 107 ff.

60 In Gilbert, 488.

61 Minturno, *L'Arte Poetica* (1564), in Gilbert, 277; Giraldi Cinthio, *On the Composition of Romances* (1549), in Gilbert, 270.

62 In Smith, I, 173.

63 See Alan D. Isler, 'Heroic Poetry and Sidney's Two *Arcadias*', *Publications of the Modern Language Association*, LXXXIII (1968), 368–79.

64 *Ben Jonson*, ed. C. H. Herford and Percy and Evelyn Simpson, 11 vols. (Oxford, 1925–52), I, 136; hereafter referred to as 'Herford and Simpson'.

65 Herford and Simpson, X, 512.

66 Herford and Simpson, VII; ll. 31, 34–5.

67 *Festival Designs by Inigo Jones* [the catalogue of an exhibition of drawings from the Devonshire Collection at Chatsworth] (International Exhibitions Foundation, 1967–8), No. 19.

68 W. Todd Furniss shows how adroitly Jonson manages to treat these warriors as part of the paneygric of the even greater king, James I, whose ideal is peace, but it is an exaggeration to say that 'the text plainly points out that revival of chivalry is a poor thing compared with the acquisition of a wisdom which sees battle as the worst way to settle difficult questions' ('Ben Jonson's Masques', in *Studies in the Renaissance* [New Haven, 1958], 126). The text is not so unequivocal; for it is equally plain that it leads up to feats of arms which complete the revival of British greatness. In this revival chivalry plays a glorious part.

69 Herford and Simpson, X, 514.

Two

Emergence

In the first decade of the seventeenth century Francis Beaumont sought to amuse an élite audience at Blackfriars, a 'private house', by bringing onstage Rafe, an apprentice, reading from a chivalric romance:

> Then Palmerin and Trineus, snatching their lances from their dwarfs and clasping their helmets, gallop'd amain after the giant; and Palmerin, having gotten a sight of him, came posting amain, saying, 'Stay, traitorous thief, for thou may'st not so carry away her that is worth the greatest lord in the world,' and with these words gave him a blow on the shoulder, that he struck him besides his elephant;. . . .[1]

Beaumont's satire bears on an early form of heroic drama in several ways. Rafe's reading is lifted from *Palmerin de Oliva*, a romance translated into English in 1588 by Antony Munday. Though Beaumont has heightened the effect by changing a horse into an elephant, and has doctored the quotation in other ways, it is not an unfair sample of the bombast and the derring-do in this story, one of a number of romances of Iberian origin, including *Amadis de Gaule*, which enjoyed great popularity in England at the close of the sixteenth century.

The fact of the continued popularity of chivalric romance is in itself worthy of comment. Despite the protests of a few men such as Roger Ascham, who considered the *Morte Darthur* a wanton product of Catholic monasteries, apt to corrupt Englishmen by its portrayal of 'open mans slaughter and bold bawdrye',[2] chivalric romances of all descriptions poured from the presses of Caxton and his followers. As some of the older romances began to lose their appeal, their places were taken by more recent ones such as

those dealing with Amadis and Palmerin, whose endless adventures filled many volumes of English translation in the last
decade of the century.[3]

In Beaumont's play the devotees of this literature are a grocer
and his wife, who have come to the theatre in hopes of seeing a
play of the same ilk, and who induce the players to let their man,
Rafe, play a part in it. His role of a grocer-knight furnishes the
title for the whole entertainment, *The Knight of the Burning Pestle*.
It is bourgeois taste that Beaumont is mocking for the amusement
of his more exclusive audience (though the sad fact is that they
were not amused),[4] and there is a great deal of evidence that
romances were increasingly read by the middle class.[5] Though
Beaumont seems to consider his grocers ideally suited for such
reading by their naïveté, we know already from Sidney's comment on *Amadis de Gaule* that not all readers of romances resembled
Beaumont's characters. *The Faerie Queene* is a massive testimony
to the hold of romance on another highly educated and sophisticated mind. To be sure, Sidney's practice in his *Arcadia* shows
that the strain of romance which appealed most to him was less
chivalric than the one we have been considering, and was heavily
indebted to the second- and third-century love-stories known as
Greek romances, in some of which the setting is pastoral. Boccaccio
and Sannazaro had both written pastoral romances, which were
followed by such works as Montemayor's *Diana* (1559) and Honoré
d'Urfé's *L'Astrée* (1608–24), both of which became the fashionable
reading matter for several generations of *literati*. It would be easy
to say that by the end of the sixteenth century chivalric romances
had become middle-class reading, while more aristocratic or
more cultivated readers turned to pastoral romances, but the
distinction cannot be drawn so neatly. Chivalric, and more
generally heroic, episodes occur in Sidney's *Arcadia*,[6] and chivalry
is ubiquitous in *The Faerie Queene*. It would probably be wiser to
settle for the unexciting conclusion that while romances of various
sorts continued to enjoy extraordinary popularity with almost
everyone, readers with good literary taste chose the ones with
more literary merit.

The same sort of conclusion seems to be warranted in the field
of drama; for while Sidney's well-known censure of romantic
plays for their disregard of classical structure[7] sounds like aristocratic disdain for popular entertainment, there is ample evidence

that the aristocracy was entertained not only by tournaments, those vestigial remnants of chivalry, but also by dramatized romances, many of which were performed at court in the seventies and eighties.[8] Most of the court plays are lost, though we have titles such as *Herpetulus the Blue Knight and Perobia*, *The Knight in the Burning Rock* and *Ariodante and Genevora*. The surviving samples of the public theatre repertory suggest that there the average romantic play may have been almost as foolish as the one in which Beaumont's Rafe plays the lead. Nevertheless, the heroic drama, which was to become an aristocratic diversion after the Restoration, owes much to the popular tradition of this early period. Ludicrous as the first romantic plays were, they are part of our story.

Stephen Gosson's comment on the popular theatre in 1582 is scathing:

> Sometime you shall see nothing but the aduentures of an amorous knight, passing from countrie to countrie for the loue of his lady, encountring many a terible monster made of broune paper, & at his retorne, is so wonderfully changed, that he can not be knowne but by some posie in his tablet, or by a broken ring, or a handkircher, or a piece of cockle shell, what learne you by that?[9]

This description hits very close to *Clyomon and Clamydes* (probably performed in 1570), the nature of which is obvious in the full title: 'The Historie of the two valiant Knights, Syr Clyomon Knight of the Golden Sheeld, sonne to the King of Denmarke: And Clamydes the white Knight, sonne to the King of Suauia'. Clamydes, who appears in the first scene, is an 'amorous knight', charged by his Juliana with the task of eliminating a flying serpent in the Forest of Marvels, where the enchanter, Brian Sans Foy, rules. Even though no 'terible monster made of broune paper' appears, there is a scene in which Clamydes enters with the serpent's head on his sword, and is charmed into a trance by Brian. Anyone who has seen Wagner's Siegfried do battle with a stage dragon will be grateful to the author of *Clyomon and Clamydes* for stopping short of the spectacle which some of his fellow playwrights apparently offered. Aristotle saw the danger of unintended humour in staging certain episodes in the epics, and for the dramatizer of marvels, awesome enough in a book, the danger is infinitely greater. Even without visual aids the episode of the flying serpent in this play is sufficiently absurd.

Another feature of *Clyomon and Clamydes* which Beaumont would have found ridiculous was its language. Here is Clyomon challenging a wicked king in terms similar to Palmerin's in the passage read by Rafe:

> Nay Traytour stay, and take with thee that mortall blow
> or stroke
> The which shall cause thy wretched corps this life for to
> reuoke.
> It ioyeth me at the hart that I haue met thee in this place.
>
> (ll. 1360–2)[10]

The relentless, bumpy rhythm of the fourteener couplets, filled out when necessary with tautologies like 'blow or stroke', was bound to offend a sensitive ear, and no great sensitivity was required to perceive that both diction and sentence structure were too feeble to support the author's attempts at elevation. Apt alliteration's artful aid is summoned for a set speech by one of the heroines as she wanders in the forest disguised as a page:

> Ah weary paces that I walke, with steps vnsteddy still,
> Of all the gripes of grislie griefes, *Neronis* hath her fill.
>
> (ll. 1597–8)

Though we know nothing about the audiences for whom this extravaganza was played, it is firmly tied to the popular tradition by its structure and by the use of a 'Vice'. David M. Bevington has traced the development of the plays performed by itinerant companies in the late-fifteenth and sixteenth centuries, and has shown how, first in the moral interludes, then in other kinds of plays, the successive encounters of the central characters with various other groups of characters were suited to performance by relatively few players.[11] The trick was accomplished by the doubling of parts and the alternation of scenes in which the same characters reappeared. This structural technique was applied to chronicle plays and to romances such as *Clyomon and Clamydes*, where the thirty-seven parts can be played by ten actors, certain groups of characters appearing in only one of the far-flung locales, which include Denmark and Macedonia, the Forest of Marvels and the Isle of Strange Marshes. As Bevington says, 'The pattern of wandering, confusion, separation, and loss leads ultimately to rediscovery and reunion, a linear process not unlike the fall from grace leading to regeneration in the moral play' (pp. 195–6).

In the company of the White Knight, the Knight of the Golden Shield, their 'peerless dames', the kings of Denmark and Suavia and Alexander the Great, it is surprising to find another borrowing from the moral interludes—the Vice, Subtle Shift. With him is introduced a most unromantic element, the 'comedy of evil', associated by Bernard Spivack with the grotesqueries of gargoyles, which, while entertaining, serve a grimly didactic purpose.[12] The prologue proclaims the purpose of the action, 'That vertue from the roote of vice, might openly be knowne', but we may question how seriously this intention is to be taken. Subtle Shift, though he has capriciously betrayed both heroes, is neither punished nor shown up in the general rejoicings at the end. The character and the 'comedy of evil' of which he is a part seem to be no more than vestiges of a dramatic formula which had been remarkably successful. Out of it a new pattern was beginning to emerge.

If *Clyomon and Clamydes* is hilariously unimpressive as a specimen of dramatic art, it commands attention as an example of how the early Elizabethan popular drama served the ideals inherited from chivalric literature. The presence of Alexander the Great is eloquent in itself, for as the hero of the first French romance and the prototypical embodiment of generosity and large-mindedness, he has every right to the title Clyomon gives him, 'chiefe of chiualrie' (l. 486). He does not enter actively into the plot, which mainly concerns the rivalry in honour and fame of the titular heroes, but he is always present in the background, and appropriately presides at the climactic encounter between them, persuading them to choose reconciliation rather than combat. At his first appearance the company's resources in costume and supernumeraries are taxed to give Alexander his full symbolic significance: '*Enter King* Alexander *the Great, as valiantly set forth as may be, and as many souldiers as can*' (l. 357). His first speech establishes him as the invincible warrior he is known to be, and shows that like other heroes of epic and romance, he is not reticent in proclaiming his power:

> Who bowes not now vnto my becke, my force who doth
>   not feare?

Who doth not of my conquests great, throughout the
world heare?
What King as to his soueraigne Lord, doth now not bow
his knee?
What Prince doth raigne vpon the earth, which yeelds
not vnto mee
Due homage for his Regall Mace? What countrey is at
libertie?
What Dukedome, iland, or Prouince else, to me now are
not tributarie?

(ll. 368–73)

In an earlier scene the King of Suavia, about to knight his son,
Clamydes, talks to him somewhat as the king talks to his son
Alexander in *Cligès*. Since he is to spend his 'youthfull dayes in
prowesse', he should know 'what to knighthood doth belong':

Know thou therefore *Clamydes* deare, to haue a knightly
name
Is first aboue all other things his God for to adore,
In truth according to the lawes prescribde to him before.
Secondly, that he be true vnto his Lord and king.
Thirdly, that he keepe his faith and troth in euery thing.
And then before all other things that else we can
commend,
That he be alwaies ready prest, his countrey to defend:
The Widow poore, and fatherlesse, or Innocent bearing
blame,
To see their cause redressed right, a faithfull knight must
frame:
In truth he alwaies must be tried, this is the totall charge,
That will receiue a knightly name, his honour to en-
large.

(ll. 222–41)

The standard emphasis upon prowess, loyalty, honour and protection of the weak and oppressed is supplemented here with religious
and patriotic injunctions found in some but not all chivalric
literature.

By means of the example of Alexander the Great and the
precepts of the King of Suavia the ideals to which both Clyomon
and Clamydes are pledged are made clear. With one exception,

Redressing the causes of poor widows does not quite cover the service to ladies performed by these knights. The ideal of love is introduced by Clamydes at the opening of the play in a rapturous encomium of the Princess Juliana, whose command to him to slay the serpent immediately places her in the category of distressed but exacting maidens. Somewhat more concern with the psychology of love is shown in the treatment of the story of Clyomon and Princess Neronis. When the princess discovers that she is in love, she expresses her feelings in a major set piece, full of the self-questionings which characterize the love soliloquies in the romances (for example in *Cligès* and *Tristan*) and prepare the way for the great soliloquies of the Elizabethan stage. Neronis's speech, giving the audience a brief respite from fourteeners, starts with short lines arranged in a stiffly symmetrical pattern which was apparently fashionable then and even appealed some years later to more gifted poets such as Kyd and Marlowe:[13]

How can that tree but withered be
That wanteth sap to moyst the roote?
How can that Vine but waste and pine,
Whose plants are troden vnder foote?
How can that spray but soone decay,
That is with wild weeds ouergrowne?
How can that wight in ought delight
Which showes, and hath no good will showne?
Or else how can that heart alasse,
But die by whom each ioy doth passe?
Neronis, ah I am the Tree, which wanteth sap to moyst
    the roote.
Neronis, ah I am the vine, whose Plants are troden vnder
    foote.
I am the spray which doth decay, and is with wild weeds
    ouergrowne,
I am the wight without delight, which shows, and hath no
    good wil showne.
Mine is the heart by whom alas, each pleasant ioy doth
    passe,
Mine is the heart which vades away, as doth the flower or
    grasse.

(ll. 990–1007)

It will be noticed that the strain of avoiding fourteeners is too great, and that in the last two lines the author has slipped comfortably into his old ways. In this measure Neronis continues for another twenty lines to probe her feelings toward the Knight of the Golden Shield.[14] Thus the theme of love is emphatically, if not subtly, presented, and is made a prime motive for the action. At the end it is trumpeted *fortissimo* ('O sudden ioyes, O heauenly sight . . .') with the double marriage of the heroes to their princesses.

Foolish as are most of the adventures (and speeches) in this play, they actualize in their way the striving of the characters toward the ideal set before them, the achievement of honour and love. The basic ingredients of heroic drama as Davenant and Dryden were to understand it nearly a century later are here.

Common Conditions is a romantic play of about the same time (1576?) and, as the title page reveals, of a very similar make-up: 'An excellent and pleasant Comedie, termed after the name of the Vice, Common Condicions, drawne out of the most famous historie of Galiarbus Duke of Arabia, and of the good and eeuill successe of him and his two children, Sedmone his sun, and Clarisia his daughter: Set foorth with delectable mirth, and pleasant shewes.'[15] The 'historie of Galiarbus' is not known today. If it were, we should be in a better position to evaluate the abrupt termination of the play by the Epilogue, who arrives at what seems a most inopportune moment to announce that there is no time to proceed further. Clarisia's beloved Lamphedon has taken poison and she is about to follow suit, while the stories of her father and brother are left incomplete. Was the action brought to a happy conclusion in the source, as some believe? Whatever explanation there may be of this whimsical no-ending, the play is well supplied with the stock episodes of romantic adventure—banishment, wandering, capture by pirates, disguise, love reciprocated and unreciprocated and combat with a wicked oppressor of ladies. Even more than *Clyomon and Clamydes*, the play is dominated by the Vice, Common Conditions, who comes near to embodying the unpredictable turns of fortune. There is less talk of chivalric ideals than in the other play, and less action in which honour and prowess are demonstrated. *Common Conditions* is therefore an example of a kind of romantic play which had relatively little direct connection with the development of heroic drama. Here the Vice is even more, in Spivack's words, 'the enemy of the play's romantic values' (p. 294) than is Subtle Shift in *Clyomon and Clamydes,* and thus anticipates in one respect at least both Touchstone and Autolycus.[16] We are reminded that the origins of romantic comedy as well as heroic drama are in these plays.

If *Common Conditions* is romantic without being markedly heroic, Thomas Preston's *Cambises,* a popular play[17] of slightly earlier date, is in part heroic without being at all romantic. It features a character-type—the extravagant boaster and threatener—who had a lengthy career on the stage, and particularly in heroic drama. Like the two plays just discussed, *Cambises* is intimately related to the morality tradition through not only its Vice, Ambidexter, but also a number of allegorical characters such as Cruelty and Murder. The main story is from Herodotus by way of Richard Taverner's Elizabethan compilation, *The Garden of Wisdom,* but to this are added the frolics of Huf, Ruf and Snuf, Meretrix, Hob and Lob, and Marian-May-Be-Good, which fully justify the odd title, 'A lamentable Tragedie, mixed full of plesant mirth, containing the life of Cambises king of Percia . . .'.[18] The play marks, as Bevington shows, an important stage of transition between the moral interlude and the history play.

The protagonist, King Cambises of Persia, whose one good deed, three evil deeds and final punishment enact the moral theme, is the ranting boaster who foreshadows some of the later heroes and thus warrants our attention. Near the end of the play, already a flamboyantly evil man, he falls in love with his cousin, instantly demands that she marry him, and when she objects, flies into a characteristic rage:

> May I not? Nay, then, I will! by all the gods I vow!
> And I will mary thee as wife. This is mine answere now!
> Who dare say nay what I pretend? Who dare the same
>   withstand
> Shal lose his head, and have reporte as traitor through
>   my land.
> There is no nay. I wil you have, and you my queene shal-
>   be!

> (ll. 919–23)

When she crosses him he orders her death and threatens two lords who intercede for her:

You villains twain! with raging force ye set my hart on
    fire!
If I consent that she shall dye, how dare ye crave her life?
You two to aske this at my hand, dooth much inlarge my
    strife.
Were it not for shame, you two should dye, that for her
    life do sue!
But favour mine from you is gone; my lords, I tell you
    true.

                            (ll. 1093–7)

His final speech expresses his frustration and despair when he has
'accidentally' received a fatal wound (it is not an accident, of
course, but an act of God):

Out! alas! What shal I doo? My life is finished!
Wounded I am by sodain chaunce; my blood is min-
    ished.
Gogs hart, what meanes might I make my life to pre-
    serve?
Is there nought to be my helpe? nor is there nought to
    serve?
Out upon the court, and lords that there remaine!

                          (ll. 1159–63)

This wilful king, ruthless when he has the power to be so,
furious when crossed, and nearly out of his mind when finally
overcome, is reminiscent of several stage figures. Distantly he
recalls the *miles gloriosus* of Roman comedy, whose great boasts
lead inevitably to discomfiture, but the tone is entirely different
there, the threat never serious, and the final frustration purely
ludicrous.

    The Senecan tyrant is a much closer analogue. Lycus in *Hercules
Furens*, Atreus in *Thyestes*, Eteocles in *Phoenissae* and Nero in
Octavia[19] all dream of absolute power, rage at everyone who
opposes them, and act with utter ruthlessness. Wolfgang Clemen
shows how Seneca's example helped the rhetoric-conscious English
playwrights to compose set speeches expressing the intense
emotions of their characters.[20] The formality of Senecan rhetoric
was especially appealing, and certainly influenced many writers
(even such as the author of *Clyomon and Clamydes*) who were not

directly imitating Senecan tragedy. To some extent, then, Seneca's tyrants may have been models for Cambises. Even in Elizabethan translations, however, the speeches in which the tyrants assert their royal prerogatives have a different ring from those of Cambises. Rebuffed by Megara, Lycus says:

> Goe to, these fierce and furious wordes thou woman mad refraine,
> And imperyes of princes learne of Hercles to sustayne.
> Though I the scepters gotten by the force of war do beare,
> In conquering hand and all do rule without the law his feare.[21]

In *Thyestes* Atreus answers the objections of an attendant:

> *Ser[vant].* Doth fame of people naught
> Adverse thee feare? *Atre[us].* The greatest good of king-dom may be thought
> That still the people are constraynd their princes deedes as well
> To prayse, as them to suffer all. . . .
> *Ser.* Let first the king will honest thinges and none the same dare nill.
> *Atre.* Where leeful are to him that rules but honest thinges alone,
> There raynes the kyng by others leave.
>
> (ll. 205–8, 213–15; I, 62)

Finally, Nero in the *Octavia* resists the pleas of Seneca:

> *Se[neca].* A soveraigne salve for feare is for to beare
> Your selfe debonair to your subjectes all.
> *Ne[ro].* Our foes to slea, a cheftaynes vertue call. . . .
> *Se.* That heavenly powers your doinges may allow.
> *Ne.* A madnes 'twere to Gods for me to bow,
> When I my selfe can make such Gods to be:
> As Claudius now ycounted is we see.
>
> (ll. 442–3, 448–9; II, 166)

Though the fourteeners of Jasper Heywood and the pentameters of Thomas Nuce are far from capturing the terseness of Seneca's style,[22] there is more definition than rage in these passages.

In some scenes Nero gives way to a more unbuttoned rhetoric, as when he contemplates punishing Rome for its resistance:

> Then shall their houses fall by force of fyre:
> What burning both, and buildings fayre decay,
> What beggerly want, and wayling hunger may
> Those villaines shal be sure to have ech day.
>
> (ll. 831–3; II, 184)

However, a closer approximation to Cambises' exclamatory style may be found in John Studley's translation of *Hercules Oetaeus*, where the hero boasts of his conquests and demands his reward from Jove:

> Thwack not about with thunder thumpes, the rebell kinges bee downe,
> The ravening tyrauntes Scepterlesse, are pulled from their crowne:
> By mee all daunted is whereon, thy boults thou shouldst bestowe.
> And yet O Father, yet the Heavens are still withhelde mee froe . . .
>
> (ll. 5–8; II, 193)

This is indeed 'Ercles' vein', as Bottom says.[23] An actor in Robert Greene's *Groatsworth of Wit* (1592) says 'The twelue labors of *Hercules* haue I terribly thundred on the stage',[24] and though we do not know what play is referred to, one sure inference is that Hercules had become a familiar ranting character. A 'thundering style' was admired in non-dramatic poetry of this period too[25]—sometimes, as in Golding's translation of Ovid, where one would least expect it. On the stage it was apparently associated with the heroic but also with the role of the tyrant, for Bottom, after reciting the lines which he describes as 'Ercles' vein' (lines quite similar to parts of Studley's translation of *Hercules Oetaeus*), goes on to say 'a tyrant's vein', though Hercules was the arch-slayer of tyrants. That a similar style was assigned to heroes and tyrants suggests that stage tyrants like Cambises, however overtly deplored and brought to fitting punishment, might nevertheless be objects of admiration. They seem to have become increasingly so as the point of view of the plays moved away from that of the moralities.

The rages of Cambises and his ilk, however, owe their tone if not their form to the Herod of the mysteries even more than to Seneca.[26] Chaucer's Miller tells us of the clerk Absolon:

> Sometime to shewe his lightnesse and maistrye,
> He playeth Herodes upon a scaffold hye.[27]

And no wonder; for this was 'a part to tear a cat in', to quote Bottom once more. In the Coventry *Shearmen and Taylors' Pageant* of the Magi, Herod and the Slaughter of the Innocents, Herod boasts that he is

> . . . the myghttyst conquerowre that eyuer
> walkid on growved;
> For I am evyn he thatt made bothe hevin and hell,
> And of my myghte powar holdith vp this world rownd.[28]

Hypocritically polite when he first greets the three kings, he becomes apoplectic with rage when he discovers that they have eluded his snare:

> Hath those fawls traytvrs done me this ded?
> I stampe! I stare! I loke all abowtt!
> Myght I them take, I schuld them bren at a glede!
> I rent! I rawe! and now run I wode!
> A! thatt these velen trayturs hath mard this my mode!
> The schalbe hangid yf I ma cum them to!
> > *Here Erode ragis in the pagond and in the strete also.*
> > (p. 27)

The stage direction indicates what an Absolon might do 'to shewe his lightnesse and maistyre'. In the Digby *Mary Magdalene* Herod is already in a rage at his first appearance, swearing by Mahomet, like many other pagans in these plays:

> In the wyld wanyng wor[l]d, pes all at onys!
> No noyse, I warne yow, for greveyng of me!
> Yff yow do, I xal hovrle of yower hedes, be Mahondes bones,
> As I am trew kyng to Mahond so fre.[29]

That this flashy character was proverbial for his rant[30] is well known from Hamlet's advice to the players. Though his ambitions were less vast than those of the Senecan tyrant, his rant, innocent of aphorism and pointed argument, was more emotional and fluent. It was the verve and the copiousness of Herod's intemperate rages which seem to have influenced Preston.

In the learned tradition which existed side by side with the popular tradition, Thomas Hughes, writing for the lawyers of Gray's Inn, fashioned a tragedy out of the 'matter of Britain', called *The Misfortunes of Arthur* (1588). In this most Senecan of all Senecan imitations, where romantic narrative is brought to a classical standstill, the villain Mordred is Lycus, Atreus, Eteocles and Nero rolled into one[31] and a surprising number of lines are transported bodily from several of Seneca's plays. It is difficult to say how important such academic experiments were in the development of the style of later ranters,[32] but in general the plays which owed most to the native mysteries and moralities had a greater influence on the major Elizabethan dramatists.[33]

During the years 1587–93 the stage was conquered by a warrior-hero who was in at least one respect a direct descendant of Herod and Cambises: like them, and like the Ercles Bottom knew, he threatened terribly, but with an eloquence far beyond their reach and at the same time utterly different from that of the Senecan tyrant in either Latin or English. His passionate outbursts were expressions of his will to achieve something beyond revenge and also beyond tyrannical power over his subordinates. In most cases he was not, strictly speaking, a tyrant. The virtuosity of the old ranters was being adapted to a different enterprise.

The exact dates of the plays in which this new figure appeared are unknown, as are the authors of several of them. Even the best and most famous of them, *Tamburlaine*, of which Part I was probably performed in 1587, was published anonymously, though Marlowe's authorship was hinted as early as 1588[34] and is now unquestioned. Robert Greene may have been the author of *Locrine*, *Alphonsus of Aragon* and *Selimus*, which may have been written in that order and may all have followed *Tamburlaine*, but not one of these possibilities has been proved. What can be said without fear of contradiction is that *Tamburlaine* is incomparably superior to the others, and since each of them resembles it in some respect, it is at least reasonable to suppose that they followed it.[35] For this reason, and because it will be a relief to come to a dramatic masterpiece after so many feeble precursors, I shall deal first with *Tamburlaine*.

The often-quoted prologue points to the most striking novelty
of the play—Marlowe's resonant poetry:

> *From iygging vaines of riming mother wits,*
> *And such conceits as clownage keepes in pay,*
> *Weele lead you to the stately tent of War,*
> *Where you shall heare the Scythian* Tamburlaine
> *Threatening the world with high astounding tearms*
> *And scourging kingdoms with his conquering sword.*
> *View but his picture in this tragicke glasse,*
> *And then applaud his fortunes as you please.*[36]

Anyone who comes to *Tamburlaine* from *Clyomon and Clamydes* or
Cambises will require no demonstration that Tamburlaine's 'high
astounding tearms' represent a significant advance. He will also
see that a world-threatening speaker is held out to the audience
as an attraction. In other words, the popular formula is not being
abandoned but improved.

In the opening lines of the play the foolish king of Persia,
Mycetes, says:

> Brother *Cosroe*, I find my selfe agreeu'd,
> Yet insufficient to expresse the same:
> For it requires a great and thundring speech: . . .
>
> (ll. 1–3)

and Tamburlaine, true to the promise of the Prologue, delivers
just such a speech at his first confrontation with the emissaries of
Mycetes. To Theridamus he says:

> Forsake thy king and do but ioine with me
> And we will triumph ouer all the world.
> I hold the Fates bound fast in yron chaines,
> And with my hand turne Fortunes wheel about,
> And sooner shall the Sun fall from his Spheare,
> Than *Tamburlaine* be slaine or ouercome.
> Draw foorth thy sword, thou mighty man at Armes,
> Intending but to rase my charmed skin:
> And *Ioue* himselfe will stretch his hand from heauen,
> To ward the blow, and shield me safe from harme.

* * *

Ioine with me now in this my meane estate,
(I cal it meane, because being yet obscure,
The Nations far remoou'd admyre me not)
And when my name and honour shall be spread,
As far as *Boreas* claps his brazen wings,
Or faire *Bootes* sends his cheerefull light,
Then shalt thou be Competitor with me,
And sit with *Tamburlaine* in all his maiestie.

(I, 2, 367–76, 397–404)

The forty-five-line speech from which these excerpts are taken is a beautifully constructed piece of persuasive oratory, in which each component section, such as the famous lines about fate, contributes to the total effect and leads to the vision of '*Tamburlaine* in all his maiestie'. It is an aria for which each audience after the first must have waited, and which is as worthy of applause at the end as many an aria in Italian opera. Some of the tricks of earlier versifiers are there, such as alliteration, though it is not allowed to run riot. There is no thwacking about with thunder thumps. The rhythms are insistent but controlled and varied by the adroit use of inversions, enjambments and parenthetical clauses, to cite only a few of Marlowe's devices. Thus the rhetorical divisions of the speech are wrought into verse paragraphs, each with its own climactic point, and the successive paragraphs are composed to form the larger rhythm of the whole oration. The hyperbolic boasting for which Marlowe became famous contributes to the impression of epic grandeur, and characterizes Tamburlaine as the perfect example of the 'over-reacher'.[37]

This threatener of the world, who is no tyrant—he is, in fact, the special enemy of tyrants—is, in the final analysis, less like Cambises, whom he resembles only superficially, than like Hercules, of whom he reminds Theridamus—and not the debased Ercles of popular tradition but his glorious original. I have proposed elsewhere that the legendary hero, especially as he appears in Greek and Roman tragedy, is an illuminating analogue to the protagonists of several English plays, including this one.[38] Hercules is the epitome of valour and courage, his ambitions are the greatest imaginable, and he is admirable without being altogether good. To the extent that characters such as Tamburlaine share these characteristics they may be called Herculean, and may elicit a similar response.

There can be no question, however, of Marlowe's imitating the form of the classical Hercules tragedies, conscious as he was of his hero's Herculean traits. The structure of *Tamburlaine*, as David Bevington has demonstrated,[39] is rooted firmly in the popular plays designed for acting by small bands of travelling players. By the 1580s some of these groups had settled in London, had permanent theatres, and had increased in size, but the old structural pattern was still useful. It had already proved effective in narrative dramas with a romantic base, such as *Clyomon and Clamydes*, or those with a historic base such as *Cambises*, and was ideally suited to chronicle the successive conquests of the Scythian shepherd. Each major episode introduces new characters and a new locale, and thus contributes to the impression of spaciousness which *Tamburlaine* gives so forcibly.

One cannot discuss the structure of this play without mentioning an unusual feature—that it is in two parts.[40] It is unlikely that this was the original plan, for the Prologue to Part II states clearly that the success of Part I encouraged the poet to write a continuation. So we have two structures to consider: a self-contained five-act play and a ten-act play to be performed on successive days. Everyone who has commented on the structure of Part I has been struck by the relative lack of complication—the progression from victory to victory until at Damascus Tamburlaine, after conquering the city, makes peace with the Soldan and marries his daughter Zenocrate. The ending is what one might expect in a romance or in such a history as that of Henry V. Part II is more tragic in that it ends with the death of the hero, preceded by his bitter grief at the death of Zenocrate and his murder of the son who refuses to follow in his martial footsteps. Despite the darker colouration of this part, however, Tamburlaine is always triumphant in battle, and the play ends on a note of transcendence as the hero contemplates the 'higher throne' with which the gods mean to invest him. As the reins of Tamburlaine's conquering chariot are handed to Amyras, the hero speaks of perpetuating himself in his sons, who may complete the conquests he has begun. The myth of Hercules' immortality as a star (alluded to at IV, 3, 4039–40) reinforces the final emphasis on continued movement towards the ideal rather than on arrest and defeat. Though the two parts differ considerably, the end of the second part, like that of the first, is the opening of a new era, a wider horizon.[41]

It is obvious that the conqueror who captures and later marries a princess betrothed to another king and refuses ransom for a defeated emperor, whom he keeps in a cage and uses as a footstool, is somewhat deficient in the courtesy expected of a knight. In fact, Tamburlaine's outrageous and often immoral behaviour, commented on throughout the two plays, is so remote in most respects from the chivalric ideal that it is surprising to find certain similarities between him and the heroes of chivalry. His unexcelled prowess is not a special bond with the knights of romance and the *chansons de geste*, since it is also the characteristic of the heroes of epic and myth. It serves, however, to distinguish him from tyrants like Herod, who accomplish less than they threaten to do. It is Tamburlaine's enemies who are cast in the roles of ineffectual blusterers—Bajazeth in Part I and the 'knot of kings' in Part II, who engage the hero in slanging matches reminiscent of the boasts in classical epic and the flyting in medieval epic and romance. Tamburlaine invariably proves himself their superior in both word and deed.

A trait which links him more closely to the tradition described in the first chapter is his liberality. It is demonstrated in a scene of great theatrical power which is a symbolic node for Part I— the banquet celebrating Tamburlaine's victory over Bajazeth (IV, 4). Not only the hero's liberality but his cruelty, his love for Zenocrate and his unswerving ambition are all presented as inseparable parts of his heroic personality. The initial stage direction sketches very briefly the spectacular opening: '*The Banquet, and to it commeth Tamburlain al in scarlet, Theridamas, Techelles, Vsumcasane,* the Turke, with others.' The banquet table with the first course on it is brought in and placed, centrally no doubt, on the large projecting stage. Then from one of the doors at the back of the stage Tamburlaine enters, followed by his faithful lieutenants and others, including Zenocrate. Behind them, as they walk in solemn procession to their places, the defeated emperor is drawn in a cage, followed by his empress. The red of Tamburlaine's robes symbolizes his wrath, and as he enters he orders 'bloody collours' to be hung outside the walls of Damascus, which his army is now besieging. We have been told that on the first day of a siege he displays white for clemency, the second day red to warn that the besieged leaders will be put to death for resisting, and the third day black to show that everyone will be killed. Against the background of the ominous second phase of the current military operations, then, we witness the celebration of the previous victory and the cruel spectacle of the humiliation of Bajazeth. Marlowe, as Douglas Cole remarks, 'has brought upon the stage, in a spectacular and sensational way, the fall of an emperor; and he has integrated that fall with the main line of action, the indomitable rise of Tamburlaine'.[42] The medieval conception of tragedy as the fall of a great man is incorporated in the stage image of cage, banquet and blood-red robes.

The first action of the scene consists in the crude humour of urging Bajazeth to eat his own flesh or his wife's while Tamburlaine's guests dine royally a few feet away. Then the fallen emperor is forced to take meat from the point of Tamburlaine's sword. Bajazeth's refusal of food and drink, his curses, his Herodian rages are all 'a goodly showe at a banquet', as Tamburlaine observes to Zenocrate. Surprisingly, she agrees.

The theme of ambition is introduced when the conqueror turns to address his lady. Noticing that she is sad, he asks what makes her so. She begs him to raise the siege of Damascus and make a truce with her father, the Soldan of Egypt, who is in command. Despite his love for her, Tamburlaine immediately refuses, but the refusal is far from routine:

> *Zenocrate*, were Egypt *Ioues* owne land,
> Yet would I with my sword make *Ioue* to stoope.
> I will confute those blind Geographers
> That make a triple region in the world,
> Excluding Regions which I mean to trace,
> And with this pen reduce them to a Map,
> Calling the Prouinces, Cities and townes
> After my name and thine *Zenocrate*:
> Here at *Damascus* will I make the Point
> That shall begin the Perpendicular.
> And wouldst thou haue me buy thy Fathers loue
> With such a losse? Tell the *Zenuerate*?
> *Zen.* Honor still waight on happy *Tamburlaine*: ...

> (IV, 4, 1713–25)

The importance of Damascus in the scheme of conquest is presented in the striking image of the sword-pen, visible in the hero's hand, and the world map, whose geometry is in his mind, actualized at present only in his words. As he speaks, the gross cruelty being meted out to Bajazeth and the imminent cruelty to the inhabitants of Damascus are metamorphosed in a bewildering way into a beautiful design to be imposed by art upon the resistant material of the earth. Zenocrate agrees that the perpendicular upon this point—the honour of Tamburlaine—must not be lost, and she begs only for her father's life, which is granted.

No sooner is this brief and strange flight into the realm of the ideal completed than the taunting of Bajazeth begins again, focusing attention on the animal necessity of feeding. But now the contrast between the man in the cage and the company at the banquet table is heightened by another piece of business: '*Enter a second course of Crownes.*' It is impossible to be sure what this direction means. The second course at an Elizabethan dinner was the main one, and we know that on state occasions food was sometimes served in ornamental shapes. In the ensuing dialogue the crowns are first referred to as 'cates' and as food for kings, which suggests that they are edible. A moment later, however, Tamburlaine actually crowns his three lieutenants as kings of Argier, Fez and Morocco, the former kingdoms of Bajazeth's vassals. No doubt the actual crowns taken from these kings are borne in, and in the dialogue they could be referred to as food, but they would hardly constitute the 'second course' of the stage direction, where no metaphors are to be expected. It seems quite possible that the gold crowns are brought to Tamburlaine and food in the shape of crowns set on the table before the guests. Such a piece of business would strengthen what is in any case the main impression given by the succeeding lines, that Tamburlaine dispenses with regal largesse the rewards of valour, which are, to the valorous, the most coveted food.

> *Theridamas*, *Techelles* and *Casane*. Here are the cates you
> desire to finger, are they not?

(ll. 1747–8)

Again the material and the immaterial are fused in a symbolic gesture. The tokens of royalty are related to the map of conquest when Tamburlaine reminds the new kings that they

> . . . marcht with happy *Tamburlaine*,
> As far as from the frozen place of heauen,
> Vnto the watry mornings ruddy bower,
> And thence by land vnto the Torrid Zone, . . .
>
> (ll. 1762–5)

The vastness of the enterprise is ultimately an expression of the vastness of the conquering mind—not only the mind of Tamburlaine, manifested in his plans and in his princely giving of crowns, but also the minds of his subordinates, whom he urges to deserve their good fortune 'By valour and by magnanimity' (l. 1767). As in the romances, largesse and greatmindedness are not wholly separable. Here this most desirable trait is juxtaposed with others which, taken by themselves, would be thoroughly despicable.

The largesse of this scene is prepared for by descriptions early in the play, stressing physical and spiritual greatness. Before Tamburlaine delivers his first 'thundring speech', Theridamas sees him as Hercules:

> His looks do menace heauen and dare the Gods,
> His fierie eies are fixt vpon the earth,
> As if he now deuis'd some Stratageme:
> Or meant to pierce *Auernas* darksome vaults,
> To pull the triple headed dog from hell.
>
> (I, 2, 353–6)

And at the opening of Act II Menaphon compares him to Atlas and Achilles in an elaborate verbal portrait: 'Of stature tall, and straightly fashioned,/Like his desire', his head a pearl, his eyes stars, his amber hair dancing 'with wanton maiestie', his arms, and fingers 'Betokening valour and excesse of strength' (II, 1 460–84). As Tamburlaine's persuasive oration to Theridamas confirms the heroic dimensions of Theridamas' description, so Menaphon's description is confirmed later in Act II by two well-known speeches:

> Is it not passing braue to be a King,
> And ride in triumph through *Persepolis*?
>
> (II, 5, 758–9)

and:

55

The thirst of raigne and sweetnes of a crown,
That causde the eldest sonne of heauenly *Ops*;
To thrust his doting father from his chaire,
And place himself in the Emperiall heauen,
Moou'd me to manage armes against thy state.
What better president than mightie *Ioue*?
Nature that fram'd vs of foure Elements,
Warring within our breasts for regiment,
Doth teach vs all to haue aspyring minds:
Our soules, whose faculties can comprehend
The wondrous Architecture of the world:
And measure euery wandring plannets course,
Still climing after knowledge infinite,
And alwaies moouing as the restless Spheares,
Wils vs to weare our selues and neuer rest,
Vntill we reach the ripest fruit of all,
That perfect blisse and sole felicite,
The sweet fruition of an earthly crowne.

(II, 6, 863–80)

The earthly crown does not limit Tamburlaine's aspirations in the way some critics have supposed. As the rest of the play shows, it is not one crown he wants but all crowns, and in the final analysis not specific kingdoms but the abstraction, 'raigne', or rulership, of which a crown is the symbol. The longing for an infinite series of conquests leading to the essence of rulership—this aspiration is the measure of his magnanimity.[43]

Our first view of Tamburlaine suggests another dimension of his character included briefly in the banquet scene—his love for Zenocrate. At its first appearance the love theme dominates the scene, as it might in romance. Tamburlaine, dressed as a Scythian shepherd, comes on stage with Zenocrate and her train, whom he has just captured with the aid of his henchmen. His heroic self-confidence is already complete, his plans for world conquest at the tip of his tongue, and before our eyes he strips off his shepherd's weeds and dons complete armour. His immediate object, however, is to impress Zenocrate, to whom he addresses a splendid speech, filled with the promises of a romantic lover who knows he can in fact present the treasures of all the world to his beloved. He does not prostrate himself at her feet or promise to gratify her every whim, but chivalric romance does not require all lovers to behave like Lancelot, and a great many of them do not. Tamburlaine offers Zenocrate a dazzling prospect of the icy mountains they will scale and of the martial prizes he will give her with himself. The speech combines the aspirations of warrior and lover, but for the moment gives priority to love.[44]

The love theme recurs intermittently in Part I amidst the din of conquest. In one scene (III, 2) Zenocrate professes her love for Tamburlaine to Agydas, one of the lords captured with her, as Tamburlaine enters and listens. Then '*Tamburlaine goes to her, & takes her away louingly by the hand, looking wrathfully on Agidas, and sayes nothing*'. Later Zenocrate shows her devotion by trading mouth-filling insults with the Turkish empress ('Disdainful Turkesse and vnreuerend Bosse . . .' III, 3, 1266 ff.), and by encouraging the further punishment of the Turks (IV, 2 and 4).

While these moments remind us briefly of the love of Tamburlaine and Zenocrate, it is the long final scene of Part I which provides the major definitive statements of the feelings of the two protagonists. The place of love in the hero's life is fixed by an action at the opening of the scene and by a long speech which follows. The action is the denial of mercy to the virgins of Damascus, who come too late, when the black colours are already flying, to plead for the city. The scheme of conquest, complete with its rules set forth in contrasting colours, must not be altered; for Tamburlaine's honour resides in its perfect geometry:

> I will not spare these proud Egyptians,
> Nor change my Martiall obseruations,
> For all the wealth of Gehons golden waues,
> Or for the loue of *Venus*, would she leaue
> The angrie God of Armes, and lie with me.
> They haue refusde the offer of their liues,
> And know my customes are as peremptory
> As wrathfull Planets, death, or destinie.
>
> (V, 2, 1902–9)

Not even love can make him bend.

His moving eulogy of Zenocrate, which follows almost immediately, must be seen in the context of this refusal, and indeed it fits perfectly. Tamburlaine admits that Zenocrate's pleas for Damascus and the Soldan have tempted him, and he then moves

with a logic which at first is not clear to a discussion of the beauty
which is beyond the descriptive power of the greatest poets. The
famous lines,

> Yet should ther houer in their restlesse heads,
> One thought, one grace, one woonder at the least,
> Which into words no vertue can digest: . . .
>
> (ll. 1952–4)

express a poetic and erotic aspiration which is exactly analogous to
Tamburlaine's martial aspiration. Their bearing on the problem
of Zenocrate's intercession appears in the remaining lines of the
speech, which present the relationship between the claims of
beauty and valour. Though the difficult syntax, possibly due to
textual corruption, obscures some details,[45] it is clear in general
that Tamburlaine, after reproaching himself for setting so much
store by beauty, makes the important concession that beauty is a
necessary stimulus to valour:

> . . . euery warrior that is rapt with loue,
> Of fame, of valour, and of victory
> Must needs haue beauty beat on his conceites, . . .
>
> (ll. 1961–3)

and finally vows, though aware of the power of beauty, which has
sidetracked even the gods, to keep on towards his goal, and show

> That Vertue solely is the sum of glorie,
> And fashions men with true nobility.
>
> (ll. 1970–1)

'Vertue' here is to be understood as *virtù*, the equivalent in Italian
Renaissance writing of *areté* or *virtus*—something not far removed
from 'prouesse'. If Tamburlaine is saying that beauty, and by
implication love, is to be subordinated to heroic achievement, he
is not departing much from what Erec or Yvain or Gawain might
have said. In those romances there is a danger in undervaluing
love as in overvaluing it, and such a danger is present at this
point in Marlowe's play. Tamburlaine is never more humanly
alive than in this long speech where, for once, he admits to a
momentary doubt and speaks so eloquently of his response
to Zenocrate's beauty. When he reproaches himself for such
sensitivity and returns to the logic of his campaign for glory, this

dominant ideal seems even more inhuman than when he condemned the virgins to death, for he has shown what he is sup-
pressing.

Zenocrate's love for Tamburlaine, as shown later in this scene,
is undiminished by her horror at the death of the virgins of
Damascus and the suicides of the Turkish emperor and empress.
Even the continuing battle against her father does not embitter
her against Tamburlaine, but only brings her to pray for a
'gentle victorie' and a 'league of honour'. Though Tamburlaine's
concession to her of the Soldan's life may seem minimal, the fact
remains that it is a concession which permits Part I—the entire
original play—to end on a note of reconciliation. Tamburlaine
crowns Zenocrate, proclaims a 'truce with al the world', and plans
for his marriage.[46]

The love theme is carried over to Part II with a difference.
Marlowe had largely exhausted his historic materials in Part I,
and therefore, as numerous commentators have pointed out,[47]
when he decided to write a continuation, was obliged to rely more
heavily on his invention and on episodes drawn from a variety of
sources. In general he followed the successful model of Part I,
devising new conquests to match those of Persia, the Turkish
empire, and Damascus. He was even freer than before, however, to
develop the play thematically. The conflict between love and
prowess as seen in Tamburlaine's long soliloquy and in the surrounding action of the ending of Part I provided him with a
major theme.

Zenocrate appears for the first time in Act I, Scene 4, asking
Tamburlaine when he will give up war; for of course his 'truce
with al the world' has ended, and he is once more in hot pursuit
of earthly crowns. His answer is that he will stop 'When heauen
shal cease to mooue on both the poles' (l. 2581). 'Alwaies moouing
as the restles Spheares', we recall from Part I. Endless movement
towards an ever-receding horizon is Tamburlaine's destiny, which
up to now he accepts with joy. A moment later he observes with
displeasure that his young sons look more 'amorous' than 'mar-
tiall', but Zenocrate assures him that their hearts are like his even
if they have 'their mothers looks'. Two of them, Celebinus and
Amyras, assure him that they wish to be world conquerors, but
Calyphas, the eldest, absurdly asks to stay with his mother and
let his brothers help Tamburlaine with the world. Tamburlaine is

not amused: only the courageous, the wrathful and the cruel may inherit from him (ll. 2638–53).

This scene is the beginning of what would now be called a 'black comedy' which stretches over three scenes and ends with the murder of Calyphas in Act IV, Scene 1. In all of these scenes the boy is so effeminate, trivial and self-indulgent that until the last horrible moment he is more a figure of fun than an object of compassion. At the same time he is Tamburlaine's son, the product of his love for Zenocrate, and more like Zenocrate than either of his brothers. Looked at genetically, psychologically or allegorically, Calyphas seems to represent that part of Tamburlaine which is most attracted to Zenocrate, and which made him, if only for a moment, hesitate before the walls of Damascus.

Before the terrible comedy of Tamburlaine's rage at Calyphas is played out, the hero receives in the death of Zenocrate what all readers of the play have seen as his first blow. Though he has carefully limited the role she is to play in his life, his love for her and even need of her is very great. Hence her illness prompts another impassioned statement of his love (II, 3, 2969–3005), and her death an outburst which Cole properly qualifies as 'Herodian', though he goes on to say that 'there is much more involved here than out-Heroding Herod'.[48] In the extremity of his grief he threatens to 'wound the earth' and 'breake the frame of heauen' (ll. 3065, 3072). He has often spoken of himself as an instrument of divine vengeance, 'the scourge of God', and sometimes as the equal of the gods; now that Zenocrate's death has deprived him of an outlet for the most warmly human of his emotions, he is left with his superhuman aspirations, his will to power and the closely related passion for abstraction, which makes him see world conquest as a map redrawn by his sword. This strange passion is also manifested in his determination to preserve the body of Zenocrate, embalmed and encased in gold,—transformed into an art-object—Tamburlaine's Zenocrate, who may continue to accompany him on his conquests. The town where she died is burnt to the ground, and in its place are put an inscribed pillar, a 'streamer' with her arms, a tablet recording her virtues, and her picture, all ceremoniously set up on the stage as the gold-sheathed body is drawn past the burning town (III, 2, 3191–232).

This striking piece of symbolic action is followed by another in the same scene. Tamburlaine, infuriated by another display of cowardice by Calyphas, cuts his own arm to show that 'Blood is the God of Wars rich liuery' (l. 3306). He then compares the wound to a regal robe in which he might sit upon a jewelled throne. Again violence is bracketed with art, and both are manifestations of Tamburlaine's will. In this case, however, the cruelty is self-inflicted, the power of the will imposed upon the self. It is not fanciful to see here a suggestion of the self-destruction that accompanies Tamburlaine's increasing contempt for everything human.

The killing of Calyphas may be seen as the final extirpation of whatever in Tamburlaine's nature Zenocrate had tempted him to display. With shame he recognizes in his effeminate son something of himself, but something unworthy to be Tamburlaine. As he stabs the boy in front of his other sons, his army and the kings he has just defeated, he says:

> Here, *Ioue*, receiue his fainting soule againe,
> A forme not meet to giue that subiect essence,
> Whose matter is the flesh of *Tamburlain*,
> Wherein an incorporeall spirit mooues,
> Made of the mould whereof thy self consists,
> Which makes me valiant, proud, ambitious,
> Ready to leuie power against thy throne,
> That I might mooue the turning Spheares of heauen,
> For earth and al this aery region
> Cannot containe the state of *Tamburlaine*.
>
> (IV, 1, 3785–94)

With these words he turns his back on humanity and commits himself to the most grandiose of his ideals, prompted by what he takes to be his 'incorporeall spirit'. The suggestion of self-destruction is even stronger here than before, and combined with the reassertion of his 'thirst of raigne', it presents a stern paradox: death is a precondition to success.

Immediately after this scene comes the dénouement of a subplot in which Theridamas has attempted to win or force the affections of Olympia, the widow of an enemy captain fatally wounded in battle. Before her capture she has seen her husband die, has killed her son to save him from torture and humiliation and has longed for her own death. Now, to defend herself from Theridamus, she tricks him into killing her. The juxtaposition of these scenes with Tamburlaine's murder of his son is brilliantly theat-rical.[49] 'Look here upon this picture and on this.' In one the murder of a child out of love, in the other out of disgust; in one self-destruction out of loyalty to a past love, in the other a gesture of loveless self-assertion which is also self-destroying. The Olympia episode, derived from *Orlando Furioso*, is based on purely romantic ideals. In the scene from the main plot the ideals of romance have been perverted and transformed:

> Villaines, these terrours and these tyrannies
> (If tyrannies wars iustice ye repute)
> I execute, enioin'd me from aboue:
> To scourge the pride of such as heauen abhors,
> Nor am I made Arch-monark of the world,
> Crown'd and inuested by the hand of *Ioue*
> For deeds of bounty or nobility:
> But since I exercise a greater name,
> The Scourge of God and terrour of the world,
> I must apply myselfe to fit those tearmes,
> In war, in blood, in death, in crueltie, . . .
>
> (ll. 3820–30)

The scene following Olympia's death is the climactic scene of Part II, corresponding exactly to the banquet scene of Part I. It is the scene that everyone remembered: captive kings 'with bittes in their mouthes' draw Tamburlaine in his chariot, as he shouts:

> Holla, ye pampered Iades of *Asia*:
> What, can ye draw but twenty miles a day,
> And haue so proud a chariot at your heeles,
> And such a Coachman as great *Tamburlaine*?
>
> (IV, 3, 3980–3)

The king-drawn chariot is an even more effective image than those of the banquet table and cage, for the reins and the whip in Tamburlaine's hands relate his dreams of conquest to his concept of himself as the scourge of God and to his ideal of imposing perfect order on the world. In fact, the image is appropriate in so many ways that, though its full power could be felt only in the theatre, no single performance could exhaust its meaning. If, on the one hand, it seems to say that despite the increasingly destructive and self-destructive manifestations of the hero's nature, his ambitions have largely been achieved, it suggests, on the other hand, by being in motion, that Tamburlaine 'never is but always to be blest'. Tamburlaine himself envisions riding in his chariot until his soul, 'disseuered from this flesh,/Shall mount the milk-white way . . .' (ll. 4110–11). There is no fulfilment in this world.

The final blow for Tamburlaine, after the death of Zenocrate and the unheroic behaviour of Calyphas, is his own mortality. Though death is not presented here, as in *Cambises*, as retribution for misdeeds,[50] it imposes a limitation which Tamburlaine has never accepted. After a brief but stormy defiance of death he acquiesces even to the point of seeming to will it as a release for his 'fiery spirit' (V, 3, 4562). He dies surrounded by the most potent symbols of his aspiration—a map showing yet unconquered kingdoms, the coffin containing gold-shrouded Zenocrate, and the chariot, in which he has seated his son Amyras, bestowing on him his crown and scourge. Everything that we see and hear in this scene contributes to a powerful impression of pathos and yet allows us to think, if we will, that the fierce spirit has not yet been extinguished. The questions the play has raised about the pursuit of power and beauty, about self-assertion and self-destruction, about cruelty and idealism, are now subordinated to wonder that such greatness could have been in a man:

> Let earth and heauen his timeless death deplore,
> For both their woorths wil equall him no more.
>
> (V, 3, 4645–6)

The prominence given to this impression, not only at the end but throughout both parts, is what makes *Tamburlaine* the first important heroic drama. It is in some ways a model for the heroic plays which follow it, but like all great works of art, it is not typical of anything. No other heroic play is really like it. Its importance is to have given powerful artistic expression to the themes with which all heroic plays must deal.

A number of the hero's characteristics are closely related to the tradition of chivalric romance, and yet Tamburlaine is as unlike the knight in shining armour as it is possible to be. In some ways he resembles the tyrants in Cambises' line, and in many ways the classical Hercules, but it would be foolishly culinary to speak of combinations of all of these, as if Marlowe had made him according to a recipe. The exact genesis of such a creation must always remain a mystery. The significance of the connections with romance is that they establish for the historian the origins of the characteristics most directly responsible for the impression Tamburlaine makes. The romance took over from epic a concern with the wonder of human potentiality, expressing it in the extraordinary adventures of its heroes and in their attempts to live up to the ideals discussed in the first chapter. Even though some of Tamburlaine's ideals are very different from these, his endless striving to attain them is typical of the romance hero. As he contemplates the world map he says:

> And from the Antartique Pole, Eastward behold
> As much more land, which neuer was descried,
> Wherein are rockes of Pearle, that shine as bright
> As all the Lamps that beautifie the Sky,
> And shal I die, and this vnconquered?
>
> (V, 3, 4547–51)

Such longings are the stuff of romance.

Ethel Seaton once asked what Marlowe read in his off-time— that is, when he was not reading the classics, to which he gives us constant allusions throughout his works. Her answer was, romances, and she cited a number of passages in *Tamburlaine* and other plays to prove her contention.[51] The shape of *Tamburlaine*, she thought, was that of the 'old bottle' of medieval romance, even if it held 'the new wine of Renaissance thought' (p. 35). This is well said. With a shift of metaphor one might add that it was undoubtedly difficult for Marlowe and his contemporaries, all of whom seem to have indulged in similar light reading, to see the epic tradition uncoloured by medieval romance. This colouration adheres to heroic drama.

The three plays mentioned earlier as closely associated with each other and with *Tamburlaine* share many characteristics with Marlowe's play. *Locrine*, which may be the earliest of them, is interesting as a combination of elements of the popular dramatic tradition with elements of that more learned tradition of 'classical plays' written for the Inns of Court, such as *Gorboduc* (1562), *Jocasta* (1566) and the previously discussed *Misfortunes of Arthur* (1588).[52] Like the last-named play, *Locrine* is based on legendary British history, and like all of them it depends heavily on set speeches, has certain Senecan features and introduces each act with an emblematic dumb show.[53] Unlike the classical plays, *Locrine* has a low-comic subplot and a good deal of action, including several battles. The sons of Brutus, the legendary Trojan founder of Britain, are fighting the Scythians (or Huns, as they are variously called), led by Humber and his son Hubba. Though Locrine is king, his youngest brother, Albanact, is the hero of the first two acts, called by his father 'A perfect patterne of all chiualrie' (I, 1, 206).[54] Here is a description of the enemy by one of the Britons:

> There might we see the valiant minded knights
> Fetching careers along the spatious plaines.
> *Humber* and *Hubba* arm'd in azure blew,
> Mounted vpon their coursers white as snow, . . .
>
> (II, 3, 27–30)

There is no doubt that we are in the world of chivalric romance. Sometimes the language is very similar to that of *Tamburlaine*, as when Humber says:

> But I will frustrate all their foolish hope,
> And teach them that the *Scithian* Emperour
> Leades fortune tied in a chaine of gold,
> Constraining her to yeeld vnto his will
> And grace him with their regall diademe,
> Which I will haue maugre their treble hoasts,
> And all the power their pettie kings can make.
>
> (II, 1, 13–19)

His description of the British hero might easily be assigned to *Tamburlaine*:

> How brauely this yoong Brittain, *Albanact*,
> Darteth abroad the thunderbolts of warre,
> Beating downe millions with his furious moode,
> And in his glorie triumphs ouer all,
> Mouing the massie squadrants of the ground;
> Heape[s] hills on hills, to scale the starrie skie,
> As when *Briareus*, armed with an hundreth hands,
> Floong forth an hundredth mountains at great *Ioue*, . . .
>
> (II, 5, 1–8)

It is illuminating to discover that lines 2, 3 and 6 of this last speech were lifted, almost intact, from Spenser's *Ruins of Rome*,[55] a translation from the French of Du Bellay. The language which Marlowe and his contemporaries began to use for heroic drama, and which rescued the popular stage from the 'iygging vaines of riming mother wits', was not far removed from that which some non-dramatic poets were devising for the treatment of heroic themes, whether classical or medieval. Another striking instance of this phenomenon is Tamburlaine's description of his helmet (Part II, IV, 3, 4098–103), which is almost identical with the description of Prince Arthur's helmet in *The Faerie Queene* (I, VII, 32).[56] The wealth of classical allusion which characterizes the new style reflects the desire of all these English poets (and of Du Bellay, whom Spenser was translating) to make the literary language of their native tongue less provincial by drawing on the great literature of the past. Classical precept also encouraged them to find a suitably elevated style for heroic matter, though no one classical poet served as a model for the soaring lines of *Tamburlaine*, *Locrine* and other heroic poems of the period, dramatic and non-dramatic.[57] The shared objectives of these writers of the late eighties and early nineties, and their habits of borrowing from the classics, from Continental literature, and from each other, combine to make it very difficult to assign *Locrine* and several other plays to a specific date or a specific author. *Tamburlaine* was probably responsible for lines such as 'the *Scithian* Emperour/ Leades fortune tied in a chaine of gold' and the later 'our regall minde,/Which aimes at nothing but a golden crowne' (III, 2, 43–4), but *Locrine* as a whole is neither Marlovian nor purely imitation-Marlowe. It testifies to a broader movement of which Marlowe was the most distinguished exponent.

Locrine is not so rigorously organized as *Tamburlaine*. The first three acts concern the death of Albanact and the subsequent defeat of the invader Humber, pursued by the ghost of Albanact, crying for revenge. By this time Locrine has taken over the leadership of the British army and has assumed more heroic proportions. The remainder of the play deals largely with the fatal consequences of his passion for Humber's widow, Estrild, with whom he commits suicide when they are defeated in battle by his wife Guendoline. Mixed with the serious plots is a series of low-comic turns for the cobbler, Strumbo.[58]

The onset of Locrine's ruinous love affair is presented much as it would be in a romance: his first sight of Estrild is so overwhelming that '*at one side of the stage*' he soliloquizes about the power of Cupid, and enumerates her charms which 'Haue so entrapt poore *Locrines* louesick heart' (IV, 1, 81–102). When the end comes, some years later, their daughter Sabren is on hand to call the dead lovers '*Locrine*, the map of magnanimitie' and '*Estrild*, the perfect pattern of renowne' (V, 4, 139, 141), though they have done little in the play to merit this chivalric eulogy. Sabren then drowns herself, to re-emerge in happier circumstances in Milton's *Comus*.

The dumb shows preceding the fourth and fifth acts make it plain that Locrine's passion is heroic. The first presents Hercules and Omphale, to whom Ate, as commentator, specifically compares Locrine and Estrild. In the second, Medea takes revenge on Jason to show what may happen to unfaithful heroes. In the main action Locrine, equating his desire for Estrild with his regal will, rages even more heroically than Cambises at the members of his court who try to reason with him. To his cousin he says:

> What! prat'st thou, pesant, to thy soueraigne?
> Or art thou strooken in some extasie?
> Doest thou not tremble at our royall lookes?
> Dost thou not quake, when mighty *Locrine* frowns?
>
> (V, 1, 41–4)

Locrine is thus one of the first of the many characters in heroic drama whose love is tyrannical, vast and cataclysmic.

Love is less crucial in *Alphonsus King of Aragon*, almost certainly by Robert Greene. Alphonsus, like Tamburlaine, is more interested in conquering kingdoms, and successively overcomes the usurping King of Aragon, the King of Naples and Amurack, the Turkish King. Nevertheless, each act is presented by Venus, and at the end Alphonsus falls in love with Iphigina, the Turk's daughter, who challenges him on the field of battle after her father's defeat, like the Amazonian heroines of Ariosto, Tasso and Spenser. When she does not succumb to his blandishments (he addresses her as his 'sweet mouse'), he has at her, and drives her from the field, but shortly afterward accepts her apologies and marries her. Though it is not a tender episode, it brings the play to an end with the celebration of marriage. Greene seems to have intended to write a second part, for Venus says in the Epilogue that she will return 'to finish vp his life', but there is no evidence that such a part was ever written. What we have is properly called a 'comical history'.

Alphonsus is a more light-hearted Tamburlaine, delighting in the distribution of crowns to his faithful followers, and insulting his enemies with more zest than rancour ('How now, sir boy?' he says on two occasions). Even when he hurls a defiance at Amurack, a note of humour creeps in:

> Pagan I say, thou greatly art deceiu'd,
> I clap vp Fortune in a cage of gold,
> To make her turne her wheele as I thinke best.
> And as for *Mars* whom you do say will change,
> He moping sits behind the kitchin doore,
> Prest at commaund of euery Skullians mouth:
> Who dares not stir, nor once to moue a whit,
> For feare *Alphonsus* then should stomack it.
>
> (IV, 3, 1613–20)[59]

In *Orlando Furioso*, probably written between *Alphonsus* and *Selimus*, Greene appears to go a step further and make fun of the heroic conventions.[60] The play is based on the central episode of Orlando's madness in Ariosto's romantic epic, though the story is so altered that it bears little resemblance to the original. Here an assortment of kings and nobles sue the Emperor of Africa for the hand of his daughter Angelica, who chooses Orlando. The villain of the piece is the absurdly proud Count Sacrepant, a rejected suitor who plants 'evidence' of Angelica's faithlessness, and thus drives Orlando mad. When Sacrepant receives his death blow from Orlando, near the end of the play, he invokes universal disaster in an absurdly grandiose speech:

> Phoebus put on thy sable suted wreath,
> Cladde all thy spheres in darke and mourning weedes.
> Parcht be the earth to drinke vp euery spring,
> Let corne and trees be blasted from aboue,
> Heauen turne to brasse, & earth to wedge of steel
> The worlde to cinders, Mars come thundering downe,
> And neuer sheath thy swift reuenging swoorde,
> Till like the deluge in Dewcalions daies,

The higgest mountaines swimme in streames of bloud.
Heauen, earth, men, beasts, & euerie liuing thing
Consume and end with countie Sacrepant.

(ll. 1419–31)[61]

Nothing Sacrepant has said or done previously has prepared us for this. We have seen him display his ambition and vanity to his servant in lines such as:

And when I set my bonnet on my head,
Me thinkes I fit my forhead for a Crowne: . . .

(ll. 260–1)

And we have seen him in a temper tantrum with Angelica when she rebuffs him:

Stand I on loue? Stoop I to Venus lure,
That neuer yet did feare the God of Warre?

(ll. 496–7)

He has tricked Orlando in an underhanded way by hanging on the trees roundelays supposedly written to Angelica by another lover. For a brief moment we have seen him wearing the crown he has wrested from the emperor just before Orlando enters and defeats him. Thus it is impossible to see him as a great-souled warrior. He is a more eloquent Cambises with even less to be eloquent about, so that his soaring rhetoric has the effect of parody, whether or not it was so intended.

The hero himself fares little better. The representation of his madness onstage is inevitably ludicrous, as when he pulls a man offstage by the leg, and shortly rushes on again, using the leg as a club to beat the Duke of Aquitaine and his soldiers. Since this scene is in the manuscript actor's part as well as in the printed text it is undoubtedly genuine, though some of the clowning in other scenes with Orlando may be a later addition. Orlando's language, even when he is sane, sometimes lacks heroic conviction in the same way as that of Alphonsus:

Tell him his walls shall serue him for no proofe,
But as the sonne of Saturne in his wrath
Pasht all the mountaines at Typheus head,
And topsie turuie turnd the bottome vp,

So shall the Castle of proud Rodamant:
And so braue Lords of France, lets to the fight.

(ll. 434–9)

Such lines as these are either misrepresentations of what Greene
wrote, or they are parodies of heroic rant, or miscalculations like
'Thwack not about with thunder thumpes' in the translation of
Hercules Oetaeus. As a whole, at least in the state in which it has
come down to us, *Orlando Foolioso* (as Sir John Harington, the
translator of Ariosto, called it) cannot be taken seriously as
heroic drama, but sheds some light on the outstanding characteristics of the genre.

The example of *Orlando Furioso* may make it more likely that
Greene was partly playful in *Alphonsus of Aragon* in the speeches he
devised for his hero. There is nothing so ludicrous as the more
extreme examples from the other play, and the rise to power of
Alphonsus is a properly heroic theme. Yet at no point do the
ambitious and threatening speeches of Alphonsus carry total
conviction. No vast and terrible vision inspires them; they lack
'the language of awe', which Thomas Greene considers essential
to epic poetry.[62] Without it, Alphonsus often seems to be no more
than a very mischievous boy, and at such moments one may sus-
pect that some of the mischief is Robert Greene's.

Selimus creates a very different impression. The hero sets forth
at his first appearance a grand design that shows him to be grimly
earnest, thoroughly evil, more aspiring than Alphonsus, and more
imaginative than Sacrepant. After proclaiming himself an
atheist and 'The perfect picture of right tyrannie' (l. 284),[63] he
denounces all conventional ethics, particularly the notion of
familial devotion—'the foolish names,/Of father, mother, brother,
and such like' (ll. 340–1):

Indeed I must confesse they are not bad,
Because they keepe the baser sort in feare:
But we, whose minde in heauenly thoughts is clad,
Whose bodie doth a glorious spirit beare,
That hath no bounds, but flieth euery where.
Why should we seeke to make that soule a slaue,
To which dame Nature so large freedome gaue.

(ll. 347–53)

As Cole acutely remarks, the light and dark sides of Tamburlaine's nature are represented respectively by Alphonsus and Selimus.[64]

Though the fire of Selimus' first speech does not burn equally bright throughout the play, there are flashes, as in the lines just quoted, which approach the intensity of *Tamburlaine*. Because the author's imaginative commitment to the character of Selimus seems to be much greater than the commitment to Alphonsus, Sacrepant or Orlando, all of whom are at times treated rather cavalierly, Selimus comes through as a much more formidable character. That his atheistic sentiments carried conviction to Elizabethan spectators and readers is proved by a curious piece of evidence. Many years later fifty-nine lines of his opening speech were copied out with very few alterations and attributed to Sir Walter Ralegh in an effort to discredit him when he was on trial for treason.[65]

The first acts of *Selimus* show even more clearly than *Locrine* the close connection between the style of this group of plays and that of contemporary non-dramatic poetry, for here the author frequently uses the stanza forms current in the lyric—rhyme royal in Selimus' soliloquy, six- and eight-line stanzas elsewhere. In the latter part of the play, though blank verse becomes the rule, a certain formality, similar to that of the rhyming stanzas, is maintained. With the stanza quoted may be compared the following lines from a later speech by Selimus:

> Now sit I like the arme-strong son of *Ioue*,
> When after he had all his monsters quell'd,
> He was receiu'd in heauen mongst the gods,
> And had faire *Hebe* for his louely bride.
> As many labours *Selimus* hath had,
> And now at length attained to the crowne,
> This is my *Hebe*, and this is my heauen.

(ll. 1671–7)

The one scene of low comedy in *Selimus*, directly inspired, it would seem, by a scene in *Locrine*,[66] is in the tradition of popular clowning illustrated by the comic scenes in *Cambises* and *Orlando Furioso*. High and low style exist side by side as they continued to do in popular Elizabethan drama for many years, to the dismay of the admirers of classical decorum.

The presentation of the character of the hero in *Selimus*,

while not so subtle as Marlowe's presentation of Tamburlaine, is more complex than anything in the other plays in this group. Clearly reprehensible, he glows with heroic energy which commands admiration. He is the youngest son of the ageing emperor of the Turks, Bajazeth, a wise and noble monarch, who establishes a Christian-Stoic frame of reference in the long opening soliloquy, deploring the perils and worries of kingship and lamenting the decline of his own fortunes.[67] Corcut, the oldest of his sons, is a philosopher, ill suited to take over the empire. Acomat, the next, though a sybarite, is his favourite, whom he wants to succeed him. But Selimus (or Selim, as he is often called) is a menace to this arrangement, since his father knows him to be a warrior, ambitious and loved by the people. News is now brought that Selimus has married the daughter of one of Bajazeth's enemies and has come with a large army to visit his father. Thus the general outlines of his character have been traced before he gives his long self-description, and some ambiguity has already been introduced into the problem of appraising him. Bajazeth calls him 'a friend to chiualrie' (1. 97), but also 'wicked' (1. 211). Compared to his philosopher-brother he is a doer rather than a thinker, and compared to his luxury-loving brother, he has the self-discipline of the warrior. Though his 'loue of rule, and kingly soueraigntie' (1. 196) marks him as culpably ambitious, his father's preference for Acomat is obviously impractical and self-indulgent.

Selimus' soliloquy is a strong brew of almost everything a God-fearing Elizabethan disapproved of. Its central point is that Bajazeth, being 'weake and old', had better be dispatched, though not without a little subterfuge. Selimus even confides his plans to a follower, who argues with him like the attendant on a Senecan tyrant, and receives equally tart answers from his master. The playwright fully exploits his audience's stock responses to atheists, tyrants, parricides and Machiavellian schemers to emphasize the depravity of his protagonist, and yet at the same time he begins the process of building up Selim's demonic attractiveness. This is accomplished not only through the poetry of his speeches but also through the continuing comparison with his two brothers.

Corcut is thoroughly commendable. When both his brothers are trying to snatch their father's throne, he refrains from doing so, and urges the old man to keep it till he dies. He is even converted

to Christianity, to become a mouthpiece for unassailable ortho-
doxy. Nevertheless, as he flees in shepherd's clothing from wicked
Selimus and begs meat from the clownish Bullithrumble, he cuts
a sorry figure. When he is strangled, after prophesying Selimus'
doom, one has no sense of irremediable loss.

Acomat, the second son, rouses himself from his luxurious life
when Selimus fails in his first attempt to capture the throne. In
emulation of his brother, who 'through his manly deeds,/Hath
lifted vp his fame vnto the skies' (ll. 741–2), Acomat transforms
himself into a warrior, and demands the throne. At this point
Bajazeth's followers, though they have helped to defeat Selimus,
prefer him to Acomat because of his proved valour. It soon turns
out that Acomat rivals his brother less in bravery than in cruelty
and treachery. In short order he has his nephew tossed on to
spears from the walls of a city, has his niece strangled, and both
puts out the eyes and cuts off the hands of an emissary from his
father. In sheer monstrosity he rapidly catches up with Selimus,
but we are now given proof of the difference between these two
brothers. When Selimus is called by Bajazeth to fight Acomat, he
gets himself 'elected' emperor, and proceeds with plans to poison
his father and do away with his brothers. It is when he is making
these plans that he compares himself to Hercules in a speech
quoted earlier, and in the same scene he says:

> For th'onely things that wrought our Empirie
> Were open wrongs, and hidden trecherie.
> Oh, th'are two wings wherewith I vse to flie
> And soare aboue the common sort.

> (ll. 1739–42)

Acomat never displays quite this relish of his misdeeds, nor,
ambitious as he is, does he have Selimus' heroic image of himself.
If two such criminals were to be judged in real life, there would
be little to choose between them, but by the different standards
which the theatre imposes, the zest, the style, the imagination of
Selimus become points in his favour. They signify a capacity
which can be contemplated without counting the human cost of
such perverted heroism.[68]

Not much can be confidently deduced from the ending of the
play, since there was to be a second part, which apparently was
never written. Whether Selimus, after more victories, was simply

to die like Tamburlaine, or to pay the price for his sins is hard to guess. The play we have is called *The First part of the Tragicall raigne of Selimus* . . ., and the Prologue calls it 'a most lamentable historie', but these terms tell us little. The 'Conclusion' is slightly more specific:

> Thus haue we brought victorious Selimus,
> Vnto the Crowne of great Arabia:
> Next shall you see him with triumphant sword,
> Diuiding kingdomes into equall shares,
> And giue them to their warlike followers.
> If this first part Gentles, do like you well,
> The second part, shall greater murthers tell.

But even here there is no clear indication of what the end will be.

As the first part ends, even Selimus' enemies refer to him as 'A matchlesse knight' and 'this heroicke Emperour' (ll. 2467, 2474). The last four lines, consciously or unconsciously echoing the prologue to *The Canterbury Tales*, look forward to spring and a pilgrimage of sorts:

> But soone as *Zephyrus* sweete smelling blast
> Shall greatly creep ouer the flourie meades,
> Wee'll haue a fling at the Ægyptian crowne,
> And ioyne it vnto ours, or loose our owne.

It is a cheerfully heroic note on which to pause.

Possibly earlier than *Tamburlaine* and the plays closely associated with it was *The Wars of Cyrus*, which may have been performed in 1578 at the first Elizabethan 'private house', Blackfriars Theatre, by the Children of the Chapel Royal.[69] If so, it was, at least in its original form (for some alterations were made), probably written by Richard Farrant, the choirmaster who eagerly promoted the dramatic activities of his boy-musicians. It is a difficult play to categorize. Based on classical history, it neither points the stern morals of *Cambises* nor concerns itself much with the political issues which dominate many plays based on classical, foreign or English history. Some critics, who have dated the play in its present form at least ten years later, have called it a 'conqueror play', and have seen the influence of *Tamburlaine*, but as James Brawner says, the differences between the two plays are 'sub-stantial'.[70] *The Wars of Cyrus* tells a story from the life of the conqueror, Cyrus the Great, but the centre of interest is Panthea and her loyalty to her husband, Abradates, King of Susa. The victories of Cyrus are pushed into the background. Brawner classifies it as 'classical narrative drama', noting that it is the sole surviving exemplar of a genre which was apparently popular at court in the seventies and eighties.[71]

Though not what can properly be called a heroic play, *The Wars of Cyrus* in certain respects anticipates heroic plays which glorify a protagonist very different from Tamburlaine. The portrayal of Cyrus, the nominal hero, is taken (as is a good deal of the plot) from Xenophon's *Cyropedia*, the exemplary biography referred to in the previous chapter. Accordingly, he appears as all that a great king might be. His portrait is painted by Ctesiphon, a nobleman sent by the Assyrian king to murder Cyrus, but smitten by remorse:

> How wise and gracious is this Persian king,
> Who by his wisdome winnes his followers hearts,
> Letting them march in armour wrought with gold,
> And he girt in a coate of complete steele!
> O *Cyrus*, politique and liberall,
> How honourable and magnanimious!
> Rewarding vertue, and reuenging wrongs!
> How full of temperance and fortitude,
> Daring to menace Fortune with his sworde,
> Yet mercifull in all his victories!

> (ll. 676–85)

The roster of chivalric virtues is long, and though some of them (notably prowess and largesse) are virtues also attributed to Tamburlaine, the conspicuous difference between the two con-querors is that Cyrus is benevolent rather than terrifying. No conflict appears to exist between individual aspiration and the public weal, and the cruelty of an enemy king is contrasted with the mercy of Cyrus.

Violence rarely comes to the surface in *The Wars of Cyrus*. One murder is performed on stage by a loyal page who has changed clothes with his mistress to allow her to escape from the cruel Assyrian king. But even this act is accomplished in a way which hardly disturbs the polite atmosphere of the play: the disguised page sings his mistress's lover to sleep and then, reluctantly, stabs him in order to save his own life. In the court of Cyrus restraint and courtesy are especially noticeable. The one threatened infraction comes to nothing when Panthea, the captive queen, reports to Cyrus that his nobleman, Araspas, is trying to seduce her by force. The sovereign lectures Araspas, sends him away, and restores the rule of ceremonious good behaviour.

The theme of love gradually comes to dominate the play. Araspas first describes the beautiful captive to Cyrus at the end of Act I in a long speech packed with the conceits of Elizabethan love poetry—'haire as radiant as is Tag[u]s sand', 'lillie cheekes, all died with ruddie blush', eyes which rival the stars (ll. 285–96). It is too much for Cyrus, who refuses to see her, for fear he will fall in love, and 'Men are in folly when they are in loue' (l. 336). Araspas, designated as guardian, promptly falls in love and folly, and hires a magician to bewitch Panthea into forgetting her husband and loving her guardian. Panthea's reason overcomes the magician's charms, however, and it is then that Araspas threatens force. He repents and apologizes when reproved by Cyrus, and is forgiven with characteristic generosity. Panthea's husband then comes over to Cyrus, but is killed in battle. In the final episode of the play Panthea, overcome by grief, commits suicide. Cyrus pronounces the eulogy of her husband, 'Mirrour of honor and true Nobilitie', and of '*Panthea*, chast, vertuous, and amiable' (ll. 1673, 1678). Panthea's love is somewhat like Olympia's in *Tamburlaine*, though manifested less spectacularly. In its quiet way it is a heroic love, recognized at its true worth by the warrior Cyrus, and thus lifted above the category of folly in which he had earlier placed all love.

The subject of George Peele's *The Battle of Alcazar*, probably written late in 1588, was a battle which had occurred ten years before, and had shocked all of Europe.[72] In it had died two claimants to the throne of Barbary, Abd-el-Malek and Mohammed el-Mesloukh (Peele's Abdelmelec and Muly Mahamet), King Sebastian of Portugal and Thomas Stukley, the English adventurer.[73] To stage this momentous event and the steps leading up to it Peele borrowed from the academic tradition the device of spectacular dumb shows explained by a presenter before each act. However, the play was popular, not merely in the sense of being performed at a public theatre by one of the chief London companies, but also in the sense of being one of the long-run hits of its day. For many years it received, along with *Tamburlaine*, the tribute of parody by the leading playwrights.[74]

The favourite object of parody was a scene in which the Moor, Muly Mahamet, enters with a piece of raw meat on his sword, and offers it to his starving wife with the words:

> Hold thee Calypolis feed and faint no more,
> This flesh I forced from a lyonesse,
> Meate of a princesse, for a princesse meate, . . .

> *   *   *

> Feed then and faint not faire Calypolis,
> For rather than fierce famine shall prevaile,
> To gnaw thy intrailes with her thornie teeth,
> The conquering lyonesse shall attend on thee,
> And laie huge heapes of slaughtered carcases
> As bulwarkes in her waie to keepe her back.
> I will provide thee of a princely ospraie,
> That as she flyeth over fish in pooles,
> The fish shall turne their glistering bellies up,
> And thou shalt take thy liberall choice of all,
> Joves stately bird with wide commanding wings
> Shall hover still about thy princely head,
> And beate downe fowle by sholes into thy lap,
> Feede then and faint not faire Calypolis.

> *   *   *

> Feede and be fat that we may meete the foe
> With strength and terror to revenge our wrong.

> (ll. 537–9, 548–61, 568–9)

Ripe for parody, the lines and the stage image have a certain grotesque brilliance of their own, heightened by the reminders of *Tamburlaine*. The royal creatures who are to provide Calypolis with such abundance of raw food recall the hundreds of servants who are to wait on Zenocrate, the milk-white harts to draw her ivory sled, and the martial prizes she is to be offered (I, 2, 289–301). At the same time, the spectacle of the queen feeding on raw meat suggests the cruel treatment of the Turkish emperor and empress. Muly Mahamet's ability to translate a degrading situation into the glorious preparation of revenge is the key to his character.

77

It is made clear in the first dumb show and the accompanying
presenter's speech that Muly Mahamet is a wicked tyrant, wrong-
fully put on the throne by his father in place of the uncle, Abdelmelec, who was the rightful successor. Abdelmelec has sought aid
from the Emperor of the East and, by the end of the first act, has
ousted Muly Mahamet from the throne. In his effort to regain it,
Muly Mahamet wins the support of King Sebastian of Portugal,
who in turn persuades Thomas Stukley to join in the fight. As
Selimus is contrasted with his father and brothers, so Muly
Mahamet is set against his uncle and his two allies, but these three
are much more than foils. Each is a hero in his own right.[75]
Heroic interest is thus much more diffused than in *Tamburlaine*,
Alphonsus or even *Selimus*.

Abdelmelec, like Bajazeth in *Selimus*, is an entirely commendable character, but he is also younger, more energetic, and less
given to lamentation. God-fearing, 'Curteous and honourable'
(l. 73), he is victorious early in the play, and is prevented only by
death from enjoying the victory of his side in the great battle at
the end. In contrast to his goodness Muly Mahamet's villainy is
especially striking. Not only is he a ruthless usurper, who has
killed one uncle and two brothers, but also he has every intention
of doing away with his ally, King Sebastian, once the throne has
been regained. Nevertheless, he bears 'a princely heart unvan-
quishable' (l. 868), as one of the Christian officers says, and
expresses the scope of his ambitions in passionate rhetoric. He
opens the scene of starvation in the desert by identifying his misfortunes with world-wide disaster:

> Fight earth-quakes in the intrailes of the earth,
> And Easterne whirl-windes in the hellish shades,
> Some foule contagion of the infected heaven,
> Blast all the trees, and in their cursed tops,
> The dismall night raven and tragike owle
> Breed, and become fore-tellers of my fall, . . .
>
> (ll. 472–7)[76]

It is 'Ercles' vein' once more, well adapted to the new dramatic
style, but without the poetic power by which Marlowe made such
speeches more than rant.

King Sebastian's reasons for supporting this disreputable
schemer reveal another aspect of heroism. He is a man of noble

intentions, as even his enemies agree, and we know that the good Abdelmelec has warned him of the injustice of Muly Mahamet's cause, but Sebastian behaves like a knight sent out to win fame where he can find it. The presenter is explicit about this at the very opening:

> Honor the spurre that pricks the princely minde,
> To followe rule and climbe the stately chaire,
> With great desire inflames the Portingall,
> An honorable and couragious king,
> To undertake a dangerous dreadfull warre, . . .
>
> (ll. 1–5)

Before Act III the Presenter indicates a fault:

> . . . sweet Sebastian.
> Who surfetting in prime time of his youth,
> Upon ambitious poison dies thereon.
>
> (ll. 744–6)

but chiefly shows that Sebastian is misled not only by the Moor but by the king of Spain, who offers help he never means to send. Sebastian has revealed his outlook on the enterprise by addressing Muly Mahamet's envoys as 'warlike lords and men of chivalrie,/ Honorable Embassadors of this high regent, . . . your distressed Lord' (ll. 572–3). He has persuaded himself that he will be ful-filling that most respected of knightly functions, relieving the distressed, while also winning fame and securing the kingdom of Morocco, which the Moor has promised him. Peele never lets us forget the discrepancy between the seamy truth and Sebastian's chivalric view of his undertaking. In comparison with the model king, Abdelmelec, whose personal ambitions coincide with what is best for his kingdom, Sebastian appears somewhat irresponsible and egotistic, though innocent of Muly Mahamet's ruthlessness and immorality. The 'couragious king' is a heroic dreamer.

In Captain Thomas Stukley the heroic dream is still farther removed from concern for the common weal, and yet uncontamin-ated by malice. The historical Tom Stukley became a legend in his own lifetime. A younger son of Sir Hugh Stukley of Devon, born in about 1520, he made a financially advantageous marriage in 1552, and spent all his money in the following ten years. By that time he had already been involved in a conspiracy at home, had served in foreign armies, and done some privateering. He now embarked on some adventures in Ireland which led eventually to his fleeing to the court of Philip II of Spain and then to the Papal court at Rome. Here, in 1578, a small expedition against Ireland was fitted out by the Pope with Stukley in command. For some reason, however, he stopped in Lisbon, where King Sebastian persuaded him to join forces with him and sail to Africa.[77]

In the play he first appears when he is being welcomed by the Governor of Lisbon and asked why he, an Englishman, should attack Ireland, a country belonging to England. Stukley replies by asserting his liberty to go where he pleases and above all to do whatever is necessary 'to win a crowne':

> King of a mole-hill had I rather be,
> Than the richest subject of a monarchie,
> Huffe it brave minde, and never cease t'aspire,
> Before thou raigne sole king of thy desire.
>
> (ll. 464–7)

Here is a home-grown Tamburlaine, whose aspiration seems more nakedly egotistical, unornamented by Asiatic references. Seeking a crown in Persepolis or Samarkand seems more symbolic than a crown in Ireland. Once he has been persuaded by Sebastian to alter his course, however, his heroic vision of himself takes on the colouring of Sebastian's vision. In this part of the play (at least as it has come down to us) Peele gives him little to say until the moment of his death. Killed by his own soldiers when the battle turns against Muly Mahamet and his allies, Stukley cries, again like Tamburlaine:

> Strike on, strike downe this body to the earth
> Whose mounting minde stoopes to no feeble stroke.
>
> (ll. 1319–20)

In a long dying speech he reviews his entire life, hopes that his country will think kindly of him, reaffirms his bond with 'brave Sebastian', now dead also, and accepts his destiny:

> Here endeth Fortune, rule, and bitter rage:
> Heere ends Tom Stukleys pilgrimage.
>
> (ll. 1371–2)

As Yoklavich says, 'Peele slighted the guilt of his hero and consistently avoided emphasis on Stukley's traitorous designs against his own country.'[78]

The Battle of Alcazar is in some ways a crude piece of dramatic art, and it is true, as Clemen says, that there is little real dramatic conflict, since opposing characters rarely encounter one another.[79] Nevertheless, the play succeeds by genuinely theatrical means[80] in presenting four variations on heroism, distinguished from one another with some subtlety. Effective juxtaposition presents a conflict of ideas which takes the place of physical confrontation.

Of the four heroic characters Stukley's is the least fully portrayed, though 'the death of Captaine Stukley' is important enough to be mentioned on the title page. Stukley's career was the sole concern of another play, *The Famous History of the life and death of Captaine Thomas Stukeley*—an example of the biographical play which was also on occasion a form of heroic drama. An earlier version of this play may have been in existence when Peele wrote *The Battle of Alcazar*, but much of the extant version appears to be later, and there is no proof that either author borrowed from the other.[81] With the exception of a few passages of prose, the language is blank verse which is usually competent but colourless. The chief interest of the play is the portrayal of Stukley.

In the first series of episodes we see him in domestic surroundings before he has launched upon his military adventures. A suitor of Anne Curtis, whose father is an alderman, withdraws in favour of Stukley because he knows of the girl's love. The advantage of love in marriage is weighed against Stukley's reputation as a spendthrift and a quarreller, but the parents reluctantly agree to their daughter's preference. The atmosphere is what one might expect in either domestic tragedy or a comedy of city life, and so it continues after the marriage, as Stukley pays off his creditors while his father-in-law looks on, appalled at the rapid disposal of so much money. The scene leads to a comic confrontation between Curtis and Stukley. 'Shall I not pay my debts?' Stukley asks. 'Not with my money son, not with my money,' Curtis replies, the epitome of bourgeois possessiveness. We then get a first glimpse of Stukley's image of himself:

> It is mine own, and Stukley of his own
> Will be as frank as shall the Emperor.

I scorn this trash, betrayer of mens souls;
I'll spurn it with my foot; and with my hand
Rain showers of plenty on this barren land.
Were it my fortune could exceed the clouds
Yet would I bear a mind surmounting that.

(ll. 632–8)[82]

Absurd as this attitude seems in the context in which it is placed, it prepares for a description of Stukley's liberality by his lieutenant a few moments later:

Nay if you look but on his mind
Much more occasion shall ye find to love him
He's liberal, and goes not to the wars
To make a gain of his poor soldiers spoil,
But spoil the foe to make his soldiers gain—

(ll. 675–9)

Prodigality has turned into largesse.

A conflict between two standards of judgement is also implicit in the treatment of his departure for Ireland. Having spent all his wife's dowry, he abruptly leaves her, answering her pathetic, affectionate entreaties with the callous statement that he wants no 'chambering' and 'belly-cheer', but only honour (ll. 701–8). Though the two fathers are dismayed by his actions, Old Stukley says that his son's resolution is 'heroical' (l. 788).

In this play, then, we watch Stukley emerge from the world of good county families and city aldermen into which he was born, into the world of heroic adventure. The remaining scenes show him in Ireland, Spain, Portugal and Africa, where he is much the same Stukley we have seen in Peele's play. Though he is always brave, ambitious and liberal, the cost of these virtues to his family at home is never overlooked. Vernon, his former rival, reappears in Ireland, rebuking him for the treatment of his wife. When Stukley brushes him off he reflects:

Doubtless if ever man was misbegot
It is this Stukley; of a boundless mind
Undaunted spirit, and uncontrolled spleen,
Lavish as is the liquid Ocean,
That drops his crowns even as the clouds drop rain.

(ll. 1013–17)

In Spain, when Vernon brings news of Anne's death, Stukley is untouched and unrepentant for the money he squandered: 'What's twenty-thousand pound to a free heart?' (l. 2055). Once more Vernon meets Stukley on the battlefield of Alcazar, where they are reconciled on Vernon's initiative. He even attempts to defend Stukley from his murderers. The final emphasis is on the qualities that elicit respect and even affection from the man Stukley has injured most. It is consonant with the tone of the whole play that his last tribute to the hero is personal and intimate, unaccompanied by the fanfares which end *Tamburlaine* and *The Battle of Alcazar*.

To an Englishman the high points of English history had a more obvious claim to heroic treatment than classical history or recent foreign history. In the mind of Thomas Heywood, writing his *Apology for Actors* (1612) English heroes ranked with Achilles, Alexander and other notables whose representation on the stage would 'mooue the spirits of the beholder to admiration'.[83] In a remarkable passage he traces a line of heroic emulation beginning with the inspiration of Hercules by a performance of 'the worthy and memorable acts of his father *Iupiter*', and extending through Theseus, Achilles and Alexander to Julius Caesar. Then, turning to 'our domesticke hystories', he asks:

> . . . what English blood seeing the person of any bold English man presented and doth not hugge his fame, and hunnye at his valor, pursuing him in his enterprise with his best wishes, and as beeing wrapt in contemplation, offers to him in his hart all prosperous performance, as if the Personater were the man Personated, so bewitching a thing is liuely and well spirited action, that it hath power to new mold the harts of the spectators and fashion them to the shape of any noble and notable attempt. What coward to see his contryman valiant would not bee ashamed of his owne cowardise? What English Prince should hee behold the true portrature of that [f]amous King *Edward* the third, foraging France, taking so great a King captiue in his owne country, quartering the English Lyons with the French Flower-delyce, and would not bee suddenly Inflam'd with so royall a spectacle, being made apt and fit for the like atchievement. So of *Henry* the fift: . . .

(sigs. B3–B4)

Edward III, probably performed in the early 1590s, breathes
something of this spirit. In style it is sufficiently Shakespearian
to have been ascribed very credibly to Shakespeare,[84] though it
does not appear in editions of his works. The subject of the play,
as of *The Wars of Cyrus*, is 'love and valour', though with an exact
reversal of the relative importance of the two and of the order of
presenting them. Here love interrupts valour early in the play
and takes over the first two acts, while the last three present the
glories of Crécy and Poitiers, shared by King Edward and the
Black Prince. On the verge of departure for France to try to
make good his claim to the throne, Edward hears that the Scots
have invaded England and are besieging the Countess of Salisbury
in Roxborough Castle. Putting off his expedition, he goes to her
assistance, routs the Scots, and falls in love with the countess,
who is the daughter of one of his nobles and the wife of another.
We hear of his infatuation, in the familiar figures of Elizabethan
love poetry—first from a courtier:

> I might perceiue his eye in her eye lost,
> His eare to drinke her sweet tongues vtterance,
> And changing passion, like inconstant clouds.
> That racke vpon the carriage of the windes,
> Increase and die in his disturbed cheekes.
>
> (II, 1, 1–5)[85]

and then from him:

> There is no summer but in her cheerful lookes,
> Nor frosty winter but in her disdayne.
>
> (II, 1, 42–3)

Virtuous disdain is all the king wins, despite his desperate venture
of sending the countess's father to persuade her. The alternatives
of love and war are forcibly dramatized when Prince Edward
tells his father that the army is ready to leave for France and the
king seems about to abandon his siege. A smile from the countess
raises his hopes, however, and the war is again deferred. Only
when the countess in her defence shows him two daggers, one to
kill his queen, the other to 'dispatch' the love in her heart, does
the king give orders for departure, saying 'I am awaked from this
idle dreame' (II, 2, 200). The king's love, though offered with the
forms of romantic courtship, is always seen as an ignoble alterna-
tive to prowess and even, metaphorically, as an unchivalric

1 St George's Portico
Reproduced by permission of the Trustees of the Chatsworth Settlement

2 Horace and Curiace

Reproduced by courtesy of the Harvard College Library

attack on the very person he has come to protect. Thus the countess's loyal love for her husband, also transformed by the military metaphor, becomes a heroic defence, even nobler than her earlier defence of the castle against the Scots.

The English victories in France are seen largely as a triumph of chivalry over tyranny. The first series of episodes leads up to the knighting of the Prince of Wales. The English arrive, King John of France exchanges threats with King Edward in the established manner of heroes in epic and romance, and before the battle of Crécy the prince is armed in a formal ceremony which gives great dramatic importance to the traditional symbolic value of armour. During the battle the king refuses to rescue his son from a tight spot, preferring to test his valour. 'Hees close incompast with a world of odds!' comes one report. 'Then will he win a world of honor to', says the king (III, 5, 20–1). And so he does. Following the victory at Crécy comes another ceremony in which the prince, having entered in triumph with a broken lance in hand, is knighted by his father.

The king is both liberal and stern, taking pity on 'six poore Frenchmen' turned out of the besieged city of Calais, but also insisting upon unconditional surrender of the city. He is a much less active figure, however, than the prince, who goes on from his victory at Crécy to the final one at Poitiers in which the French king is captured.

King John, a tyrannous usurper from the English point of view, is the antithesis of the two Edwards. His deplorable failings are brought out in a sub plot centred on the chivalric custom of ransom. The Earl of Salisbury captures Villiers, a French lord, whom he releases on the understanding that he will obtain a pass for Salisbury through territory held by the French to Calais, where King Edward is. Villiers wins the consent of the French king's son, Charles of Normandy, by insisting that without it, he must in honour return to captivity. When Salisbury attempts to go through the French lines, however, King John tries to force Charles to go back on his word, and is only persuaded to honour the ransom agreement when Charles shames him by saying that King Edward would never disgrace the Prince of Wales in a similar way.

In the concluding action the discredited French king is pitted against Prince Edward at Poitiers. Outnumbered and surrounded, the prince refuses to capitulate and, aided by an ominous darkness and 'A flight of vgly rauens', disrupts the French force. Leading King John captive, he returns to his father at Calais when hope for him has been almost lost. Here the English king has just shown mercy to the defeated city, so that the final impression is of power and generosity conjoined. The prince's speech offers a heroic prospect of victories to come:

> As not the territories of France alone,
> But likewise Spain, Turkie, and what countries els
> That iustly would prouoke faire Englands ire,
> Might, at their presence, tremble and retire.
>
> (V, 232–5)

Whether or not Shakespeare had anything to do with *Edward III*, he wrote a few years later about the other famous warrior-king of England, Henry V. Before he came to the plays in which this figure emerges, he had already created three characters touched in different ways by the heroic. In *Titus Andronicus*, a revenge tragedy of the early 1590s, there are two of them—Aaron the Moor and Titus.[86] Aaron is unambiguously wicked like the Moor, Muly Mahamet, but only occasionally reveals any extraordinary scope to his ambition. The lover of the Gothic queen Tamora, and brought with her to Rome in captivity, he sees a sudden improvement in his fortune when she unexpectedly becomes the wife of the emperor:

> Away with slavish weeds and servile thoughts!
> I will be bright, and shine in pearl and gold,
> To wait upon this new-made empress.
> To wait, said I? to wanton with this queen,
> This goddess, this Semiramis, this nymph,
> This siren, that will charm Rome's Saturnine,
> And see his shipwrack and his commonweal's.
>
> (II, 1, 18–24)

One or two later speeches have some of the fire to be expected of a heroic villain:

> . . . but if you brave the Moor,
> The chafed boar, the mountain lioness,
> The ocean swells not so as Aaron storms.
>
> (IV, 2, 137–9)

But Aaron is also a sly schemer, a satirical commentator, and a fiercely protective father. He is more humanly understandable than Muly Mahamet and less heroic.

Titus, the revenger *par excellence*, who bakes and serves to Tamora the bodies of two of her sons, appears at the opening of the play as a brave general and devoted servant of Rome, whose only fault is stern inflexibility. Unmoved by Tamora's pleas, he has her eldest son sacrificed to the *manes* of the Andronici killed in battle. His cruelty is shown equally to his own family a short time later in a quarrel over who shall marry his daughter Lavinia. Titus, having promised her to the emperor, kills one of his own sons who favours the emperor's brother. The irony of this sacrifice is that the emperor then humiliates Titus by choosing the captive queen as his bride.

When Aaron, on behalf of Tamora, takes outrageous revenge on Titus by arranging the rape and mutilation of Lavinia, the deaths of two of Titus' sons, and the cutting off of his hand, we witness the transformation of a man into a monster. The story of his revenge on Tamora is a re-enactment of the revenge of Philomela and Procne upon Tereus as told by Ovid in the *Metamorphoses*, where all three persons are transformed into birds, as if to symbolize the metamorphic power of the intense emotions they feel as the revenge is consummated. The metamorphosis of Titus is similar. An essentially reasonable and public-spirited man is driven first into a realm of lunatic fantasy, but finally to so total an obsession with revenge that he is carried beyond the normal limits of humanity.[87] By emphasizing in an Ovidian way the strangeness even more than the immorality of this transforming passion, the play makes its own sort of appeal to that response of admiration which was intimately associated with the heroic genre.

Shakespeare's Richard III is also in part a heroic figure, but never wholly so. In *III Henry VI* (1591–2) he displays regal ambitions reminiscent of Tamburlaine:

> I'll make my heaven to dream upon the crown;
> And, whiles I live, t'account this world but hell,
> Until my misshap'd trunk that bears this head
> Be round impaled with a glorious crown.

> (III, 2, 168–71)

and a commitment to evil like that of Selimus:

87

I'll drown more sailors than the Mermaid shall;
I'll slay more gazers than the basilisk;
I'll play the orator as well as Nestor,
Deceive more slily than Ulysses could,
And, like a Sinon, take another Troy.
I can add colours to the chameleon,
Change shapes with Proteus for advantages,
And set the murderous Machiavel to school.

(III, 2, 186–93)

In these last lines he also resembles Marlowe's Jew of Malta, whose evil scheming sometimes rises to heroic proportions, but Richard, again like Barabas, is often less visionary and more concerned with the tactics of the next move than with a grand design. Only at moments is either of these Machiavellians an aspiring character like Selimus or Muly Mahamet. Richard's rise and fall in *III Henry VI* and *Richard III* (1592–3) are beautifully adjusted to the moral scheme of the first tetralogy, in which the anarchy produced during years of struggle by warring factions is ended by the providential victory of the Earl of Richmond, the future Henry VII, at Bosworth Field. The crookback king, who wades through blood to the throne, seems to concentrate in his person all the selfish evil of the preceding era, and therefore, fascinating as he is in himself, to point to a pattern of meaning which has less to do with the human potentiality for good or evil than with the political problems of usurpation, weak rulers, and rival claims to the throne. Twice, however, he is given statements of heroic self-sufficiency which are quintessential in their simplicity. Near the end of *III Henry VI* he says 'I am myself alone' (V, 6, 83), and in his self-catechism in *Richard III*, 'Richard loves Richard: that is, I am I' (V, 3, 184).

The character of Henry V clearly called for heroic treatment and, as we know, had received it from the early biographers. Henry's life was appealing not only because of his 'famous victories', which furnished the title for a pre-Shakespearian play about him, but also because of the youthful escapades attributed to him from the first.[88] The transformation of scapegrace into hero had obvious dramatic potential. The old play of *The Famous Victories of Henry the Fifth* (1586?) makes comparatively little of the contrast, since the undistinguished prose gives a sameness of tone to both comic and serious scenes, but Shakespeare exploits the contrast to the full. He prepares for it in a soliloquy in *I Henry IV* (ll. 596–7) which has proved a stumbling-block to some critics. The young Hal, at the conclusion of his first scene with Falstaff and Poins, says:

> I know you all, and will awhile uphold
> The unyok'd humour of your idleness.
> Yet herein will I imitate the sun,
> Who doth permit the base contagious clouds
> To smother up his beauty from the world,
> That, when he please again to be himself,
> Being wanted he may be more wonder'd at
> By breaking through the foul and ugly mists
> Of vapours that did seem to strangle him.

> * * *

> And like bright metal on a sullen ground,
> My reformation, glitt'ring o'er my fault,
> Shall show more goodly, and attract more eyes
> Than that which hath no foil to set it off.
> I'll so offend, to make offence a skill,
> Redeeming time when men think least I will.
>
> (I, 2, 190–8, 207–12)

Dr Johnson saw the point: 'This speech is very artfully introduced to keep the prince from appearing vile in the opinion of the audience: it prepares them for his future reformation, and, what is yet more valuable, exhibits a natural picture of a great mind offering excuses to itself, and palliating those follies which it can neither justify nor forsake.'[89] One need not press psychological analysis further. To do so is to be embarrassed with the problems of Hal's sincerity to his drinking companions and with the extent to which his calculation is Machiavellian. These are not the issues here, and the speech is only in part 'a natural picture' of the prince. More important is the anticipation of the glorious character into which this unpromising youth will turn. The effect of the soliloquy, set apart by its blank verse from the preceding prose dialogue, is to create a regal portrait which we seem to see beside the figure of the young prince as he speaks—a vision of the future which is more Shakespeare's than his. More precisely, this vision anticipates an extraordinary description of the prince in the fourth act, at the moment of his metamorphosis.

Before this important moment arrives, we are given contrasting images of several other characters surrounding the prince, for *I Henry IV* is a veritable hall of mirrors.[90] It has become a commonplace of critical interpretation to note that Hal is poised between Hotspur, the embodiment of one concept of Honour, and Falstaff, the engagingly dishonourable companion with whom he spends most of his time.[91] In the first scene of the play the king wishes that his son were more like Hotspur, who seems to have more of the princely graces than Hal. When Hotspur grows angry after a quarrel with the king over the disposition of some prisoners of war, his emotional commitment to the canons of chivalry appears. His uncles, Northumberland and Worcester, are eager to harness his energy to their political scheming, but Hotspur will hardly listen. 'Imagination of some great exploit/Drives him beyond the bounds of patience', says Northumberland, and Hotspur rushes on:

> By heaven, methinks it were an easy leap
> To pluck bright honour from the pale-fac'd moon,
> Or dive into the bottom of the deep,
> Where fathom-line could never touch the ground,
> And pluck up drowned honour by the locks,
> So he that doth redeem her thence might wear
> Without corrival all her dignities: . . .
>
> (I, 3, 199–205)

Beaumont gives this speech, very slightly altered, to the romance-fed apprentice, Rafe, 'the Knight of the Burning Pestle', as proof that he 'can speak a huffing part', and Shakespeare makes a point of the extravagance by having Worcester comment,

> He apprehends a world of figures here,
> But not the form of what he should attend: . . .
>
> (ll. 207–8)

In a sense, but only in a sense, Hotspur is what the prince should be, totally committed to the noblest ideals. His rashness and naïveté, however, compare unfavourably with the self-possession shown by Hal even at his most irresponsible, and the limitations of the soldierly code of honour are brought out in the caricature of Hotspur given by the prince in Act II, Scene 4. Here Hotspur appears as a mindless killer of 'some six or seven dozen of Scots at a breakfast', complaining to his wife that he hasn't enough to do.

Later in the same scene Falstaff and Hal entertain each other with impersonations of the king. Falstaff promises to do his 'in King Cambyses' vein', and though his style is closer in detail to Lyly, Greene and Kyd than to Preston, it obviously parodies a kind of 'ludicrous rant', as Arthur Humphreys says,[92] which had become associated with the old play of *Cambises*. Since the occasion for Falstaff's game with Hal is a summons from the king to his son, the underlying issue is the king's disapproval of Hal. The mock-heroic portrait of the king is also a defence of an unheroic way of life, as Falstaff makes clear in yet another impersonation. Playing the part of the prince in his imaginary interview with his father, Falstaff begs the king never to banish 'sweet Jack Falstaff' from his son's company: 'banish plump Jack, and banish all the world' (II, 4, 460–74). As brilliant as they are hilarious, these distorted images, like the prince's caricature of his rival Hotspur, suggest the dangers of taking oneself and one's mission too seriously, though they never succeed in justifying Hal's failure to act responsibly. However, when Hal, taking the part of the king, replies to Falstaff, 'I do, I will', he gives another promise of reformation.

To force him to behave more properly is the king's object in the interview to which he summons Hal, and for this purpose he uses another image of a prince—his unsympathetic portrait of his predecessor, the 'skipping King', who 'ambled up and down,/ With shallow jesters and rash bavin wits,/Soon kindled and soon burnt' (III, 2, 60–2). As the king pursues his strategy of likening the prince to Richard II ('For all the world/As thou art to this hour was Richard then') the complexity of the relationship between these various portraits becomes increasingly apparent. None of them wholly faithful, most of them distorted by malice or self-love, each captures an aspect of the subject's personality and simultaneously reveals something about the speaker. Here Henry IV, the opportunist, the clever politician, the usurper, describes the king who in the play of *Richard II* appeared as the impractical player of the role of king, obsessed with the glory of his title and afraid that if he was not treated like a king he might no longer be one.[93] Yet Henry is accusing him of disregard of his prerogatives and of the distance he should have kept in order to make majesty revered. Though Richard would hardly recognize his portrait, something of his indulgent frivolity is caught. More to the king's point, the reflection of Hal's behaviour is a palpable hit. And ironically, the king's craving for legitimacy enshrined in ceremony is revealed:

> Thus did I keep my person fresh and new,
> My presence, like a robe pontifical,
> Ne'er seen but wonder'd at, and so my state,
> Seldom, but sumptuous, show'd like a feast,
> And wan by rareness such solemnity.

(III, 2, 55–9)

On one other moving occasion this craving appears again, as the king lies on his death-bed. It is the famous episode, recorded by the chroniclers, in which the king mistakenly suspects his son of having snatched the crown in his impatience to succeed his yet living father. Once more the prince seems to have fallen into gross impropriety, and the old man conjures up a nightmare vision of the England of the fifth Harry: 'For now a time is come to mock at form' (*II Henry IV*, IV, 5, 118). The loss of ceremony leads in his despairing thoughts to total disorder and a return of the kingdom to a state of wilderness.

By the time of this bitter speculation it is clear that the king's interpretation of his son's behaviour is mistaken, but in the earlier interview the king is more right than wrong. However fully Hal may be planning to reform, he admits his fault in not having already done so when he says 'I shall hereafter, my thrice gracious lord,/Be more myself' (*I Henry IV*, III, 2, 92–3). To be himself, the play implies, is to be more like that regal figure he has promised to become, startling the world by his sudden appearance from behind a cloud. The wonder he hopes to inspire is almost exactly what his father describes as the proper response to a king, and Hal now proposes to become this awe-inspiring figure by the practical means of defeating Hotspur, the leader of the rebels.

The confrontation occurs at the Battle of Shrewsbury. As Hotspur is waiting for reinforcements which never arrive, Sir Richard Vernon comes with news that the king is approaching with his army. Hotspur asks:

> . . . where is his son,
> The nimble-footed madcap Prince of Wales,
> And his comrades that daft the world aside
> And bid it pass?
>
> (IV, 1, 94–7)

Vernon's reply is as unwelcome as it is unexpected:

> All furnish'd, all in arms;
> All plum'd like estridges that with the wind
> Bated, like eagles having lately bath'd,
> Glittering in golden coats like images,
> As full of spirit as the month of May,
> And gorgeous as the sun at midsummer;
> Wanton as youthful goats, wild as young bulls.
> I saw young Harry with his beaver on,
> His cushes on his thighs, gallantly arm'd,
> Rise from the ground like feather'd Mercury,
> And vaulted with such ease into his seat
> As if an angel dropp'd down from the clouds
> To turn and wind a fiery Pegasus,
> And witch the world with noble horsemanship.
>
> (IV, 1, 97–110)

Symbolically the promised transformation has already taken place: the 'nimble-footed madcap' has turned into the fully armed and mounted knight of romance.[94] The prince we see in the battle is, of course, a more practical knight, and his defeat of Hotspur is, in part, the triumph of a stable, practical honour over honour which is idealistic, rash and easily misled. Nevertheless, the prince's grasp of political reality never leads him to the practicality of Falstaff in his famous disquisition on honour and his preference for discretion over valour. These comparisons come to life on the stage in the brilliant moment when the prince kills Hotspur and, turning, sees Falstaff, apparently dead. To his former rival he first addresses a eulogy in which he laments that so great a spirit was undone by 'ill-weav'd ambition'; then, in a gesture of chivalric courtesy, places his 'favours'—very likely some of the plumes from his helmet—over Hotspur's 'mangled face'.[95] To the body of his drinking-companion he says:

I could have better spar'd a better man:
O, I should have a heavy miss of thee
If I were much in love with vanity: . . .

$$(V, 4, 103-5)$$

Affection and cool appraisal mingle. The appraisal is confirmed
the instant after his exit when Falstaff stops playing dead and, in a
piece of ugly clowning, sticks his sword in the dead Hotspur, hoists
the body on to his shoulder, and proceeds to boast of his victory.
After this scene the rejection of Falstaff, though it couldn't come
until the end of *II Henry IV*, is inevitable.

What has been called 'the education of the prince' is virtually
complete. The process has also been seen, in morality-play terms,
as the triumph over temptation. It is both of these things and
something else as well. We have seen how the ideals of chivalry
could be dramatized in even so crude a play as *Clyomon and Clamydes* by a ceremony of knighting, and, far more effectively in
Edward III, by two successive ceremonies of the investiture and
knighting of the Black Prince, separated by his testing in the battle
of Crécy. In *I Henry IV* the pattern is even more fully worked out
in the movement of the prince from what his frivolous behaviour
shows him to be to what he immediately promises to become. By
means of a succession of contrasting views of Hotspur, Falstaff,
King Henry and King Richard the significance of the prince's
development is clarified and heroic kingship is established as his
goal—the energy and idealism of Hotspur mixed with the responsibility and practicality of King Henry. To be this kind of king
he must first demonstrate the chivalric virtues. This part of Shakespeare's tetralogy, though it contains no ceremony of knighthood,
presents the making of a knight.

In Part II (1597–8) there is, somewhat surprisingly, a repetition
of the process.[96] Hal is once again playing with Falstaff in the
tavern scene of Act II, as if there had been no Battle of Shrewsbury
and no capture of Hotspur's honour. Impossible as this is psychologically or historically, it is dramatically effective as a foil to the
last scenes of the play, in which the prince once more persuades
his father that he is not an irresponsible scape-grace, and then,
after being crowned as Henry V, rejects Falstaff. Harold Jenkins
puts the matter admirably when he says, 'there is a type of hero
whose adventures always can recur. Robin Hood has no sooner

plundered one rich man than another comes along. . . . In folk-lore, that is to say, though not in history, you can be at the same point twice. And it seems as if Prince Hal may be sufficient of a folklore hero to be permitted to go again through the cycle of riot and reform.'[97]

It is no longer necessary to justify the rejection of Falstaff. Most critics, however captivated by Falstaff, however disposed to argue in favour of instinctual life and rich though erring humanity, agree that the new king could no longer dally with his old drinking companion. Shakespeare has made such a conclusion inevitable by showing Falstaff in Part II sparring with the Lord Chief Justice and boasting to the foolish Justice Shallow, when news comes that the prince is now king: 'I am Fortune's steward! . . . the laws of England are at my commandment. Blessed are they that have been my friends, and woe to my Lord Chief Justice!' (V, 3, 126–34). The scene in which this bold claim is made immediately follows one in which the new king praises the Lord Chief Justice for having punished him severely when he was a riotous prince. Thus the scene of the rejection is prepared for by our knowledge of what use Falstaff plans to make of his friendship and our certainty that his friend is (once again) a new man.

If the transformation in Part I was the making of a knight, its counterpart in Part II is the making of a king. The final scene opens with the spectacular passage of the coronation procession across the stage. Falstaff then takes his place with the bystanders and begins promising what he will do with the power he expects to have. When the king and his train enter again with the Lord Chief Justice, Falstaff's jocular greeting is met with the stern 'I know thee not, old man' (V, 5, 47), which grieves Falstaff's literary admirers almost as much as it does him. It is indeed a sharp blow, but effective for the very reason that it is so unexpected by the recipient. Hotspur was similarly staggered by Vernon's description of the prince in armour, when he expected the latest scandalous report. The king leaves no doubt about the meaning of the rebuff:

> Presume not that I am the thing I was;
> For God doth know, so shall the world perceive,
> That I have turn'd away my former self; . . .
>
> (V, 5, 56–8)

The play ends with anticipation of the war in France in which the king is to prove himself a hero.

Knight, king and hero. The three facets of Henry V are not truly separable, and yet each play builds up to a striking demonstration of one of the three. Though the heroic is clearly the province of the last play, the second part of *Henry IV* prepares for it by introducing, before the main statement of the theme, a comic variation on it: Pistol is a travesty of the conqueror King Henry will become. The title page of the play, which was, in the manner of the time, part publisher's blurb, recognized the importance of Pistol as well as Falstaff by announcing 'The Second part of Henrie the fourth, continuing to his death, and coronation of Henrie the fift. With the humours of sir Iohn Falstaffe, and swaggering Pistoll.' Pistol's humours are given their first airing in the second-act tavern scene, which is one of the theatrical strong points of the play. It gets under way with a quarrel between Falstaff and the loud-mouthed Doll Tearsheet, his equal in coarseness if not in wit. When Falstaff's 'ancient' (ensign) is announced, Doll, immediately protests against admitting such a swaggering, foul-mouthed fellow (fearing, perhaps, to be outdone), and the Hostess, whose pretensions to gentility are her greatest comic asset, adds her protest, for fear of what the neighbours may say. But Falstaff insists, and Ancient Pistol strides into a tense situation— the ideal sort for him, offering very little real danger with maximal opportunity for bluster. Shakespeare begins the scene by exploiting the military and sexual puns lurking in Pistol's name as the first verbal shots are exchanged. Doll so infuriates him that he tears her ruff and even draws his sword as the Hostess in her best Malapropian vein begs him to 'aggravate' his choler. Then come verbal fireworks of a different sort, calculated to enchant a theatre audience familiar with the great hits of the previous decade. 'These be good humours indeed!' says Pistol:

> Shall pack-horses,
> And hollow pamper'd jades of Asia,
> Which cannot go but thirty mile a day,
> Compare with Caesars and with Cannibals,
> And Troyant Greeks? Nay, rather damn them with
> King Cerberus, and let the welkin roar!

*   *   *

Then feed and be fat, my fair Calipolis!

(II, 4, 160-5, 175)

The great ranting speeches of *Tamburlaine, The Battle of Alcazar* and probably of other plays now lost are chopped up and combined with bits of fustian from a contemporary depiction of 'The Bragger'[98] to give a devastating and exceedingly funny picture of heroic pretension based on nothing but words. Soon after his extravagant threats Pistol is forced out of the room by Falstaff and Bardolph, and the scene finishes with a prank played on Falstaff by the prince and Poins.

Henry V (1598-9), the last play in this historical tetralogy and the third of the plays concerned with the victor of Agincourt, is written in a different style from its predecessors. The new note is sounded in the opening lines of the Prologue, which have become deservedly famous:

> O, for a Muse of fire, that would ascend
> The brightest heaven of invention;
> A kingdom for a stage, princes to act
> And monarchs to behold the swelling scene!

As J. H. Walter says in his New Arden edition, 'Shakespeare's epic-like invocation embraces the fiery, warlike nature of his theme, the divine origins of poetry, and the sublimity of the conception he hopes to achieve' (p. 5n.). The heroic elevation of this Prologue, only briefly anticipated in earlier passages such as Vernon's description of the prince, recurs in the choruses which precede each act and in many speeches. The fact that some of these speeches, notably the king's at Harfleur and at Agincourt, have also become anthology pieces like the Prologue, indicates something of the distinctive quality of the play. Individual speeches assume greater importance here than in the preceding plays, because *Henry V* is more formal and its action less fluid. Moments of crisis are rendered in stirring oratory on the battlefield and in diplomatic exchanges shaped by the courtesy of court protocol. The tone of the play is largely determined by these elevated and formal utterances by characters in the play and by their presenters.

The association in the Prologue of poetic imagination with heroic vigour ('Piece out our imperfections with your thoughts' —l. 23) not only prepares for Henry's eloquence but points to the

97

visionary aspect of heroism seen in Tamburlaine, whose sword is a pen for redrawing the map of the world.[99] Henry's designs on the world map are less grandiose, but the imaginative appeal to an English audience of his revival of Edward III's claim to all of France is obvious. Shakespeare thus makes the imaginative effort to which he summons the audience an analogue of the ambitious vision of his hero. If the 'unworthy scaffold' of the stage can be transformed into England and France, the audience can participate in the enterprise of 'warlike Harry'.

Having been converted to honour twice, Henry cannot be converted again, but the ghost of his unconverted self haunts the play, keeping the old contrast alive. In the first scene the Bishop of Ely discusses the extraordinary transformation with the Archbishop of Canterbury, who treats it as quasi-miraculous:

> Consideration like an angel came,
> And whipp'd th'offending Adam out of him,
> Leaving his body as a Paradise, . . .
>
> (I, 1, 28–30)

Ely gives a more homely explanation, that 'wholesome berries thrive and ripen best/Neighbour'd by fruit of lesser quality' (ll. 61–2), recalling Warwick's defence of the prince in *II Henry IV* (IV, 4, 67–78), that he was educating himself by studying his low companions, and thereby benefiting from his unsavoury association. Canterbury agrees with Ely that the conversion cannot be the miracle it seems, but the introduction of this possibility has already contributed to the elevation of King Henry's character. He is a hero who appears to have received divine favour.

The old reputation for wildness functions in another way in the episode of the tennis balls sent by the Dauphin. Here the fact that the French are so ill-informed about recent developments is made to seem an indication of their folly and triviality. Henry's reply, earnest, pious and energetic, shows how completely he has taken on his father's view of the office of kingship:

> But tell the Dauphin I will keep my state,
> Be like a king and show my sail of greatness
> When I do rouse me in my throne of France: . . .
>
> (I, 2, 273–5)

In *Henry V* Shakespeare adds another dimension to his hero's character—his utter devotion to the cause of his country. Even more conspicuously than Edward III, Henry is the patriot hero, the polar opposite of the tyrant heroes and also opposed to Tamburlaine, whose empire is his brain-child and never the object of his veneration nor a master whom he serves. After Canterbury, in the second scene, has explained to the king the justness of his claim to the throne of France, he explains how England may be defended while the king is fighting abroad, if every citizen is assigned a task and all work for the good of the whole. Referring to those favourite models of corporate enterprise, the bees, Canterbury gives a long and fanciful account of their ideal commonwealth. One remarkable line carries a large percentage of his meaning: 'The singing masons building roofs of gold' (I, 2, 198). In this complex image architecture and music are joined as in the legend of Amphion, whose music raised the walls of Thebes. The construction of the golden honeycomb-palace is a triumph of harmony and design from which an entire community is to benefit. The prominence given to these ideas strongly fortifies the impression made by the king in asking whether his cause is just, and if so, how he can best carry out the French campaign without leaving England unprotected. His ambitions are completely identified with the common good.

The episode in which he punishes the traitors who were plotting to murder him provides further evidence of his subordination of personal feeling to patriotic concern. Although he rebukes them in a fervent speech, he specifically abjures personal revenge and orders their deaths for contriving the ruin of the kingdom (II, 2, 79–144, 166–93). The same spirit breathes in the familiar 'Once more unto the breach, dear friends' (III, 1, 1–34) and the St Crispin's day oration with its stress on the 'happy few' privileged to fight for their country (IV, 3, 19–67).

The king's speeches are fluent and often moving but never so extravagant as Hotspur's 'By heaven, methinks it were an easy leap/To pluck bright honour from the pale-fac'd moon,' not to mention the soaring eloquence of Tamburlaine. In the most passionate of them all, the exhortation of the army on St Crispin's day, Henry boasts of no hold over fate, and offers no crowns to loyal followers:

By Jove, I am not covetous for gold,
Nor care I who doth feed upon my cost;
It earns me not if men my garments wear;
Such outward things dwell not in my desires:
But if it be a sin to covet honour,
I am the most offending soul alive.

(IV, 3, 24–9)

In his disregard for gold and longing for honour he is the perfect chivalric hero, but despite his high aspirations he retains a kind of simplicity and even humility conspicuously lacking in other aspiring heroes.

Pistol's boasts and threats are the perfect foil, and though he never quite rises to the absurd heights of his scene in *II Henry IV*, his quarrel with Nym in Act II, Scene 1, is an excellent reminder of his style. On one occasion the king exchanges brags with the French king's herald, but not only does he apologize for doing so, blaming the air of France for such boastfulness, but his brags are only of the bravery of his sick men.

If Pistol, Bardolph and Nym, the bad soldiers, serve as a contrast to Henry's solid virtues, the good soldiers, Gower, Fluellen, Macmorris and Jamy, representing England, Wales, Ireland and Scotland, act as reflectors of his valour and discipline. Fluellen also discusses the king and works out an ingenious parallel between Henry and Alexander the Great (IV, 7, 11–52). In this way the good soldiers provide within the body of the play a point of view similar to that of the prologue and the choruses between the acts. The chorus preceding Act IV praises the king, in fact, for the very quality traditionally associated with Alexander: 'A Largess universal like the sun/His liberal eye doth give to everyone' (ll. 43–4). It is characteristic of Shakespeare's presentation of Henry that largesse is made to mean here a giving of self and not of material gifts.

The scene in which the king in disguise dispenses this largesse, cheering the troops on the even of the Battle of Agincourt with 'A little touch of Harry in the night', presents a fundamental problem about Henry's role as king and hero. He promises his father to 'be more himself' in taking on the chivalric virtues, and he seems to shed some outer layer of himself when, on becoming king, he rejects Falstaff. In this play he performs as warrior-king with

The Indian Queen

J. Smith ex.   W. Vincent fe

3 'The Indian Queen'
   Reproduced by courtesy of the Harvard Theatre Collection

4 Muly Labas and Morena in Prison
Reproduced by courtesy of the Beinecke Rare Book and Manuscript Library, Yale University

complete assurance as if, indeed, this were the essential Henry, but now we are obliged to see at least what the transformation has cost him, and perhaps to question whether what we have been seeing is the whole man or a part he has elected to play. In other words, the conversion, already put to such effective dramatic use, is now made the basis of a further probing of character and of a concept of heroism.

When Henry tells Bates and Williams that 'the king is but a man as I am: . . . his ceremonies laid by, in his nakedness he appears but a man' (IV, 1, 101–2, 105–6), it is not mere comic irony. He is deliberately presenting himself to his men as a man. In response to his comments they raise the problem of the king's moral responsibility for his men if his 'cause be not good', and Henry partially evades this question by answering only that the king cannot be responsible for the state of each man's soul. That he nevertheless feels his responsibility deeply is apparent when he is left alone to reflect:

> Upon the king! let us our lives, our souls,
> Our debts, our careful wives,
> Our children, and our sins lay on the king!
> We must bear all. O hard condition!
> Twin-born with greatness, subject to the breath
> Of every fool, whose sense no more can feel
> But his own wringing. What infinite heart's ease
> Must kings neglect that private men enjoy!
> And what have kings that privates have not too,
> Save ceremony, save general ceremony?
>
> (IV, 1, 236–45)

In his mind the problem of his moral responsibility is brought into line with the still more general problem, which plagued his father also, of the cares of kingship. This is not only a very general problem; it is also a cliché of Stoical and Christian thought. In Henry V's case, however, it has the special applicability that he has assumed these cares so consciously and so abruptly. The contrast between private man and king is also the contrast between Prince Hal and King Henry, and the questioning of the intrinsic worth of ceremony which follows the lines quoted is a questioning of what he has made himself.

Although the soliloquy ends on a seemingly unfavourable

comparison of the king to the commoner, Henry's prayer a few lines later indicates that he accepts the penalties and responsibilities of his office. He prays for courage for his soldiers and forgiveness of his father's usurpation, for which he has tried to atone in part by reburying the body of Richard II and building two chantries. In the same spirit in which he takes on his inherited share of Henry IV's guilt he prepares to do all that is required of him as king. When we next see him he is delivering the St Crispin's Day oration, where he appeals to his followers to join him in an aristocracy based on heroic deeds.

The distinction he seeks for himself is now seen to be what he can earn rather than what ceremony accords him; yet at this moment he is playing to the hilt his role as warrior-king. Rather than choose either horn of his dilemma, he seems determined to annihilate the dichotomy of private man and king by conducting the battle as both a leader and a comrade.

The astounding triumph of the ragged, ill-fed English over the well-equipped and far more numerous French is given its full dramatic value and provides the high point of the play. The king attributes the victory to God, but in human terms it is, of course, the victory of the patriot hero who has sacrificed his personal pleasures but not his humanity to be a chivalric king. In a sense it is also a victory of morale over ceremony.

The contrast between rough strength and hollow formality carries over into the fifth act and gives a certain thematic relevance to the wooing of the French princess, which is in other respects a disappointing conclusion. After the intoxicating statistics of French nobles captured or dead, the king's hearty teasing of Princess Katharine is undeniably a come-down:

> *K. Hen.* . . . Do you like me, Kate?
> *Kath.* Pardonnez-moi, I cannot tell wat is 'like me.'
> *K. Hen.* An angel is like you, Kate, and you are like an
> angel.
>
> (V, 2, 107–10)

Yet in its way—a not altogether satisfactory way—this scene completes the pattern of Shakespeare's portrayal of Henry V. Abandoning the formal language of court and the rhetorical devices of his battlefield oratory, Henry adopts a conversational

idiom which is much more personal. He presents himself to
Katharine as both a man and a king:

> I speak to thee plain soldier: if thou canst love me for this,
> take me; if not, to say to thee that I shall die, is true; but
> for thy love, by the Lord, no; yet I love thee too. . . . If
> thou would have such a one, take me; and take me, take
> a soldier; take a soldier, take a king.
>
> (V, 2, 152-6, 170-2)

It seems to us today somewhat arch, as if he were making rather
too much of being plain Harry while knowing that he is a conquering king, able to dictate terms, but in Elizabethan times
it may have seemed more like the true simplicity of a great man.
If the king as lover can be seen in this light, the wooing scene resolves some of the problems raised by the earlier speeches on
ceremony. Here, with 'ceremonies laid by', is a more genuine
personal relationship than the casual contact, in disguise, with
Bates and Williams, and a less dangerous relationship than the
long since abandoned friendship with Falstaff. Henry does not
so much escape from the restraints of ceremony as rise above it,
when, in defiance of French protocol, he offers to kiss the princess,
and at her hesitation says:

> O Kate! nice customs curtsy to great kings. Dear Kate,
> you and I cannot be confined within the weak list of a
> country's fashion: we are the makers of manners, Kate.
>
> (V, 2, 284-7)

Having denied himself the simple pleasures of the citizen and
shouldered his regal responsibilities, Henry is now entitled to
amuse himself in the planning of a dynastic match with a pretty
girl.

When Henry's success in reducing Katharine to wordless
compliance is followed by the arrival of the entire French court, a
ceremonial confirmation of the match also confirms the English
victory and promises the union of the two kingdoms. The pattern
of romance asserts itself powerfully here in preparations for a
marriage to reward the efforts of the hero and to symbolize the
attainment of harmony. Even in Renaissance treatises on kingship, as J. H. Walter points out in his introduction (p. xxxi),
marriage is the proper completion of the virtues of a Christian

prince, and such a conclusion is especially fitting in a history so much affected as this one is by the ideals of chivalric romance. Starting as a novice, Henry has learned the lessons of knighthood, won his spurs, been tested in battle and now wins the lady. But Shakespeare has used this pattern along with others to make the play both a fitting culmination to his historical tetralogy and an analysis of the meaning of heroic kingship.

Between *Henry V* and *Antony and Cleopatra* Shakespeare wrote no play dominated by a heroic ideal, but three of the major tragedies of this period are affected by heroic concepts which condition the protagonists' views of themselves. Hamlet is literally haunted by a heroic ideal in the person of his dead father, whose accomplishments he reveres but cannot equal. The image of 'that fair and warlike form' appears in the first scene, 'armed at point exactly, cap-a-pe', and we are told of the single combat, 'well ratified by law and heraldry', in which Hamlet Senior defeated the king of Norway. That Prince Hamlet can never translate into action the ideal for which his father stands is at the centre of his tragedy, for neither will he totally relinquish the ideal and scheme against his uncle with the fiendish ingenuity of other revengers in contemporary plays and stories. When the players come, he hears an echo of the heroism he admires in the curiously elevated diction of the speech based on Aeneas' description of the death of Priam in Virgil. The actor's ability to mime this scene and even weep for Hecuba seems to Hamlet like an indictment of his inability to rise to the challenge that life has presented to him. Opportunities for heroic action are offered but not taken, and the not-taking of heroic action is one of the many themes of the play. Hamlet's last concern is for the 'wounded name' that may live after him if his part in the unheroic wholesale slaughter at the end is not understood.

The warrior Othello has a heroic image of himself, the shattering of which in the last act brings on his suicide. Only the perfection he insists upon explains the violence of his disillusionment when he is made to believe that he has been betrayed by Desdemona. At one blow his reputation seems to have been impaired and the basis of his emotional life destroyed. But even at the moment of the murder he believes that he is being true to his love of justice despite the temptation to be merciful. Discovery of the truth forces him to see how miserably far from heroic he has been.

When Othello's nobility and idealism are underplayed, as they occasionally are, an important dimension of the play is lost. Shakespeare makes dramatic capital out of Othello's high-mindedness by exploiting the familiarity of the audience with wicked Moors such as Muly Mahamet and Aaron. He even opens the play with Iago's distortion of Othello's character, in which the lechery, pride and crude extravagance of these stage Moors are featured. The actual Othello who then appears on the stage is therefore the more remarkable for being precisely the opposite of what is expected. His views of both love and war are idealized in the manner characteristic of romance, as some of the more familiar quotations show:

> . . . when I love thee not,
> Chaos is come again.
>
> (III, 3, 92–3)

> . . . nay, had she been true,
> If heaven would make me such another world,
> Of one entire and perfect chrysolite,
> I'ld not have sold her for it.
>
> (V, 2, 144–7)

> Farewell the plumed troop, and the big wars,
> That makes ambition virtue: O farewell,
> Farewell the neighing steed, and the shrill trump,
> The spirit-stirring drum, the ear-piercing fife;
> The royal banner, and all quality,
> Pride, pomp, and circumstance of glorious war!
>
> (III, 3, 355–60)

Thus heroic ideals are built into his character and determine part of the expected response to his tragedy. Yet the play as a whole is not heroic drama, since its emphasis is so clearly upon limitation, and specifically upon a man's failure to be the hero he thought himself to be.

King Lear is a play which is even further removed from the heroic by its dominating pattern of error, suffering and repentance leading to increased self-knowledge. But the implications of this pattern are so extensively modified by other elements in the play that the significance of the tragedy, culminating in the murder of the innocent heroine and the death of the repentant hero, continues to be debated. The periodic recurrence of heroic self-assertion, interrupting Lear's pilgrimage from error to enlightenment and from pride to humility, is one of these complicating elements. The old king's claim on our respect is partly due to his elemental rages at what he considers injustice; if the first of them, directed at Cordelia, is clearly based on blindness to true worth, the last, when he shouts, 'Howl, howl, howl' as he carries on stage the body of Cordelia, expresses an acknowledged truth, that the worthy are not always rewarded. Between these two outpourings come his cursing of Goneril and Regan and his vying with the storm on the heath, to which differing amounts of approval or sympathy may be due, but in each instance the powerful statement of conviction testifies to extraordinary strength. Lear never loses, even after his disillusionment, his vision of himself as 'every inch a king'. The hero of the earlier, anonymous *King Leir*, who weeps more than he rages, is more pathetic than admirable. Though his repentance for the injustice done to his good daughter is rewarded by reconciliation with her and total victory over his evil daughters, he never attains the stature of Shakespeare's Lear. One of several responses a reader or spectator may have to Shakespearer's final scene is summed up in Kent's words at the death of Lear, 'The wonder is he hath endur'd so long', and this wonder at a capacity greater than one could expect is the feeling most often inspired by the heroic. To the extent that the play emphasizes such individual capacity it touches on the realm of heroic drama.

Lear, who at times sees himself as a heroic defender of his principles, has a greater heroic dimension for the audience than either Hamlet or Othello. Macbeth is heroic in a different way from any of the three, for one's sense of his extraordinary capacity has relatively little to do with his view of himself. Like Richard III, he is ambitious for power, unscrupulous in getting it and tyrannical in using it; yet the 'fruition of an earthly crown' does not obsess his imagination as it does Tamburlaine's or Richard's. His visions are of another order. The 'horrid image' of murder both excites and terrifies him, but a moral sense quite foreign to either of them restrains him until Lady Macbeth persuades him to repress it. The progressive deadening of this impulse is, from one point of view, the refusal of opportunities once offered and the diminution of potential greatness. But it is not entirely so. His total commitment to Lady Macbeth's concept of manliness as naked valour, unqualified by moral scruple, is remarkable in one who begins with his awareness.[100] The very success in stifling conscience reveals strength, and there is, as Matthew Proser says, 'something awesome' about his choice of fighting at the end, when he at last understands the meaning of the riddling prophecies. 'Untouched by remorse or repentance he becomes his own victim, his own damnation.'[101] Looked at from this point of view, Macbeth's development has a Satanic grandeur and leads to what Clifford Leech has called his achievement of 'a profound mode of being'[102] through his progressive knowledge of evil.

In *Antony and Cleopatra* (1606–7) a heroic concept of character once more assumes major importance in the total meaning of a Shakespearian play. Antony is another of those heroes, more great than good, whom I have called Herculean.[103] Unlike Henry V, he refuses to subordinate his desires to the common weal, and since the great distraction of his life in Cleopatra, it is possible to view him as Shakespeare's Romans do (and as Plutarch mainly does) as a man ruined by sensual indulgence. But the play, while presenting this view forcefully in many scenes, works towards a revaluation of Antony's nature, in which his faults seem almost inseparable from his virtues, and his virtues those of a demigod. It is Cleopatra's description of the dead Antony in Act V which completes this process and leaves with the spectator an image of mythic proportions:

> His legs bestrid the ocean, his rear'd arm
> Crested the world: his voice was propertied
> As all the tuned spheres, and that to friends:
> But when he meant to quail, and shake the orb,
> He was as rattling thunder.
>
> (V, 2, 82–6)

Meanwhile Octavius Caesar, the triumvir who tends to the business of the empire with ascetic concentration, seems to shrink until one can almost accept at face value Cleopatra's ' 'tis paltry to be Caesar' (V, 2, 2). Here the determination to rule is given none of the noble overtones it has in other plays. Instead, it seems a little mean, as if mere control of men and territories were for the less imaginative sort of man.

The magic by which Shakespeare accomplishes this revaluation is essentially a manipulation of perspective, in which certain characteristics are seen at very close range while others are distanced. The effect of a readjustment of dimensions is reinforced by the fact that one of Antony's characteristics which is brought closest to us is in itself a matter of spiritual dimension. This is his liberality, which, like the largesse of certain heroes of romance, implies both magnificence and magnanimity. Cleopatra continues her description by saying:

> For his bounty,
> There was no winter in 't: an autumn 'twas
> That grew the more by reaping: his delights
> Were dolphin-like, they show'd his back above
> The element they lived in: in his livery
> Walk'd crowns and crownets: realms and islands were
> As plates dropp'd from his pocket.
>
> (V, 2, 86–92)

Antony's first display of this trait in its most concrete sense occurs when he is at his lowest point, following the ignominious defeat at Actium for which his bad judgment was to blame. Overcome with shame, he reproaches himself for his loss of leadership ('for indeed I have lost command'), and dismisses his men, offering them a ship 'laden with gold' (III, 11, 1–24). When Cleopatra approaches in a contrite mood, begging forgiveness for her share in the débâcle, he shows another kind of generosity by telling her that one kiss will repay him (ll. 69–71). Both gestures are so obviously the products of despair that they alarm as much as they comfort those who love him, and yet in their very excessiveness they are typical of Antony. At his first appearance on the stage he replies to a teasing question of Cleopatra's by insisting that his love for her can have no limits—'There's beggary in the love that can be reckon'd' (I, 1, 15). Somewhat later Cleopatra says of him:

> Be'st thou sad, or merry,
> The violence of either thee becomes,
> So does it no man else.
>
> (I, 5, 59–61)[104]

From the Roman point of view these violent extremes, whether 'lascivious wassails' or sudden rages, are the very things which destroy Antony's effectiveness as a general and triumvir, and indeed Antony seems to perform these duties less and less according to Roman rules. The soothsayer makes the curious observation that Antony is bound to lose at any game he plays with Caesar, and that his demon or spirit, though nobler than Caesar's, is daunted in Caesar's presence. He sums up:

> Thy lustre thickens,
> When he shines by: I say again, thy spirit
> Is all afraid to govern thee near him;
> But he away, 'tis noble.

(II, 3, 26–9)

If the defeat at Actium seems to be due quite simply to the faults of which the Romans accuse Antony, the soothsayer's superstitious talk of a spirit which is only great when far from Caesar suggests something positive about Antony's excesses, and thus mirrors Cleopatra's admiring comment on the violence of his moods. By the time of Actium, if not earlier, the extremes to which Antony goes can be seen paradoxically as evidence of both an unstable character and a certain largeness of spirit.

After he has offered his treasure to his officers and has forgiven Cleopatra, Antony displays the excessiveness of his violent demon in several ways. He sends a cringing message to Caesar, who is then encouraged to demand that Cleopatra turn Antony over to him. At this Antony is so incensed that he challenges Caesar to single combat—a heroic gesture which provokes Enobarbus' scornful comment: 'Caesar, thou hast subdued/His judgement too' (III, 13, 36–7). Cleopatra, clearly bewildered by her lover's behaviour, receives Caesar's messenger, and without making any commitment, seems to leave the way open to a settlement. As the messenger kisses her hand Antony enters. Enraged at what he sees, he orders the messenger whipped, and, turning on Cleopatra, reviles her with a brutality as fierce as his earlier forgiveness was mild. Cleopatra's response is unexpected. Antony's torrent of abuse, and perhaps also his cruelty to the messenger (for she, too, has violent ways with messengers), prompts a moving statement of her love to him—the most outright commitment she has made—and leads to their plan for 'one other gaudy night'.

At Antony's low point his generosity seems to extend almost to a giving away of himself and thus to a diminution of his stature, whereas his angry self-assertion once more augments his stature, at least in the eyes of Cleopatra. And it is more and more from her point of view that we are led to see him.

To Enobarbus is given the chief responsibility for reminding us of the Roman point of view, as he comments satirically on the scene just described and decides to desert Antony (III, 13, 195–201). Shakespeare's manipulation of perspective is nowhere more apparent than in his way of discrediting the unfavourable conclusions of this commentator. Told of Enobarbus' desertion, Antony sends his treasure after him, and Enobarbus, crushed by this generosity, pays an agonized tribute to his former master:

> O Antony,
> Thou mine of bounty, how wouldst thou have paid
> My better service, when my turpitude
> Thou dost so crown with gold!
>
> (IV, 6, 31–4)

Bounty clearly betokens here, not weakness, but largeness of spirit.

Antony's momentary victory is not militarily significant, but it is a demonstration of personal valour, and that, increasingly, is what counts for the audience. Cleopatra helps to arm him for the battle, and retires to her chamber wishing that her lord were headed for single combat with Caesar (IV, 4, 36–8). In another era she might have gone to a castle window to watch the tournament, and precisely this chivalric atmosphere pervades the scenes of Antony's arming. At his victorious return he is greeted by his lady:

> Lord of lords,
> O infinite virtue, com'st thou smiling from
> The world's great snare uncaught?
>
> (IV, 8, 16–18)

The ultimate defeat brings Antony to another moment of disillusionment with Cleopatra and loss of confidence in himself. In his famous comparison of himself to 'a cloud that's dragonish' but quickly loses its shape, his image seems once more in danger of being not only diminished but dissipated, but the process is suddenly reversed by the false news of Cleopatra's suicide.[105] On this occasion his heroic resolution is prompted not by suspicion, but by emulation of a noble act. In one case Cleopatra's seeming betrayal stings him into a reassertion of himself; in the other her nobility heartens him to take his life as a defiance of Caesar and a pledge of his love. In comparison to the values of this love and of the individual courage it inspires, the importance of success in Caesar's world shrinks steadily in the latter part of the play until at the end both the hero and the heroine seem to have transcended such mundane considerations.

Cleopatra, by committing suicide 'after the high Roman fashion' but also after a very Egyptian fashion in all her regal finery, becomes heroic in her own right. She is also the living emblem of a love that, by the last act, is more 'fine amor' than lechery. She is the chief means by which the character of Antony is finely elevated, even as his dying body is hoisted by Cleopatra and her women into her monument. It is she who expresses most fully the colossal proportions of the man, juxtaposing in successive clauses of her description the cosmic harmony of his voice to friends, the thunder of his rages, the active play of his sensuality and the magnificence of his bounty.

In Coriolanus Shakespeare created another colossus and the last (1608) of his tragic heroes. Again the trait of generosity is stressed: when the mutinous citizens are enumerating Caius Marcius' faults in the opening scene, one of them has the honesty to insist, 'You must in no way say he is covetous' (I, 1, 39–40),[106] and at the battle of Corioli the implied estimate is confirmed. The hero shows his scorn for material rewards in his harsh words to some Roman looters (I, 5, 4–8) and in his refusal to accept more than his share of the spoils (I, 9, 38–40). In most respects Coriolanus, as he is named after his victory, is as different from Antony as it is possible to be, and even this generosity, though reminiscent of Antony, has a harder edge. If it commands respect it does not move anyone to tears, as Antony's does when he gives money to all his household servants on the eve of battle, making even Enobarbus 'onion-ey'd' (IV, 2, 10–45). Coriolanus does not actually give anything of his own, but refuses to take anything he does not deserve. Considering captured horses and treasure beneath his deserts, he says:

> I thank you, general,
> But cannot make my heart consent to take
> A bribe to pay my sword.
>
> (I, 9, 36–8)

His greatness is decidedly forbidding. It is manifested not in human excesses but in inhuman superiority, with all that word connotes of both inherent worth and scornfulness.

Negative generosity is characteristic of Coriolanus, but the real key to his character is inflexibility, a trait Shakespeare had touched on in *Titus Andronicus*. Here it is carried to extraordinary lengths. We know from the start that Caius Marcius is the epitome of valour, and that Rome has greatly benefited from his fighting, though some of the angry citizens think he is more interested in pleasing his mother and himself than in serving Rome. In the battle of Corioli, which takes place early in the play, his accomplishments include the seemingly superhuman feat of winning a single-handed fight inside the walls of the enemy city, whose fall is attributable solely to him. Unyielding in battle, he is also unyielding in his devotion to a code of heroic behaviour in which Roman *virtus* is the virtue of virtues.

The consequences of such inflexibility are the subject of the tragedy. The prickly character of the hero brings him into conflict with the citizenry of Rome, with their scheming representatives, the tribunes, and even with his mother, Volumnia, an archetypal Roman parent, worthy to be classed with Lucius Junius Brutus and the mother of the Gracchi. Each confrontation challenges the assumptions by which Coriolanus lives, and thus contributes to a continuous dialectic which accompanies the story of the hero's rise and fall. The play is more analytical than any other Shakespearian tragedy, and yet through it all runs a thread of wonder at an excellence which defies analysis.

The first scene is not calculated to make the audience love the hero. Arriving just when Menenius has cajoled the rebellious citizens into a relative calm, Coriolanus showers his scorn on them with a spectacular disregard for tact and tactics. We are immediately aware of his aristocratic prejudice, but there is also a more solid basis for his attitude. He accuses the crowd of cowardliness, injustice and inconstancy, and here we can begin to see in the midst of his apparent faults the virtues he not only admires but possesses—bravery, justice and constancy. Though Shakespeare portrays some of the citizens as reasonable, humane individuals, their behaviour as a group in the ensuing action substantiates the accusations of Coriolanus. At the battle of Corioli they run away until Coriolanus drives them back; in Rome they give him their

votes, then banish him, and finally claim they were opposed to
the banishment. These confirmations of the hero's view come to us
one by one in the course of the play, qualifying the initial impression of pride and intemperate anger made by his outburst in
the first scene. But even this reappraisal hardly makes him a
character to whom our hearts go out.

The revelation of Coriolanus' contempt for the citizens is
immediately followed by another, the full significance of which
cannot be appreciated until the latter half of the play. News comes
that the Volsces are in arms, and Coriolanus, delighted by the
prospect of a change from political wrangling to outright war,
dilates upon the virtues of the enemy general, Tullus Aufidius:

> They have a leader,
> Tullus Aufidius, that will put you to't.
> I sin in envying his nobility;
> And were I any thing but what I am,
> I would wish me only he. . . .
> Were half to half the world by th' ears and he
> Upon my party, I'd revolt, to make
> Only my wars with him. He is a lion
> That I am proud to hunt.
>
> (I, 1, 223–31)

Like Antony, Coriolanus would prefer to test his valour in single
combat, but so great is his devotion to the ideal of individual
prowess that loyalty to any group is of secondary importance. He
is permitting himself an extravagance, of course, when he speaks
in this way, and does not intend to be taken at his word, but his
fantasy provides a true insight into his nature. When Rome
banishes him, Tullus Aufidius is the man he goes to, seeking an
alliance with him or death at his hands.

The episode in which the victor of Corioli is asked to show his
wounds to the people and to solicit their votes for his consulship
moves him toward the complete break with Rome. Compliance
with this ancient custom is repellent to him not only because it
makes him ask favours from people whom he despises, but also
because he believes in absolute justice. If he deserves the consulship for having saved the city, he should not have to sue for it.
The truth of the situation is the brave deeds he has performed,
which cannot be enhanced by a ritual in which kind words he

does not mean are repaid by flattery. He only half complies, and the people are easily persuaded by the tribunes to withdraw the assent they have given Coriolanus. He then speaks once more as he thinks, giving the tribunes the pretext they need for another uprising. Menenius' comment on this disastrous turn relates Coriolanus' intransigent honesty to nobility:

> His nature is too noble for the world.
> He would not flatter Neptune for his trident,
> Or Jove for's power to thunder. His heart's his mouth.
> What his breast forges, that his tongue must vent; . . .
>
> (III, 1, 255–8)

His eccentricity is more than simple pride; it is heroic devotion to principle, to the point where the world and the people in it count very little. He insists that the words he speaks must mirror his feelings with absolute fidelity—must be projections of himself rather than mere instruments to advance his interests.[107] He is a very different sort of speaker from Tamburlaine, who is no less of an egotist, but uses oratory to stir the sympathies of others. So far is Coriolanus from any fellow feeling with his auditors or concern for what they think of him that one of the tribunes remarks sarcastically, but also shrewdly:

> You speak o' th' people
> As if you were a god to punish, not
> A man of their infirmity.
>
> (III, 1, 80–2)

Among those with whom Coriolanus is contrasted in the first three acts the people are fickle, the tribunes devious and Menenius, who supports Coriolanus, a practical politician, willing to cajole and compromise to achieve patrician goals. To the hero's amazement his mother ranks herself with those who urge him to veil his feelings and make peace with his opponents. Volumnia has brought her son up to feel as he does about the plebeians and to cherish manly valour above all else, but in two respects she differs from him: she is eminently practical, and the end in view is always the glory of Rome. By stressing these differences, Shakespeare pushes the situation of Coriolanus towards its first major crisis in the episode of his candidacy for the consulship. For Volumnia believes that in order to become consul he should dissemble if necessary. She even gives him a model speech for the occasion, applauded by Menenius. But Coriolanus is crushed. Having told her that he only wants to 'play the man I am', he finally agrees with great bitterness to be as insincere as a whore or a mountebank. Unfortunately for Volumnia's plan, he is unable to carry it through. The moment he is baited by the tribunes he reverts to speaking what is in his heart, which is enough to get him banished. His honesty has opposed him to his native city.

When Coriolanus leaves Rome, 'alone,/Like to a lonely dragon' (IV, 1, 29–30), despising the city which has rejected him, and seeking 'a world elsewhere' (III, 3, 134–6), he is the perfect example of the hero as lonegoer. Neither a villain who defies accepted morality to gain power over his world nor a benefactor willing to sacrifice himself for the public weal, he risks everything in order to be what he is. His old enemy Aufidius, to whom he now turns, sums up his character with remarkable objectivity in a long speech in which he sees as one explanation of Coriolanus' behaviour a nature which will not 'be other than one thing' (IV, 7, 41–2). In the second stage of his career this determination leads to a far more basic conflict than any he has envisaged.

The 'world elsewhere' is not an actual place but a world of Coriolanus' heroic imagining, where former enemies may join hands and fight for the vindication of the brave and the true. In this light he seems to see his alliance with the Volscians and his planned revenge on Rome, though to Aufidius it is a much more down-to-earth matter of exploiting the great general's pique in order to get the upper hand over traditional enemies. The legendary invincibility of Coriolanus brings Volscian victories, and Rome, helpless in the path of the advancing army, begins sending envoys to plead with him. Reports come to the city of Coriolanus leading the Volscians like a god, or 'like a thing/Made by some other deity than nature,/That shapes man better (IV 6, 91–3). He is portrayed as seated on a gold throne, 'his eye as red as 'twould burn Rome' (V, 1, 63–4)—an icon of revenging divinity. 'He wants nothing of a god but eternity, and a heaven to throne in' (V, 4, 23–4). He has almost made himself into the sort of superhuman being who might inhabit his imaginary world.

Almost, but not quite; for complete success would mean the denial of Coriolanus' humanity. Only when Volumnia comes, accompanied by his wife and child, does he realize that the course

he has chosen opposes him not only to Rome but to nature.[108]
As he sees them approach he says:

> But out, affection!
> All bond and privilege of nature, break!
> Let it be virtuous to be obstinate.

(V, 3, 24–6)

> . . . my young boy
> Hath an aspect of intercession which
> Great nature cries, 'Deny not!'

(ll. 31–3)

and then:

> I'll never
> Be such a gosling to obey instinct, but stand
> As if a man were author of himself
> And knew no other kin.

(ll. 34–7)

Volumnia, as might be expected, subjects him to her most
moving rhetoric, appealing to his patriotism and to his love for his
family, not hesitating to suggest what will happen to her in the
flaming ruins of Rome. In this scene, one of Shakespeare's most
powerful, the issues are clear but complex. Natural feeling is
opposed to absolute justice, since nothing Volumnia says mitigates
the excessive severity of banishing Coriolanus. Oratory is opposed
to logic, a mixture of good and bad to neat distinctions between
them, and second thoughts to total consistency. When Coriolanus
gives in, he does not so much bend as break. The inflexible
character, reflected in the hard, metallic imagery of which G.
Wilson Knight has written,[109] shatters as the pressure for change
mounts. As he tells his mother, hers is a happy victory for Rome but
'most mortal' to him (V, 3, 185–9).

The stage picture of the broken hero is ironically sandwiched
between some of the reports of his god-like superiority. The last of
these is followed by the scene in which Aufidius incites the Volscians to murder Coriolanus as a traitor to his word and a boy
dominated by his mother. There is nothing transcendent in this
death, but the greatness of Coriolanus is reaffirmed by his response
to the accusations of his enemy. At 'traitor' and 'boy of tears' he
speaks what is in his heart for one final time, reminding the

Volscians with magnificent folly that he once took their city of Corioli alone. It is as if he had for a moment reassembled the shattered pieces of his heroic image. Once he is dead, even his enemies realize that nothing so remarkable remains as what they have destroyed.

But the Volscians merely complete a process for which they are not mainly responsible. Nor is Volumnia truly responsible. Coriolanus destroys himself by pursuing an ideal so absolute that it exceeds human bounds and is even denied by one part of his own nature. The final conflict between Volumnia and Coriolanus is more truly a conflict within himself. Thus he is the most paradoxical of heroes. Antony's excessiveness has both good and bad manifestations, but one can distinguish between them with some assurance. In Coriolanus the opposed traits nearly cancel each other out, leaving the beholder not only awed but bewildered. The difference between the impressions made by the two heroes is suggested perfectly by the difference between Cleopatra's description of Antony bestriding the ocean and Aufidius' analysis of Coriolanus, ending with the couplet:

> One fire drives out one fire; one nail, one nail;
> Rights by rights founder, strengths by strengths do fail.
>
> (IV, 7, 54–5)

Notes

1 *The Knight of the Burning Pestle*, ed. John Doebler (Lincon, Neb., 1967), I, 215–21. The play was probably performed in 1607 (see Doebler, xi–xiii). It is impossible to be sure whether Beaumont had seen *Don Quixote*, published in 1605 (first translated into English in 1612, the year before the printing of *The Knight of the Burning Pestle*), but it is probable that he had not (see the edition of the·play by H. S. Murch [New York, 1908], xxxii–lviii, and Charles M. Gayley, *Francis Beaumont: Dramatist* [London, 1941], 313–31).

2 *The Scholemaster* (published posthumously in 1570), in Smith, I, 4.

3 See Ronald S. Crane, *The Vogue of Medieval Chivalric Romance during the English Renaissance* (Menasha, Wis., 1919).

4 Alfred Harbage discusses the taste of the audience in the 'private houses' as opposed to that of the public-theatre audience in *Shakespeare and the Rival Traditions* (New York, 1952), and comments on this play specifically (pp. 106–8).

5 See Louis Wright, *Middle-Class Culture in Elizabethan England* (Ithaca, N.Y., 1963; orig. 1935), 81–118, 375–417.

6 Alan Isler shows that by Elizabethan criteria both the old and the revised Arcadia qualified as heroic poetry (*PMLA*, LXXXIII [1968], 368–79).

7 'An Apology for Poetry', in Smith, I, 197.

8 Records for the nineties are fragmentary; see Lee M. Ellison, *The Early Romantic Drama at the English Court* (Menasha, Wis., 1917); Marion Jones, 'The Court and the Dramatists', *Elizabethan Theatre*, ed. J. R. Brown and B. Harris (London, 1966), 173–4.

9 *Plays Confuted in Five Actions* [1582] in *The English Drama and Stage*, ed. W. C. Hazlitt (New York, n.d.; orig. 1869), 181.

10 All quotations are taken from *Clyomon and Clamydes* (Malone Society Reprints, 1913).

11 *From Mankind to Marlowe* (Cambridge, Mass., 1962), esp. 68–85, 190–8. See also Harbage, *Rival Traditions*, 62, 343.

12 *Shakespeare and the Allegory of Evil* (New York, 1958), 121. Spivack traces the development of this important character type; see esp. 289–303; see also Patricia Russell, 'Romantic Narrative Plays: 1570–1590', *Elizabethan Theatre*, 126.

13 See *The Spanish Tragedy*, ed. Philip Edwards (London, 1959), III, 2, 1–22; *II Tamburlaine*, II, 3, 2983–3001 in *The Works of Christopher Marlowe*, ed. C. F. Tucker Brooke (Oxford, 1910).

14 See Patricia Russell's good comment on the function served by this soliloquy (*Elizabethan Theatre*, 126).

15 All quotations are taken from *Common Conditions*, ed. Tucker Brooke (New Haven and London, 1915).

16 See Patricia Russell on the Vice and Autolycus (*Elizabethan Theatre*, 120).

17 The fact that it was probably performed at court does not make it a play for an élite audience; for, as Harbage has shown, many plays in the popular repertory were performed at the houses of noblemen and at court (*Rival Traditions*, 56, 61). See also Bevington, *From Mankind to Marlowe*, 65–7, 183–9.

18 The Tudor Facsimile Texts, 1910. Later quotations are taken from *Chief Pre-Shakespearean Dramas*, ed. J. Q. Adams (Boston, 1924).

19 Seneca's authorship of *Octavia*, accepted in the Renaissance, is usually denied today.

20 *English Tragedy Before Shakespeare*, tr. T. S. Dorsch (London, 1961), esp. 23–39, 47–55, 215–25.

21 *Hercules Furens*, ll. 397–400. Line references to Seneca's plays are to *Seneca's Tragedies*, Loeb Classical Library, 2 vols. (London and Cambridge Mass., 1953; orig. 1917); the Elizabethan translations are from *Seneca His Tenne Tragedies*, ed. Thomas Newton (1581), 2 vols. in 1 (Bloomington, Ind. and London, 1964; orig. 1927), I, 21.

22 C. S. Lewis has excellent illustrations of his acid comment, 'the Drab poets were of all men the least able to reproduce the epigrammatic' in *English Literature in the Sixteenth Century*, *The Oxford History of English Literature*, III (Oxford, 1954), 253–4.

23 *A Midsummer Night's Dream*, I, 2, 42.

24 E. K. Chambers, *The Elizabethan Stage*, 4 vols. (Oxford, 1923), IV, 241.
25 See C. S. Lewis, *English Literature in the Sixteenth Century*, 248–52.
26 See Harry Levin, *The Overreacher* (Cambridge, Mass., 1952), 31; Douglas Cole discusses both Herod and the Senecan Hercules in *Suffering and Evil in the Plays of Christopher Marlowe* (Princeton, N.J., 1962), 11–23, 49–56.
27 'The Miller's Tale', ll. 197–8; *Chaucer's Poetry*, ed. E. T. Donaldson (New York, 1958), 114.
28 *Two Coventry Corpus Christi Plays*, ed. Hardin Craig, The Early English Text Society (London, 1902), 17.
29 Adams, *Pre-Shakespearean Dramas*, 228.
30 See Warren E. Tomlinson, *Der Herodes-Charakter im englischen Drama* (Leipzig, 1934).
31 He is given lines of all four and also of several other Senecan characters.
32 W. A. Armstrong discusses various influences on the evolving tyrant-figure in 'The Elizabethan Conception of the Tyrant', *Review of English Studies*, XXII (1946), 161–81; and 'The Influence of Seneca and Machiavelli on the Elizabethan Tyrant', *RES*, XXIV (1948), 19–35.
33 It would be inappropriate to enter any further here into the broad question of Senecan influence on Elizabethan tragedy. G. K. Hunter indicates the complexities of the problem and the importance of non-Senecan influences, both classical and medieval, in 'Seneca and the Elizabethans: A Case-Study in "Influence"', *Shakespeare Survey*, XX (1967), 17–26. Werner Habicht shows how the nature of the interlude in the mid-sixteenth century encouraged borrowing from Seneca in 'Sénèque et le théâtre populaire pré-Shakespearien', *Les Tragédies de Sénèque et le théâtre de la Renaissance*, ed. J. Jacquot (Paris, 1964), 175–87.
34 In Greene's epistle prefixed to *Perimides the Blacksmith*.
35 There is an extensive literature on this topic. I make no attempt to summarize or add to it since I am not primarily concerned here with the dates, authors or sequence of these plays. Irving Ribner refers to the principal books and articles in his discussion of the plays in *The English History Play in the Age of Shakespeare* (Princeton, N. J., 1957), 236–41.
36 All quotations from Marlowe are taken from Tucker Brooke's one-volume edition of *The Works of Christopher Marlowe* (Oxford, 1910).
37 In his brilliant analysis of Marlowe's style and its relation to the plays, *The Overreacher*, Harry Levin points to the extraordinary appropriateness of this term of Puttenham's for hyperbole.
38 *The Herculean Hero* (London and New York, 1962).
39 *From Mankind to Marlowe*, 199–217.
40 See Clifford Leech, 'The Two-Part Play: Marlowe and the Early Shakespeare', *Shakespeare Jahrbuch*, XCIV (1958), 90–106.
41 I reserve the question of Tamburlaine's death as punishment for his misdeeds for discussion at a later point.
42 *Suffering and Evil*, 94.
43 I have discussed this point at greater length in *The Herculean Hero*, 67–68.
44 See also *The Herculean Hero*, 64–5.
45 See Una Ellis-Fermor's note on the passage in her edition of *Tamburlaine the Great*, 2nd ed. (London, 1951), 163–4.

46 See G. I. Duthie, 'The Dramatic Structure of Marlowe's "Tamburlaine the Great", Parts I and II', *English Studies (Essays and Studies*, New Series), I (1948), 101–26).

47 See Miss Ellis-Fermor's introduction to *Tamburlaine*, 41–8.

48 *Suffering and Evil*, 105.

49 Douglas Cole makes this point in *Suffering and Evil*, 119.

50 This point has been much debated in relation to Tamburlaine's blasphemies and his burning of the Koran. See Bevington, *From Mankind to Marlowe*, 214—15, and Cole, *Suffering and Evil*, 116.

51 'Marlowe's Light Reading', *Elizabethan and Jacobean Studies* (Oxford, 1959), 17–35.

52 For discussions of the date and authorship of *Locrine* and its relationship to the other plays see Baldwin Maxwell, *Studies in the Shakespeare Apocrypha* (New York, 1956), 22–71; C. F. Tucker Brooke, ed. *The Shakespeare Apocrypha* (Oxford, 1908), xvi–xx; and Ribner, *English History Play*, 236–41.

53 For discussion of the origins of the dumb show and its uses in these plays see Dieter Mehl, *The Elizabethan Dumb Show* (Cambridge, Mass., 1966). The best treatment of the set-speeches is Clemen's in *English Tragedy Before Shakespeare*, 92–9.

54 Quotations are taken from *The Shakespeare Apocrypha*, ed. Brooke.

55 The borrowing was noted many years ago; see Maxwell, *Studies*, 53 ff.

56 In this instance it is impossible to be sure who was the borrower. If Marlowe was, he must have seen Spenser's stanza in MS., since it was not in print till 1590.

57 Harry Levin discusses the formation of a heroic style and the influence of Lucan and Ovid on Marlowe (*Overreacher*, 10–17); Virgil and Seneca were also important influences on heroic poetry of this period.

58 Though no such comic plot survives in *Tamburlaine*, we know from the printer's address 'To the Gentlemen Readers' that he omitted 'some fond and friuolous Iestures' which had been applauded on the stage, but were in his opinion unworthy digressions. The clownery of Strumbo suggests what these 'gestures' may have been like.

59 All quotations are taken from *Alphonsus King of Aragon* (Malone Society Reprints, 1926).

60 Any such comments on *Orlando Furioso* are necessarily tentative, since the quarto from which later editions derived is corrupt. Comparison with the actor's part for Orlando, which has survived by rare good fortune, shows that some cuts have been made and also additions to the low-comic scenes. See *Two Elizabethan Stage Abridgements*, ed. W. W. Greg (Malone Society, Extra Volume, 1922), 125–364.

61 All quotations are taken from *The History of Orlando Furioso* (Malone Society Reprints, 1907). See Clemen, *English Tragedy*, 180–1.

62 'The Norms of Epic', *Comparative Literature*, XIII (1961), 206. See also Clemen, *English Tragedy*, 179–80.

63 All quotations are taken from *The Tragical Reign of Selimus* (Malone Society Reprints, 1908).

64 *Suffering and Evil*, 99–100.

65 See Jean Jacquot, 'Ralegh's "Hellish Verses" and the "Tragicall Raigne of Selimus" ', *Modern Language Review*, XLVIII (1953), 1–9.

66 Several passages of poetry in *Selimus* also appear to be borrowed from *Locrine*, including some in which *Locrine* borrows from Spenser. The relationship between these plays is susceptible of many explanations: see Maxwell, *Studies*, 61–71. For the borrowings from Locrine see *The Tragical Reign of Selimus*, ed. A. F. Hopkinson (London, 1916), xxii–xxx.

67 Clemen and Cole both discuss the importance of complaints in these plays. Clemen is concerned with the rhetorical tradition and Cole with the expression of suffering in relation to evil.

68 Ruthlessness and great capability were traits of the historical Selim I, whose conquests ushered in the most glorious period of the Ottoman Empire. His son was Suleiman the Magnificent.

69 See *The Wars of Cyrus*, ed. J. P. Brawner (Urbana, Ill., 1942), 10–20, from which all quotations are taken. G. K. Hunter points to several lines stylistically very similar to *Tamburlaine* and associated plays. He is sceptical of the early date for the play as it stands (*Notes and Queries*, n.s. VIII [1961], 395–6).

70 *Wars of Cyrus*, 10–11.

71 The titles of several similar-sounding plays performed at court are known. See *Wars of Cyrus*, 61–71.

72 *The Battle of Alcazar* is therefore one of many plays which dramatize incidents from foreign or English history. *Tamburlaine, Locrine, Alphonsus of Aragon* and *Selimus* do so too. Whether any or all of these plays should be called 'history plays' is a more difficult question than it seems. The term is best reserved for plays such as Shakespeare's English history plays, primarily concerned with political problems and the lessons history can teach. *Tamburlaine*, though based on history and concerned with some of these problems, is even more concerned with the portrayal of a heroic personality. *The Battle of Alcazar*, presenting the conflict between several outstanding men and focusing attention on one historic event, lies somewhere between the extremes represented by *Tamburlaine* and Shakespeare's histories. However, since it is my aim to show that some history plays are also vehicles for the expression of heroic ideals, I do not wish to make any rigid distinctions nor to complicate the issue with arbitrary terminology.

73 See *The Battle of Alcazar*, ed. John Yoklavich in *The Dramatic Works of George Peele*, gen. ed. C. T. Prouty, II (New Haven and London, 1961), 226–9. All quotations are taken from this edition, hereafter referred to as 'Peele'.

74 See P. H. Cheffaud, *George Peele* (Paris, 1913), 62–70; Peele, II, 221–5.

75 Some gauge of this relative prominence is given by Yoklavich's line count: 'Of the 1452 lines in the quarto text, Sebastian has 223 lines: Muly Mahamet, 210; Abdelmelec, 181, and Stukley, 132' (Peele, II, 223 n. 12).

76 In Ben Jonson's *Poetaster* (III, 4) a boy recites these lines almost *verbatim* to show that he can 'do the Moor'.

77 For the full story of Stukley's life see Richard Simpson, *The School of Shakspere* (London, 1878), 1–139; it is well summarized by Yoklavich (Peele, II, 248–52).

78 Peele, II, 269.

79 *English Tragedy*, 172. Some of the crudity is probably due to cutting; see Peele, II, 286–7.

80 One of the rare playhouse documents of the period, the manuscript 'plot' of the play, gives fuller stage directions than are included in the printed edition.

81 See Peele, II, 256–61.

82 Simpson, *School of Shakspere*, 183–4. All quotations are taken from this edition.

83 (New York: Scholars' Facsimiles & Reprints, 1941), sig B3v.

84 For a discussion of critical opinion up to 1908 see Brooke, *The Shakespeare Apocrypha*, xx–xxiii; all quotations are taken from the edition in this collection. For more recent opinions see Kenneth Muir, 'A Reconsideration of *Edward III*', *Shakespeare Survey*, VI (1953), 39–48; Karl Paul Wentersdorf, *The Authorship of Edward III* (Doctoral Dissertation, University of Cincinnati, (1960); Inna Koskenniemi, 'Themes and Imagery in Edward III', *Neophilologische Mitteilung*, LXV (1964), 446–80.

85 All quotations are taken from *The Shakespeare Apocrypha*, ed. Brooke.

86 Shakespeare's authorship of the entire play is still seriously questioned, but there is general agreement that he was largely responsible for it: see J. Dover Wilson's introduction to the New Cambridge edition (Cambridge, 1948), vii–l; and J. C. Maxwell's introduction to the New Arden edition (London, 1953), xxiv–xxxiv. In the following section all quotations from Shakespeare are taken from the New Arden editions unless otherwise noted.

87 I have discussed the Ovidian elements of the play in 'The Metamorphosis of Violence in *Titus Andronicus*', *Shakespeare Survey*, X (1957), 39–49.

88 See Arthur Humphreys' introduction to the New Arden edition of *I Henry IV* (London, 1960), xxix–xxxi.

89 Quoted in the New Arden edition, 20.

90 See John Shaw, 'The Staging of Parody and Parallels in "I Henry IV" ', *Shakespeare Survey*, XX (1967), 61–73.

91 J. Dover Wilson discusses the morality pattern, in which Falstaff is a tempter, in *The Fortunes of Falstaff* (Cambridge, 1944), esp. Chapters II and IV; see also C. L. Barber, 'Rule and Misrule in *Henry IV*', *Shakespeare's Festive Comedy* (Princeton, N.J., 1959), 192–221.

92 *I Henry IV*, New Arden edition, 77n.382.

93 See esp. III, 2.

94 One possible source of this remarkable description is Spenser's description of the Red Cross Knight, miraculously restored by the Well of Life and ready for battle (*Faerie Queene*, I, xi, 34; quoted by Humphreys, Appendix VII, 201.

95 See Humphreys' note and John Lawlor, *The Tragic Sense in Shakespeare* (London, 1960), 26–7. Dover Wilson comments that it is 'a gesture worthy of Sir Philip Sidney himself' (*Fortunes of Falstaff*, 66); I am indebted to his entire chapter, 'The Prince Grows Up'.

96 Whether Shakespeare originally planned a second part and a separate play of *Henry V*, and whether the plays as they stand are independent

entities are questions that have been debated ever since the eighteenth century. See Humphreys' introduction to *II Henry IV*, xxi–xxviii. Regardless of whether Shakespeare intended to divide the material about Henry V into three plays, he must from the first have intended to treat both the wild youth and the 'famous victories'. The soliloquy in Act I of *I Henry IV* is almost sufficient proof of this.

97 *The Structural Problem in Shakespeare's Henry the Fourth* (London, 1956), reprinted in *Discussions of Shakespare's Histories*, ed. R. J. Dorius (Boston, 1964), 54; partially quoted by Humphreys, *II Henry IV*, xxvi.

98 In John Eliot, *Ortho-epia Gallica* (1593), 139. See J. W. Lever, 'Shakespeare's French Fruits', *Shakespeare Survey*, VI (1953), 85; quoted by Humphreys, *II Henry IV*, 231–2. There may be an echo of *Locrine* a few lines later; see Humphreys' note to ll. 193–5.

99 See Robert Egan, 'A Muse of Fire: *Henry V* in the light of *Tamburlaine*', *Modern Language Quarterly*, XXIX (1968), 15–28.

100 See my 'Manhood and Valor in Two Shakespearean Tragedies', *English Literary History*, XVII (1950), 262–73.

101 *The Heroic Image in Five Shakespearean Tragedies* (Princeton, N.J., 1965), 89.

102 In a paper on 'The Dark Side of Macbeth', read to the Modern Language Association in 1965.

103 See the discussion of this play in *The Herculean Hero*, 113–21.

104 See M. R. Ridley's note on these lines in the New Arden edition.

105 I discuss the connection of this speech with the imagery of melting in *The Herculean Hero*, 115–16.

106 Ed. Harry Levin, the Pelican Shakespeare (Baltimore, Md., 1956). All quotations from *Coriolanus* are taken from this edition.

107 James L. Calderwood has advanced the interesting idea that Coriolanus, because of his distrust of a fluctuating 'verbal currency', seeks to create his own verbal standard and finds this a futile venture, since his private language is not understood by others; see '*Coriolanus:* Wordless Meanings and Meaningless Words', *Studies in English Literature*, VI (1966), 217. See also my discussion of a speech in this scene in *The Herculean Hero*, 126–7.

108 See Hermann Heuer, 'From Plutarch to Shakespeare: A Study of *Coriolanus*', *Shakespeare Survey*, X (1957), 54–8.

109 *The Imperial Theme* (London, 1951), 154–98.

Three

The Early Seventeenth Century

No dramatist of the period before 1642 was more explicitly concerned with the heroic tradition than George Chapman, the translator of Homer. Though only one of his tragedies, *Bussy D'Ambois*, seems to have enjoyed any measure of success on the stage,[1] all of them are interesting as attempts to dramatize various heroic ideals. Even before Chapman wrote *Bussy D'Ambois*, the first of his tragedies, he presented a great hero in parody in *The Blind Beggar of Alexandria* (1596). The protagonist of this play is Irus, named after the bragging beggar who rashly challenges Ulysses to a fight in the last book of the *Odyssey*—a man with a 'cow-herd soul' (as Chapman was later to translate it), who pays for his impudence with a broken jaw. The beggar of the play is fully as impudent, but also gloriously successful in imposing his view of himself on the world. Born a 'shepherd's son at Memphis', he has adopted several identities, of which the blind beggar is the lowliest, and Duke Cleanthes the highest. In between are the usurer Leon, and Count Hermes, whose name suggests the hero's brilliance and changefulness. His eye is set on the crown of Egypt, as he announces in an early soliloquy, but until he can claim his throne, he plans to enjoy the 'sports of love'. Thus he contains many dramatic types just as, in the story, he plays many roles. He is a comic braggart, a scheming Machiavel, an insatiable seducer, and an aspiring warrior. His parodic relationship to Tamburlaine is revealed not only in his rise from shepherd to king but in several verbal echoes, such as 'Why, what is dalliance, says my servant then?' (Scene 1, l. 160),[2] which perfectly catches the intonation of Tamburlaine's famous 'What is beauty saith my sufferings, then?' In the last scene, after an improbable series of events in which the king of Egypt is slain, Irus enters as the newly chosen king, Cleanthes, leading four captured enemy kings. This military triumph succeeds his equally brilliant sexual conquests of the queen and of two sisters whom he has married in two of his disguises, and with whom he has cuckolded himself by switching roles. He has also provided his man Pego[3] with a third sister, and at the end he disposes of the first two (both pregnant) to two of his captured kings. The energetic hero of this farce is a witty reflection of Tamburlaine, Alphonsus and the rest, with his major activity shifted from the battlefield to the bed. Performed by the Admiral's Men, who had also done *Tamburlaine*, the play was a great success, and presumably established Chapman's reputation as a playwright with the very crowd whom he, as a poet, claimed to despise—'the prophane multitude'.[4] When, as sometimes happens, commentators refer to Chapman's tragedies as the labours of a scholar who knew little about writing for the theatre, *The Blind Beggar* (and also some of the other comedies) should be borne in mind.

The comic treatment of a conquering hero provides a useful introduction to Chapman's most impressive play, *Bussy D'Ambois*, where the attitude of the playwright towards his hero has proved to be a critical puzzle. Somewhat neglected for many years, the tragedy has recently attracted the attention of a number of critics, each of whom has been dissatisfied with the interpretations of his predecessors, and yet has failed to persuade others of the validity of his own.[5] The chief problem is the seeming discrepancy between the actions of the hero and what is said about him. The historical Bussy D'Ambois was a nobleman whose stormy career at the court of Henri III came to an end with his death in 1579, when Chapman was twenty. In the play, which is mainly but not entirely true to historical fact, Bussy is seen chiefly as an extraordinary fighter and the lover of a countess whose husband finally has him murdered. The story might seem sordid or romantic or morally instructive. What is surprising is to find it presented as heroic. This is less surprising, however, coming from a man who had already amused himself with the resemblances between a rogue and a hero. Though Bussy D'Ambois is entirely serious, it is characterized by a wit that loves paradox—the wit which links Chapman to the metaphysical poets.[6]

There are four major episodes, each of which can be read in at least two different ways: Bussy's decision to come to court as the servant of the king's brother, Monsieur; his quarrel with the

Duke of Guise; his affair with Tamyra, the Countess of Montsurry; and his death. We first see Bussy, dressed as a poor man, in
a 'green retreat' (as Monsieur later calls it), from which he looks
at the world of 'great' men with a Stoic's eye. In his opening
soliloquy mere outward greatness is represented by a striking
image, borrowed from Plutarch, of the colossal statue which is
filled with rubbish.[7] Great men are also likened to ocean-going
ships which, at the end of the voyage, must be guided into port
by a 'poor fisherman', a characteristically Stoic image for virtue
or inner worth. Equating himself with lowly virtue, Bussy lies
down, just as Monsieur arrives with an offer of advancement at
court. To Monsieur, Bussy's contempt of greatness is an instance
of sour grapes, and, in fact, Bussy is soon persuaded to accept
1,000 crowns and follow Monsieur. Temptation or challenge?
Bussy regards it as the latter, as, perfectly aware that he might
seem to be deserting his principles, he determines to show the
world that it is possible to 'rise in Court with virtue' (I, 1, 126).[8]

The Bussy who arrives in court in the next scene seems like
another man. By braving the Guise and brazenly courting his
duchess Bussy shows his contempt for 'great' men but signally
fails to set an opposing example of virtuous conduct. Yet Monsieur's comment on his protégé shows how even such brashness
can be given a heroic colouring:

> His great heart will not down, 'tis like the sea
> That partly by his own internal heart
> Partly the stars' daily and nightly motion,
> Ardour and light, and partly of the place
> The divers frames, and chiefly by the Moon,
> Bristled with surges, never will be won
> (No, not when th'hearts of all those powers are burst)
> To make retreat into his settled home,
> Till he be crown'd with his own quiet foam.
>
> (I, 2, 138–46)

The imagery marks a subtle but important shift in the concept of
virtue associated with the hero. The inner greatness symbolized
here by the sea is finally as unaccountable to the outside world as
the poor fisherman of Bussy's first speech, but the quiet foam
which crowns the calm testifies to the terrifying energy of the
bristling surges, and thus makes self-possession appear far more

dynamic than it does in the fisherman or in the supine figure of the hero in his green retreat.

Hardly less startling than the application of such richly suggestive poetry to a crude display of effrontery is the messenger's account of the triple duel which grows out of Bussy's quarrel with the Guise (II, 1, 25–104). A foolish affair, occasioned by the jeers of some courtiers who are astonished at Bussy's conduct, it is described in the form of a Senecan set piece, with diction and similes appropriate to an epic encounter. This was the 'full and height'ned style' which led John Webster, a few years later, to place 'Master Chapman' first in a list of the tragic playwrights he admired.[9] The style, by recalling not only classical epic but especially classical tragedy, transforms the duelling adventurer into a legendary hero, the very spirit of valour.[10]

Once more Bussy girds at the Guise (III, 2, 61 ff.), and again his action is glorified, this time by the king, a shadowy figure of authority, whose views, like those of the messenger, cannot be explained as the product of any desire to flatter. If Bussy speaks with exceptional freedom, says the king, it is because he represents man in the golden age before the restrictions of contemporary society were necessary:

> A man so good, that only would uphold
> Man in his native noblesse, from whose fall
> All our dissensions rise; that in himself
> (Without the outward patches of our frailty,
> Riches and honour) knows he comprehends
> Worth with the greatest: . . .

> * * *

> No envy, no disjunction, had dissolv'd
> Or pluck'd out one stick of the golden faggot
> In which the world of Saturn was compris'd,
> Had all been held together with the nerves,
> The genius and th'ingenuous soul of D'Ambois.
>
> (III, 2, 90–5, 103–7)

Between offensive remarks to the Duke of Guise and bouts of derring-do Bussy has embarked on an affair with the Countess of Montsurry. Of all his actions this is the most susceptible of contrary interpretations. There is no doubt that it is morally wrong, as Tamyra is clearly aware, though Bussy sturdily refuses to admit it. And the wrong is seemingly deepened by several circumstances: Bussy is led into outright lies to conceal the affair (IV, 1, 57–8); a friar is used as a go-between; and through the friar's expertise in black magic the powers of darkness are enlisted by the lovers. Yet there is no unequivocal condemnation of the love affair. If the heroic models for Bussy were drawn exclusively from classical epic and tragedy, the affair would seem even more deplorable, but Chapman was heavily influenced, like his contemporaries, by the romance tradition with its elevation of the importance of love. The fact that Tamyra is married merely recalls heroines such as Gueniver and Isolde, and suggests that Bussy's infatuation may be 'fine amor'. The image of 'sweet courtly friends . . . A mistress and a servant' is used tellingly in the last scene of the play (V, 3, 130–1) to represent the relationship of the soul and body. Thus the affair may be justified and also the absolute secrecy, which obliges the lover to lie in order to keep faith with his lady. Once this perspective has been adopted, it becomes possible to see Tamyra's dealings with the conjuring friar as part of the lady's effort to lead her lover towards the realization of some high ideal. Chapman's interest in neo-Platonism and Hermetic lore had already appeared in his non-dramatic poetry in rhapsodic tributes to the night, with which Tamyra is associated in a striking prayer ('Now all ye peaceful regents of the night', II, 2, 157 ff.).[11] Darkness to occultists is paradoxically equated with insight—with what the contemplative or the dreamer may see, hidden though it is to ordinary mortals in the daylight world. When the friar raises the spirit Behemoth to reveal what Monsieur and Montsurry are plotting, there are powerful hints that the revelation symbolizes a penetration of profound mysteries. Behemoth proclaims:

> I am Emperor
> Of that inscrutable darkness, where are hid
> All deepest truths, and secrets never seen,
> All which I know, and command Legions
> Of knowing spirits that can do more than these: . . .

(IV, 2, 48–52)

In some sense, then, Tamyra is initiating her lover in the secret rites of the magi, not seducing him into immoral practices. At the end of the first session Bussy is granted the power to summon the spirits himself.[12]

Bussy's death is contrived by Tamyra's jealous husband, plotting with her rejected suitor, Monsieur, and Bussy's old enemy, the Guise. Lured into an ambush by a letter which Montsurry tortures his wife into writing, Bussy is shot in the back by hired assassins. Crudely summarized in this way, the death appears to be an appropriate come-uppance for an over-reaching adventurer. The impression given in the play is totally different.

In the first place, Bussy's commitment to Tamyra is made a prime cause of his death. By means of his new powers he summons Behemoth, who warns him that he will die if he obeys the next summons from his mistress. But in the face of this knowledge he asserts that he can no more disobey her commands than his body can refuse to obey his will. Like Yvain at the castle of Pesme Avanture, he decides he must do what his heart wants.

Furthermore, the manner of the death makes it the most impressive act of self-assertion in the play. After killing one of the murderers, he fights and vanquishes Montsurry, sparing his life only at Tamyra's request. Then Bussy is mortally wounded by pistol shots from assassins concealed behind him. In his dying speeches he forgives his murderers, asks Montsurry to be reconciled to Tamyra, and thereby acknowledges his fault. Yet the emphasis of the final moments is not on repentance, but on Bussy's ideals. In a sense he returns to the point of view of the the first speech, despising life which is so controlled by the caprice of fortune, but now, instead of lying down, he props himself on his sword to die standing. In a speech almost literally translated from Seneca's *Hercules Oetaeus* he prays that his fame may survive his death, and looks forward to an eternity in the company of the immortals. As a mortal, however, he regrets that his 'strength, valour, virtue', have not been adequate to achieve the goals he set for himself. He is Herculean in both his recognition of mortal limitation and his confident assertion of the immortality of his spirit; his death, like Tamburlaine's, is both defeat and transcendence.[13]

The striking complexity—even contradiction—of possible meanings is thus maintained to the end. Two interpretations of Bussy's character in the last act contribute powerfully to this complexity—the opinion expressed by Monsieur as he waits with the Guise for Bussy to arrive at the ambush, and the eulogy spoken by the friar's ghost. Bussy's former patron describes him to the Guise as an example of Nature's senseless destruction of those she has endowed most richly, comparing him to the solid tree which will blow down when the winds 'sing through a hollow tree' (V, 3, 42). The observation fits perfectly with our impression that in the world of the play the least worthy survive longest, but these sentiments are most unexpected from the man who has plotted Bussy's death. As he and the Guise stand in the balcony above the main stage in this scene they seem to lose their individual characters and to become choric commentators. Observing the murder immediately following, they are silent embodiments of the hero's 'Death and Destiny', as he himself calls them (V, 3, 124). The laudatory characterization of Bussy as the solidly virtuous man therefore has almost the force of revelation.[14]

While the speech by Monsieur presents the gloomy view that a man of heroic worth is doomed to failure in this world, the speech by the friar's ghost, concluding the play, offers the reassurance that Bussy's fiery spirit will now join with Hercules as an inspiration to mankind:

> Farewell brave relicts of a complete man:
> Look up and see thy spirit made a star,
> Join flames with Hercules: and when thou set'st
> Thy radiant forehead in the firmament,
> Make the vast continent, crack'd with thy receipt,
> Spread to a world of fire: and th'aged sky,
> Cheer with new sparks of old humanity.
>
> (V, 3, 268–74)[15]

Chapman may have considered the ambiguities of *Bussy D'Ambois* especially suited to a play performed by a boy company for an élite audience, which might enjoy puzzling them out.[16] Hiding the profounder meaning from the prying eyes of the vulgar was also an accepted poetic practice of which Chapman approved, making his style deliberately obscure for this purpose. The difficulty of some of the poetry in *Bussy D'Ambois*, the emphasis on darkness in scenes with Tamyra and the friar, and the seeming contradictions between possible interpretations of the action may all stem from Chapman's idea of how to write for an intellectual audience.

Whatever explanation there may be of Chapman's motives, the play he wrote makes an important point already suggested by some of the biographical and historical material considered earlier: that the heroic is not a kind of person or action, but a way of looking at persons and actions.[17] Chapman's adoption of this way in all his tragedies gives him a special place in the history of drama. As Peter Ure has put it, 'Chapman, by devising a drama that is controlled by an idea of heroic worth held up to us for our wonder, was exploring a new way in tragedy'.[18]

In his early comedy, *The Blind Beggar of Alexandria*, he had alluded to heroic ideals, and in his last comedy, *The Widow's Tears* (1605), he did so again, before turning back to tragedy in his later plays. The male lead, Tharsalio, is in some important respects, a comic version of Bussy. He, too, is introduced alone in the first scene, and he, too, is at odds with Fortune, who rewards only the unworthy. But Tharsalio has not gone into the forest to meditate on the state of things. In his brother's house, preparing himself for the day, a looking-glass in his hand, he pledges himself 'to a more noble deity' than Fortune—Confidence, 'sole friend to worth,/And patroness of all good spirits' (I, 1, 11–12). No Monsieur is needed to inspire in Tharsalio a plan for rising in the world, for he has already hit upon the scheme of winning the wealthy widow, Eudora, even though she has vowed to remain faithful to her dead husband. When this confident hero comes to the widow's house, he immediately quarrels with her other suitors, as Bussy quarrels with the courtiers, but although he proves himself their superior, Eudora is so offended by his pretensions that she has him thrown out of her house. Angered but undaunted, he hires a procuress to warn Eudora against him on the grounds that his extraordinary sexual prowess makes him an insatiable philanderer. This ruse has the desired effect of interesting the widow in him. They are married at the end of the third act.

By this point in the play Tharsalio is well established as a kind of anti-hero, confident of proving that people's lofty ideals are mere sham.[19] His name derives from the Greek *tharsos*, 'boldness', and doubtless suggests his special field of competence by its resemblance to 'tarse', an old word for the male sex organ. The élite audience for whom *The Widow's Tears* (like *Bussy D'Ambois*) was performed was just the one to be amused by a character with the heroic effrontery of Bussy in the role of a sceptical seducer.

In the remainder of the play Tharsalio's view of the world, and particularly of women, is further justified in a plot adapted from Petronius' story of the Ephesian matron. Tharsalio has persuaded his brother Lysander to fake his own death in order to test his wife's vow never to remarry. When Lysander disguises himself as a soldier and enters the tomb where Cynthia is mourning over his supposed corpse, he has no more difficulty in shaking her resolve than Tharsalio had with Eudora. 'La donna è mobile' and heroic vows are quickly forgotten. The hypocrisy of such postures is shown up in this part of the play not only in the action but also in an extended passage of mock-heroic poetry in which Lysander's servant tells Tharsalio how he broke the news of Lysander's death to Cynthia. It is a 'messenger speech', like the report of the duel in *Bussy D'Ambois*, with heightened language which here is patently false, applied to an action which never took place:

> 'Phoebus address'd his chariot towards the west
> To change his wearied coursers, and so forth

*   *   *

> 'Lysander drew,
> And bore himself Achilles-like in fight;
> And as a mower sweeps off th'heads of bents,
> So did Lysander's sword shave off the points
> Of their assaulting lances. . . .'

(IV, 1, 57–8, 73–7)

In the Lysander–Cynthia plot Tharsalio is no longer the active agent, but rather an unmoved mover whose manipulations direct the course of events. By revealing to Cynthia the identity of her new lover he gives her the chance to say she recognized Lysander from the first, and thus to bring him to the reconciliation expected in comedy. The hope of living happily ever after is, however, severely qualified. If any of the characters are to do so it is by accepting a 'topsy-turvy world', as several of them call it, which does not live up to its ideals.

Chapman's comic treatments of heroic ideals testify to a mental flexibility which the stiffness of his more elevated style would seem to deny. But even the tragedies show that Chapman could adopt various attitudes towards the claims of the hero. In *Bussy*

D'Ambois he points to a wonderful spirit in a man whose actions, with the possible exception of his courageous death, are unremarkable. The point is not, as in *The Widow's Tears*, that what is supposed to be heroic is in fact not so at all, but rather that genuine heroism can be found paradoxically in behaviour which most people would find reprehensible. In the two plays called *The Conspiracy and Tragedy of Charles Duke of Byron* (1608), again based on recent French history, we find another sort of paradox. Here there is no doubt that the hero is an ambitious traitor, though he justifies himself to the end as one put upon by jealous accusers. Though Byron, like Bussy, has a greatness of spirit which even his enemies recognize, it is corrupted and partly falsified. Where Bussy's estimate of himself is one (though not the only) truth about him, Byron's is in large measure self-deception. A great deal of the interest in the play lies in the repeated collisions of two contrary views.

Though the two plays taken as a whole are ponderous and static, they contain some highly effective moments. One is Byron's first entrance. We know from what precedes that the agents of Austria and Savoy are about to tempt Byron to conspire against the French King Henry IV. A rich carpet has been spread, and 'loud music' plays as Byron enters. His opening lines are an extraordinary revelation of the man:

> What place is this, what air, what region,
> In which a man may hear the harmony
> Of all things moving? Hymen marries here
> Their ends and uses, and makes me his temple.
> Hath any man been blessed, and yet liv'd?
> The blood turns in my veins; I stand on change,
> And shall dissolve in changing; 'tis so full
> Of pleasure not to be contain'd in flesh:
> To fear a violent good abuseth goodness,
> 'Tis immortality to die aspiring,
> As if a man were taken quick to heaven; . . .
>
> (I, 2, 22–32)[20]

The first line is an unmistakable recollection of Seneca's Hercules, waking from the mad fury in which he has killed his wife and children:

Quis hic locus, quae regio, quae mundi plaga?[21]

But Byron, instead of facing the horror of the real world, is enter-
ing a world of delusion, characterized by harmony. His euphoria
is the exact contrary of Hercules' despair, and yet his premonition
of failure is explicit. What is most striking of all is his commitment
to change, as opposed to the standard protests against mutability.
Byron accepts and glories in the impermanence of flesh, and
equates immortality with the movement of aspiration. In the rest
of the speech images of transformation and transcendence are
strangely combined with those of destruction. Byron compares
perfection to the charge that bursts from a cannon: imperfect
matter cannot contain perfection, and finds its function in dis-
charging it. He envies Semele her fatal glimpse of divinity, which
brought the most intense happiness in the moment of death.
Infatuated as he is with glorious ambitions, he prophetically
imagines his own death as an analogue to the happiness of
Semele and also as a futile gesture of self-assertion:

> happy Semele,
> That died compress'd with glory! Happiness
> Denies comparison of less or more,
> And not at most, is nothing: like the shaft
> Shot at the sun by angry Hercules,
> And into shivers by the thunder broken,
> Will I be burst; and in my heart
> This shall be written: 'Yet 'twas high and right.'
>
> (I, 2, 38–44)

The goal of this aspiring is not marked by 'the sweet fruition of
an earthly crown': it is infinite and inevitably fatal.

The scene is powerfully evocative. After the initial recollection
of *Hercules Furens*, Byron's ecstatic meditation may be seen as the
onset of a madness in which he, too, will play what he thinks is a
heroic part, while to others it will clearly be nothing of the sort.
The first of many examples occurs shortly after his soliloquy
when Byron praises inner strength as the only true source of
greatness at the very moment that he is succumbing to the flattery
of Picoté, who is luring him into treason with the promise of
power (I, 2, 71–164). In a later scene, when King Henry warns
Byron against another of the tempters, La Fin, Byron replies:

134

Be what he will, men in themselves entire
March safe with naked feet on coals of fire:
I build not outward, nor depend on props . . .

(III, 2, 227–9)

though he has already fallen under La Fin's power. Most moving of all is Byron's outburst when a fortune-teller sees a traitor's death in his stars:

I am a nobler substance than the stars,
And shall the baser overrule the better?

*   *   *

Give me a spirit that on this life's rough sea
Loves t'have his sails fill'd with a lusty wind,
Even till his sail-yards' tremble, his masts crack,
And his rapt ship run on her side so low
That she drinks water, and her keel plows air.
There is no danger to a man that knows
What life and death is; there's not any law
Exceeds his knowledge; neither is it lawful
That he should stoop to any other law.
He goes before them, and commands them all,
That to himself is a law rational.

(III, 3, 109–10, 135–45)

Flattering images of the hero are repeatedly introduced in such a way as to emphasize their departure from the truth. Savoy arranges to have a court painter sketch Byron's portrait so that courtiers may then praise the picture in his hearing. Savoy des-scribes his device as an aphrodisiac to stimulate the lust of Byron's ambition (III, 2, 12–21), and in the event Byron is stimulated to plan for a far more grandiose image of himself, carved in a mountain, anticipating Mount Rushmore, as MacLure points out (p. 139). In a conversation with the king, Savoy uses a heroic description of Byron astride his horse Pastrama (II, 2, 66–81) as part of a deliberate exaggeration of Byron's merits, intended to provoke the king into discounting his importance. Such portraits, statues and descriptions are the tragic counterparts of the looking-glass in which Tharsalio complacently preens himself at the beginning of *The Widow's Tears*, as he pledges allegiance to the goddess Confidence.

135

The astounding thing about Byron is the tenacity with which he clings to his dream-vision of himself. When the king, whom Chapman presents as a model of wisdom and forbearance, reveals that he knows about the conspiracy, Byron offers an eloquent rehearsal of his military victories for France as proof of his innocence. Infuriated by the king's refusal to accept this self-portrait as the whole truth, he draws his sword, and has to be restrained by another noble.

Only once, at the very end of *The Conspiracy*, does Byron admit to wrong-doing. Henry has spoken mildly, taking the blame for the plot away from Byron and placing it on those who have corrupted him. One striking simile in the king's speech epitomizes the dangers of deceptive images. Chapman characteristically introduces it as a pendant to another comparison:

> And this wind, that doth sing so in your ears,
> I know is no disease bred in yourself,
> But whisper'd in by others; who in swelling
> Your veins with empty hope of much, yet able
> To perform nothing, are like shallow streams
> That make themselves so many heavens to sight,
> Since you may see in them the moon and stars,
> The blue space of the air, as far from us,
> To our weak senses, in those shallow streams,
> As if they were as deep as heaven is high; . . .
>
> (V, 2, 67–76)

The tempters, whose words are a musical wind, are shallow reflectors in which infinite starry perspectives appear. The simile catches with some exactitude the way Byron has been encouraged to see the fulfilment of his aspirations in the plots of the king's enemies, and thus to believe in his own false estimate of himself. The suggestions of hollow reverberation and of inner corruption caused by poison are relevant to Byron's unjustified assertions of his solid worth.

At last, however, he abandons his pose. The king's statement that innocence 'makes a man in tune still in himself' (V, 2, 88) recalls the use of music at Byron's entrance; for the harmony which Bussy heard when he stepped on the rich carpet was an ironic deception. It is clear to the unprejudiced observer that he has not been 'in tune in himself'. Only now and only for a moment

is there genuine harmony as he admits his fault and asks forgiveness. Henry grants it, saying, "Tis music to my ears' (V, 2, 107).
On the note of reconciliation *The Conspiracy* ends.

By the opening of *The Tragedy* the moment has passed. Byron is
again plotting, and the king, who is always well informed, is
unable to understand how Byron can, in effect, be two such
different people:

> But far it flies my thoughts that such a spirit,
> So active, valiant, and vigilant,
> Can see itself transform'd with such wild furies,
> And like a dream it shows to my conceits,
> That he who by himself hath won such honour . . .
> Should quite against the stream of all religion,
> Honour, and reason, take a course so foul,
> And neither keep his oath, nor save his soul.
>
> > (I, 1, 55–9, 64–6)

Again Byron is summoned. The king urges him to admit his new
fault, but this time he stands firm on his innocence, committed to
his view of himself. And so he remains to the end when, after
being tried and found guilty, he mounts the scaffold. Throughout
this second play the contradiction between Byron's actions and
his statements to the king and the court is absolute. The spectator
is made to share the king's frustration in his inability to make
Byron admit what is patently true. Thus the hero's strength,
which is indeed awesome, is a persistence in error if not, as it
sometimes appears, the strength of delusion. Epernon sums up in
a passage which is often quoted:

> Oh of what contraries consists a man!
> Of what impossible mixtures! Vice and virtue,
> Corruption, and eternnesse, at one time,
> And in one subject, let together loose!
> We have not any strength but weakens us,
> No greatness but doth crush us into air.
> Our knowledges do light us but to err,
> Our ornaments are burthens, our delights
> Are our tormentors, fiends that, rais'd in fears,
> At parting shake our roofs about our ears.
>
> > (V, 3, 189–98)

Chapman liked the last six lines well enough to refashion them slightly, making them into couplets, for his poem, *The Tears of Peace*, published the next year. There (ll. 676–83) they apply to the great and rich, who, like Byron, lack the firm government of the soul which makes the healthy man harmonious and steers him to his goal (ll. 669–72). It is learning which gives the soul her ordering power (ll. 660–8), and without learning man becomes the chaotic mass of contradictions described in the quoted lines. Though Byron cannot be exactly equated with the type described in *The Tears of Peace*, he too is deficient in learning, by which Chapman means, in part, disciplined understanding.[22] In defiance of what he knows, he gives way to an irrational fantasy which finally possesses and destroys him. In these plays heroic aspiration takes the form of a will-o'-the-wisp.

The choice of so paradoxical a hero is made somewhat easier to understand by the example of Essex, which Chapman had before him. The analogy between the careers of Essex and Byron had already been noted,[23] and Chapman had, only ten years earlier, dedicated his *Seven Books of the Iliad* 'to the most honored now living instance of the Achilleian vertues eternized by divine Homere, the Earle of Essexe . . .'. In 1600 the great earl had rebelled and in the course of the following year had been tried and executed. Twice during *The Tragedy* Byron is made to refer to the parallel between himself and Essex.

In his remaining tragedies Chapman turned to heroes very different from Bussy and Byron. In *The Revenge of Bussy D'Ambois* (1610) he invented a brother, Clermont D'Ambois, who undertakes to revenge Bussy on Montsurry. Clermont, however, is the most improbable of revengers—a philosophical man, much more inclined to suffer the slings and arrows of outrageous fortune with Stoical calm than to take arms against a sea of troubles. He is said to exceed his dead brother

> because, besides his valour,
> He hath the crown of man, and all his parts,
> Which learning is; and that so true and virtuous
> That it gives power to do as well as say
> Whatever fits a most accomplish'd man;
> Which Bussy, for his valour's season, lack'd:

And so was rapt with outrage oftentimes
Beyond decorum; . . .

(II, 1, 83–90)

He even admits to his sister Charlotte that he regrets having promised to revenge Bussy, since 'never private cause/Should take on it the part of public laws' (III, 2, 115–16). This is excellent doctrine, in which Chapman may well have believed, as he may also have believed, at least by this time, if not before, that the man of 'learning' was the human ideal. In dedicating his translation of the *Odyssey* (1614) to the Earl of Somerset, he compared the two Homeric heroes, showing his preference for Ulysses:

> In one, Predominant Perturbation; in the other overruling Wisedome; in one, the Bodie's fervour and fashion of outward Fortitude to all possible height of Heroicall Action; in the other, the Mind's inward, constant and unconquered Empire, unbroken, unalterd with any most insolent and tyrannous infliction.

(ll. 63–8).[24]

Yet even here it is Achilles who embodies 'all possible height of Heroicall Action'; Ulysses, though intellectually superior, does not excel in everything. In the play the Odyssean Clermont, who is said to have both valour and learning, is reproved by the ghost of his Achillean brother for the 'tame spirits' which have kept him from executing the revenge (V, 1, 79). The same term is applied to Clermont by his sister in the earlier scene where he expresses his scruples about revenge (III, 2, 117). Only when needled by his living sister and dead brother does the 'Senecal man' finally carry out his assigned task.

It may be impossible to decide whether this seeming uncertainty about the validity of action is due to the conflict of dramatic and philosophical principles or to Chapman's effort to give their just dues to two kinds of hero. Certainly in this play his main emphasis falls on a man so self-sufficient that a struggle for advancement is out of the question, and so rigorously ethical that he merely despises the worldly scheming of others. His contempt is shown most clearly at the moment of his death. He is a loyal servant of the Guise, who in this play is purged of the Machiavellian qualities he had in *Bussy D'Ambois*. When he is murdered, Clermont

139

commits suicide rather than live 'To feed thieves, beasts, and be the slave of power' (V, 5, 192). He is that most difficult of types to project on the stage, the man of transcendent calm.

The superiority of self-control to passion is the subject of *Caesar and Pompey*, the exact date of which is uncertain.[25] Here, where Cato, revered by the Stoics, is the embodiment of a philosophical ideal, the ethical side of the ideal is firmly joined to political principle. 'But is not every just man to himself/The perfect law?' Cato asks (IV, 5, 71–2), and the answer is clearly 'yes'. To put justice first is, of course, to subordinate one's own desires to the common good as Cato invariably does and as Caesar does not. Pompey, after his defeat, learns that true greatness consists in goodness, and is said to have conquered Caesar by this moral conviction (V, 1, 201–2). In their deaths both Pompey, who is murdered, and Cato, who kills himself, are raised above the living Caesar, who has the world at his feet but does homage to his dead opponents.

In *The Revenge of Bussy D'Ambois* and *Caesar and Pompey* the heroic ideal is close to that of Bussy's opening soliloquy in his 'green retreat', before he ventures into the world of action, and neither play succeeds in making the assertion of this ideal truly dramatic. Chapman's one remaining tragedy, *Chabot, Admiral of France* (*c.* 1622), is more successful in dramatizing a character whose worth is resolutely inward. Some of the dramatic effectiveness is probably due to James Shirley, a man of the theatre *par excellence*, who apparently revised the play about a year before its publication in 1635.[26] Chabot *is* what Byron pretends to be—an innocent benefactor of his country, falsely accused of treason by those who are jealous of him. He is depicted from the first as inflexible in his virtue, and on several occasions we hear of his extraordinary confidence. Contrasted with him are his rival Montmorency, who vacillates between scheming and repentance for it, the chancellor, a more thorough-going villain, and the king, whose basic goodness is partially perverted by a false concept of his role.

The basic conflict is established during Act I, in which the king reconciles Chabot and Montmorency only to have the chancellor stir up more trouble between them. The most striking scenes in the play are the resulting confrontations between Chabot and the king. In Act II, Scene 3, the king taxes him with his refusal to sign a bill which he considers unjust, though the king favours it. To the issue of absolute justice versus royal prerogative is soon added another which becomes increasingly important: the relative values of the king's bounty and the admiral's desert; for the king insists on taking Chabot's intransigence as a sign that he is over-confident of himself and forgetful that he owes his position to the king. The point is more subtle than it at first appears. The king is not saying merely that his favour deserves a favour in return, but that it is presumptuous for a subject to rival his king in virtue (II, 3, 189–97). Since Chabot will not budge, the king allows the chancellor to bring suit. The trial judges find the admiral innocent, but in a travesty of justice are forced by the chancellor to sign his conviction. By now Montmorency, regretting his involvement, pleads with the king to save Chabot. The king is delighted by this opportunity to gain the upper hand in what he seems to see as a contest of virtue. He will now force Chabot to recognize royal bounty by graciously pardoning his fault. But Chabot destroys the king's little scene with a few simple words:

> You cannot pardon me, sir. . . .
> It is a word carries too much relation
> To an offence, of which I am not guilty.
>
> (IV, 1, 235–7)

Unable to play at beneficence, the king is finally obliged to examine the fundamental issue of Chabot's guilt, and when he does so he discovers how the false judgment has been procured. At this point a happy ending seems to be in sight: the wicked chancellor is punished and Chabot restored to full favour. But the action takes one more turn. The trial and the king's unkindness have been too much for Chabot—'the greatest souls are thus often wounded' (V, 1, 8)—and he dies of a broken heart.

His is a transcendent death like those of his Stoic forerunners, Clermont and Cato, as the king indicates when he says, 'He has his victory in's death; this world/Deserv'd him not' (V, 3, 206–7), and yet he is a less passive figure, trying even in his final illness to stand 'and look/His destiny in the face' (V, 1, 29–30). One thinks of Bussy dying, propped up on his sword, and the comparison points up the contrast between the paradoxical greatness of Chapman's first hero and the unequivocal goodness of his last. Different as they are, however, their fates in the world of the court are about equally unhappy.

Chapman's may have been the 'second pen' to which Ben Jonson refers in the address 'To the Readers' he prefixed to the 1605 quarto of *Sejanus*, explaining that the printed text was not identical with the play as performed, since he had substituted lines of his own for those of the unnamed collaborator.[27] Certainly tyranny, the struggle for power, and the duties of magistrates to the ruler and to the people are themes in which Chapman was vitally interested, and the overweening ambition of Sejanus is comparable to that of Byron. It is easy to imagine Chapman writing a speech for Sejanus at the opening of Act V, where he exults in the apparent success of his schemes with all the enthusiasm and self-congratulation of earlier aspiring heroes. Jonson has him say:

> Swell, swell, my joys, and faint not to declare
> Yourselves as ample as your causes are.
>
>   *   *   *
>
> My roof receives me not; 'tis air I tread;
> And at each step, I feel my'advancèd head
> Knock out a star in heav'n!
>
> (V, 1, 1–2, 7–9)

But whatever Chapman may have contributed to the original presentation of this character, the play as it stands gives a very different impression of him from that made by any of the Chapman heroes. Sejanus is seen too clearly as a schemer who overestimates his cleverness and who, at the very moment of his joyful outburst, is being outmanœuvred by his master, Tiberius. Undercutting a character's self-esteem in this way is quite different from pointing to a mistaken conviction, like Byron's, which may be irrational delusion or monumental obstinacy. The total effect in *Sejanus* is to diminish and delimit the ambitious character, whereas in a Chapman tragedy, no matter what kind of hero it has, the effect is determined by what Peter Ure calls 'a fiery and imaginative response to "greatness"'.[28]

Many plays of the early seventeenth century contain flashes of heroic vision, like *Sejanus*, but few reveal anything like Chapman's persistent 'response to "greatness"'. One is John Marston's *The Wonder of Women, or the Tragedy of Sophonisba*, acted (probably in 1606) by the Revels Children,[29] for whom Chapman wrote most of his plays, and who performed *The Widow's Tears* at about the same period. As the title makes clear, the topic of this play is the extraordinary capacity of a member of the weaker sex. The imaginations of several playwrights were seized in the years following by unusually wilful women, who were able to challenge the male's traditional leadership in active good and evil, but none of them is so steadily held up for admiration as Sophonisba.

The Prologue sets the tone with his promise of

> . . . a female glory
> (The wonder of a constancie so fixt
> That Fate it selfe might well grow envious).[30]

In the first act her mastery of sexual desire shows how different she is from other daughters of Eve as normally depicted by male moralists. She is introduced on the night of her marriage to Massinissa, and the significance of the occasion is emphasized by an elaborate ceremony in which bridesmaids put the bride to bed and courtiers, accompanied by dancing boys, lead in the bridegroom.[31] This ritual calls attention to the anticipated sexual event but also forces it into an unnatural pattern of courtship, as Sophonisba complains to her maid:

> I hate these figures in locution,
> These about phrases forc'd by *ceremonie*;
> We must still seeme to flie what we most seeke
> And hide our selves from that we faine would find us.
>
> (I, 2; II, 11)

After this frank admission her self-denial is the more striking when news comes that Massinissa is needed for the defence of Carthage against the Romans, who are marching on the city, aided by Sophonisba's rejected suitor, Syphax. Sophonisba has no lust but of Massinissa's glory, she says, dispatching him to the battle with a patriotic speech worthy of a general. His reply to her again sounds the dominant theme:

> Wondrous creature, even fit for Gods, not men,
> Nature made all the rest of thy faire sex
> As weake essaies, to make thee a patterne
> Of what can be in woman.
>
> (I, 2; II, 18)

Her Stoical self-mastery is matched by her constancy, which is now cruelly tested; for in the course of nefarious political manœuvrings, she is handed over to Syphax. By a combination of clever scheming and physical bravery she manages to ward off his advances, and in due time is recaptured by Massinissa. Plotted against by the Carthaginians, he has gone over to the Romans, and now, in revenge, conquers in their name. He has already fought and defeated his rival in a single combat which has more of the atmosphere of romance than of Roman history,[32] but defeated Syphax has persuaded Scipio, the Roman general, to demand that Massinissa surrender Sophonisba, lest she turn him against his new allies. At this point exemplary valour is added to Sophonisba's other virtues. In order to remain free from Roman slavery and yet allow Massinissa to obey Scipio's command, she drinks poison. In a final spectacular scene Massinissa presents her body to the Roman general. She is not only the 'wonder of women' but of men as well; for of all the principal characters she is most consistently true to her country, her love and herself.

John Webster shared several of the concerns of Chapman, Jonson and Marston. The first two men he put at the top of his list of contemporary dramatists in the address 'To the Reader' prefixed to the first edition (1612) of *The White Devil*, and paid Jonson a somewhat less candid compliment by borrowing parts of the address without acknowledgment from the address 'To the Readers' in *Sejanus*. He admired Chapman's 'full and height'ned style', would have liked to imitate Seneca more closely if there had been spectators to relish such caviar, and did in fact incorporate many *sententiae*, in the manner of Seneca, into his tragedies. Like some of Chapman's heroes and like Marston's heroine, Webster's 'white devil', Vittoria Corombona and his Duchess of Malfi display remarkable Stoic fortitude, but despite the Senecan overtones and the flashes of great heroism, these two plays are not truly in the heroic mode. Though Vittoria defends herself so admirably at her trial that one almost forgets she is guilty, and though she meets death with such 'manhood' that even her cynical brother Flamineo calls her a 'noble sister' (V, 6, 241)[33] the play as a whole dwells more on the corruption of the world than on the strength of heroic spirits. Flamineo's satirical view is pervasive, and large doses of satire tend to choke admiration in the utterance. One of the most moving comments on the world of

The White Devil is the last speech of the revenger, Lodovico, the contriver of the final blood-bath, who finds that he has gained nothing by his vengeance and yet takes pride in it as at least some assertion of himself in the midst of the chaos which makes most action meaningless:

> I do glory yet,
> That I can call this act mine own:—for my part,
> The rack, the gallows, and the torturing wheel
> Shall be but sound sleeps to me,—here's my rest—
> I limb'd this night-piece and it was my best.
>
> (V, 6, 293-7)

The Duchess of Malfi comes closer to the heroic norm, especially in the famous assertion of its heroine: 'I am Duchess of Malfi still', inspired, no doubt, by the words of Seneca's Medea when she is reminded that she has no one to help her: 'Medea superest', 'Medea remains'. But the greatness of the duchess is always balanced against her human weakness. When she resorts to a secret marriage to get around her brothers' insistence that she remain a widow, her maid says:

> Whether the spirit of greatness or of woman
> Reign most in her, I know not, but it shows
> A fearful madness; I owe her much of pity.
>
> (I, 1, 504-6)

Her deception is understandable, but it is more apt to elicit sympathy or pity than awe or wonder. Even in her death she does not, like Vittoria, strike a heroic stance. Instead, she kneels, with courage but also humility, as she says:

> Pull, and pull strongly, for your able strength
> Must pull down heaven upon me:—
> Yet stay; heaven-gates are not so highly arch'd
> As princes' palaces, they that enter there
> Must go upon their knees.
>
> (IV, 2, 230-4)

Her nobility and integrity throughout her final ordeal are remarkable, however, inspiring Bosola, the malcontent tool of her wicked brothers, to avenge her murder and thus atone for his misdeeds. The entire last act, presenting his partially successful attempt to do so, constitutes an effective tribute to the heroine's memory. The spirit of the martyred duchess is present in the minds of each of the principal characters, and is dramatized in a romantically contrived scene where her voice is heard by her husband as an echo from her grave. Nothing could make clearer the distinction between this play and what can properly be called heroic drama than the ironic fact that alive, the heroine is a victim, and only begins to exert a powerful influence over others after her death.

Middleton's portrayals of wilful women are probably the most subtle of any in the period immediately following Shakespeare, but they are quite unheroic, their emphasis falling upon the blindness of desire and the easy stages by which a person may become corrupt. Middleton's heroines are far removed not only from the 'masculine virtue' of Sophonisba, but also from the verve of 'the white devil' and the unshakable faith of the duchess.

Occasional plays of much less merit than those of Webster and Middleton contain examples of heroic behaviour or misbehaviour more obviously intended to arouse admiration. *Lust's Dominion, or The Lascivious Queen* (1600), possibly by Day, Dekker and Haughton, will serve as an example. The queen's lover in this play is Eleazar, a Moor as wicked as Muly Mahamet or Aaron, who boasts of his lineage and plans for the future in the following words:

> Although my flesh be tawny, in my veines,
> Runs blood as red, and royal as the best
> And proud'st in *Spain* . . .

>   *   *   *

> . . . now purple villany
> Sit like a Roab imperiall on my back,
> That under thee I closelyer may contrive
> My vengeance; foul deeds hid do sweetly thrive:
> Mischief erect thy throne and sit in state
> Here, here upon this head; let fools fear fate,
> Thus I defie my starrs, I care not I
> How low I tumble down, so I mount high.
>
>   (I, 1, 154–6, 172–9)[34]

When some of his plans have borne fruit, he gives this accounting of himself:

146

I rusht amongst the thickest of their crowds,
And with a countenance Majestical,
Like the Imperious Sun disperst their clouds;
I have perfum'd the rankness of their breath,
And by the magick of true eloquence,
Transform'd this many headed *Cerberus*,
This py'd Camelion, this beast multitude,
Whose power consists in number, pride in threats;
Yet melt like snow when Majestie shines forth.

(III, 4, 16–24)

To turn from Webster to this is to see how vital a part a certain kind of rhetoric plays in creating a heroic effect. Vittoria at her most heroic on the point of death says:

My soul, like to a ship in a black storm,
Is driven I know not whither.

(V, 6, 248–9)

and a moment later:

O happy they that never saw the court,
Nor ever knew great man but by report.

(V, 6, 261–2)

The imagery of the first speech and the sententiousness of the second call attention to the moral obscurity of the heroine's career. A door closes, and what seemed to be great vistas of self-assertion are now seen to have been the delusions of someone lost or trapped. In Eleazar's speeches prospects continually open up; even at the moment of his death, when his enemies have out-smarted him, he curses lustily and plans to 'out-act' the devils 'in perfect villany' when he arrives in hell (V, 3, 166). A different attitude towards the hero is implicit in lines such as these from the attitude implied by Vittoria's speeches; a different rhetorical strategy has been adopted. Eleazar's more flowing lines, orna-mented with images of sun and stars and royalty, suggest energy and freedom, as do the similar but poetically superior lines of Tamburlaine, 'I hold the Fates bound fast in yron chaines . . .'; of Hotspur, 'By heaven, methinks it were an easy leap . . .'; or of Byron, 'I am a nobler substance than the stars . . .'. Sheer ex-travagance is a breeder of admiration.

A keen awareness of the importance of rhetoric for heroic elevation characterizes John Fletcher and his collaborators in the so-called 'Beaumont and Fletcher' plays.[35] These men were also the chief purveyors of romantic ideals among the playwrights of the early seventeenth century. Within a year of satirizing the heroic rant of Hotspur and the vogue of chivalric romance in *The Knight of the Burning Pestle*, Francis Beaumont joined Fletcher in writing *Cupid's Revenge*, a highly romantic and at times extravagantly rhetorical play, based on Sidney's *Arcadia*. This was not quite the *volte face* that it might appear to be, however. It has already been pointed out that the end of the sixteenth century saw not only a revival of interest in the old chivalric romances but also the creation of many romances of a new sort. As the Amadis and Palmerin romances were being translated for the benefit of such as Rafe and his employers, Sidney was writing the *Arcadia*, inspired by such pastoral romances as Montemayor's *Diana*, and Honoré d'Urfé was writing *L'Astrée*. Montemayor concentrated on the torments of love to the exclusion of feats of arms,[36] and both Sidney and d'Urfé, while including some fighting in their romances, gave much more space to discussions of love. Hence the kind of romance to which Beaumont and Fletcher turned in *Cupid's Revenge* was quite different from the object of Beaumont's satire in *The Knight of the Burning Pestle*. In the new romances the increased preoccupation with love was accompanied by a refinement of the old ideal of courtesy. Indeed, *L'Astrée* was in part the outgrowth of a movement (called 'préciosité') to purify the manners of a court society which had become crude and debauched.[37] This new interest in polite behaviour is clearly reflected in the Beaumont and Fletcher plays.

After *Cupid's Revenge*, a tragedy, Beaumont and Fletcher collaborated on *Philaster* (1609), a tragicomedy which, according to Dryden,[38] was their first success. Though not truly heroic in the sense that *Tamburlaine* and *Bussy D'Ambois* were, it was pervaded by the assumptions which underlie heroic conduct, and, more frequently than in *Cupid's Revenge*, there were flashes of a declamatory rhetoric which was to become one of the hallmarks of the Fletcherian style. In *Philaster* can be seen the pattern for the large corpus of plays which made Beaumont and Fletcher the great playwrights of their day.[39]

Selection of a few representative examples is the only feasible way of dealing in a study of this compass with a body of some fifty plays, in which all the tragedies and tragicomedies and even some of the comedies are relevant to the development of heroic drama. This procedure is less dangerous in the case of Beaumont and Fletcher than it would be for many other playwrights, since their plays are amazingly homogeneous beneath a surface which appears to offer infinite variety. *The Knight of Malta* (*c.* 1618, probably by Fletcher, Massinger, and Field)[40] illustrates well the way heroic ideals function in many of the plays. Like *Philaster*, it is a romantic tragicomedy with a pseudo-historical setting. The knight is 'admir'd Miranda', whose fortunate name may have been found in Richard Knolles' *General History of the Turks* (1603), where one Miranda, 'a gentleman of Spain' (in the play he is Italian), is mentioned in a section on the Knights of Malta containing the names of several other characters in the play. The Turks are attacking Malta, and Miranda, not yet a knight, has already shown 'wondrous prowess', along with the Spaniard, Gomera, in defence of the island. In the first act the nobility of these two is displayed against the black background of a plot by Mountferrat, described in the *Dramatis Personae* as 'A Knight of the Order, but a villain', to punish Oriana, sister of the Grand Master, for scorning his love. The Grand Master has planned to invest both Miranda and Gomera with knighthood as a reward for their valour, but Miranda, when the honour is offered, pleads that it be deferred until he can prove himself further by relieving a brave commander who is fighting against the Turkish fleet. Knighthood for him is not a matter of accoutrements but of a spirit tried in battle. Gomera refuses for a different reason— because he is in love with Oriana, and knows that no Knight of Malta may marry. As Mountferrat now produces a forged letter to show that Oriana has been trafficking with the enemy, Gomera offers to defend her in single combat.

By this time it is clear that we are in a world of powerful moral contrasts where the lofty ideals of the good characters are as completely formulated in terms of chivalry as those of Clyomon and Clamydes. The plot now brings these strongly opposed characters into some most surprising relationships. Miranda, after triumphantly accomplishing his mission, is apparently persuaded by the villain that Oriana is guilty and that Gomera has insulted him. He therefore dons Mountferrat's armour and in his place enters the lists against Gomera as Oriana mounts the scaffold, where she will be executed if her defender loses. Gomera wins the victory in this chivalric spectacle, but Miranda, who then reveals himself, claims credit for saving Oriana by deliberately losing the fight. This raises a nice point in the comparison of two instances of noble behaviour, and at the same time throws a new light on Miranda's impassioned argument with Mountferrat in the previous scene, when Miranda first defended Oriana's virtue and then, seemingly convinced by Mountferrat, exclaimed against its loss. His rhetoric in that entire scene is now revealed as a stratagem for keeping Mountferrat out of the combat.

The Grand Master, deciding that Gomera has deserved the hand of Oriana, promises to wed Miranda to the order (though Oriana prefers him to Gomera). Much more is to happen, however, before the evil forces of Mountferrat are quelled. His Moorish mistress takes advantage of a jealous fit of Gomera's and gets him to administer a cordial to Oriana, who has fainted upon being accused of unfaithfulness with Miranda. The cordial is one of those useful potions which give the victim every appearance of death. As it often happens in such stories, Oriana awakes from her trance sooner than expected, and is rescued from the tomb by Miranda just before Mountferrat's arrival. The repentant Gomera, supposing her dead, finds Mountferrat and his Moor and, after a fight in which he is wounded, has them both arrested.

The rest of the action is even less straightforward. In a secondary plot Miranda tests Lucinda, a beauty captured from the Turks, by seeming to try to seduce her. Again the virtuous hero is made to appear for a moment as the opposite of what he is. The device is even repeated one more time in the fifth act when Miranda asks Oriana for her love, praises her for refusing him, asks her to reconsider if Gomera should die, and (to test her further) upbraids her for saying she is unworthy of him. None of these twists and turns affect the outcome of the love story: Miranda, as pure as ever, returns Oriana to Gomera as if from death. The end of the play is a ceremony of the divestiture of Mountferrat and the investiture of Miranda.

Thanks to disguise and to Miranda's penchant for testing other characters, the hero repeatedly seems to be toppling from his pedestal of nobility, but on each occasion we are soon reassured that he has never lost his balance. Though he is the polar opposite of Mountferrat, he never does anything so obvious as to fight with him. Having got the best of the villain by deception, Miranda appears in seeming conflicts with other virtuous characters, thus providing a more novel moral spectacle. Throughout the play, however, whether the conflicts are spurious or real, it is the business of the rhetoric to heighten their significance. The tone of these scenes can be illustrated from Miranda's testing of Oriana. When she finds that he is not going to pursue his courtship, she says:

> Now thou art strait, and dost enamour me,
> So far beyond a carnal earthly love;
> My very soul doats on thee, and my spirits
> Do embrace thine, my mind doth thy mind kiss,
> And in this pure conjunction we enjoy
> A heavenlier pleasure than if bodies met: . . .
>
> (V, 1; VII, 153-4)[41]

A few lines later he makes his final test:

> Hard-hearted, and uncivil *Oriana*,
> Ingrateful payer of my Industries,
> That with a soft painted hypocrisie
> Cozen'st, and jeer'st my perturbation,
> Expect a witty, and a fell revenge:
> My comfort is, all men will think thee false. . . .

At all times the standards of heroic conduct are the highest, but instead of any serious exploration of them they are almost taken for granted and by clever manipulation made the basis for a continual swirl of emotion.

Few Beaumont and Fletcher plays are so chivalric as *The Knight of Malta*, and not many carry the emotional exploitation of heroic values to such an extreme. Yet the subordination of character and theme to theatrical effect in this tragicomedy is typical of the plays as a group. In an earlier and better-known play, *A King and No King* (1611, by Beaumont and Fletcher), the situations follow more logically from the basic premise, and the play is therefore more coherent and more compelling. By an undeniably clever stroke the heroic rant of the central character is finally understandable as the speech of a pseudo-hero, whose royalty is a matter of mistaken identity. For such a character any extravagance can be justified even if it is pushed to the edge of

absurdity. Arbaces' boasting and his sudden rages are neatly
poised on a knife edge between the styles of King Cambises and of
the braggart warriors of comedy without ever falling on either
side. When, at the opening of the play, Arbaces boasts of his
victory over King Tigranes, and at the same time offers him the
hand of his sister Panthea, he is not behaving like a tyrant, for
there is genuine magnanimity in the gesture. Nor is he a mere
boaster, for his victory is real. The presence in the play of a
typically comic braggart, Bessus, points up differences as well as
parallels between this type and Arbaces.

What most of all distinguishes Arbaces from both the stage
tyrant and the buffoon is the inner torment he suffers when he
believes that he is in love with his sister. The contempt or ridicule
he would otherwise merit is mitigated by sympathy for his plight.
A modulation of his style, which is always declamatory, brings
this other dimension of his character into focus, as two of his
speeches show. Arbaces, the victorious warrior-king, says:

> To be my prisoner is to be more free
> Than you were formerly, and never think
> The man I held worthy to combat me
> Shall be us'd servilely. Thy ransom is
> To take my only sister to thy wife—
>
> (I, 1, 97–101)[42]

Arbaces, the lover, says:

> Why should there be such music in a voice
> And sin for me to hear it? All the world
> May take delight in this, and 'tis damnation
> For me to do so.—You are fair and wise
> And virtuous, I think, and he is blest
> That is so near you as your brother is;
> But you are naught to me but a disease,
> Continual torment without hope of ease.
> Such an ungodly sickness I have got,
> That he that undertakes my cure must first
> O'erthrow divinity, all moral laws,
> And leave mankind as unconfin'd as beasts,
> Allowing them to do all actions
> As freely as they drink when they desire.
>
> (III, 1, 187–200)

If the first speech borders on the mock-heroic, the second, no doubt, approaches melodrama, yet even in so doing, conveys intense suffering. And both the hubris of the first speech and the guilt of the second testify equally to Arbaces's belief in the nobility of man. Though he finally turns out to be no king, Arbaces's values are not mocked.

A King and No King, The Knight of Malta and many other Beaumont and Fletcher plays are elegant variations on a heroic theme. Three tragedies, *Bonduca, Barnavelt* and *The False One*, present heroic behaviour with less trickery and more serious concern for the issues involved. *Bonduca* (1613, by Fletcher alone), based on early British history, presents both noble Roman and noble British warriors striving for honour. The play opens with a contrast. Bonduca, the queen of the Iceni (more commonly known now as Boadicea), exults in her victory over the Romans, while her cousin, Caratach, reproves her for boasting. Both seek honour, but Caratach believes that Bonduca falls short of her aim by her unbecoming behaviour:

> Discretion
> And hardy valour are the twins of honour,
> And nurs'd together, make a Conqueror:
> Divided, but a talker.
>
> (I, 1; VI, 80)

Finally persuaded by his eloquent praise of the enemy, Bonduca thanks Caratach with these words:

> O cousin,
> From what a flight of honour hast thou checkt me!
>
> (I, 1; VI, 83)

The contrast is not between an honourable and a dishonourable person but between a right and a wrong way of attaining honour. This distinction recurs throughout the play.

A second contrast is less important but related to the central theme. The Roman Petillius, 'a merry captain', makes sport of Junius, a captain who has been made melancholy by his love for one of Bonduca's daughters. For the time being, Junius is an ineffectual officer, sinking under the influence of love to the point where he is captured by a ruse of Bonduca's daughter. However, when he is released by Caratach, who scorns the deviousness of

'a woman's wisdom', Junius makes rapid strides towards soldierly
honour. In the latter part of the tragedy the situation of Junius
and Petillius is exactly reversed, for Petillius incongruously falls in
love with Bonduca at the moment of her death (because she dies
so well), and is the butt of several pranks of Junius. Worse yet, he
is disgraced by his general, and is at the point of suicide when
Junius makes him once more 'noble and a soldier'. Since Petillius
is basically a comic character, this symmetrical sequence provides a comparatively light treatment of the all-important
honour and nobility.

The Roman general, Suetonius, is the counterpart of Caratach,
a fearless soldier who relishes battle most when it is most dangerous. The third contrast in the play is between him and Penius,
a brave commander who refuses to obey what he considers a
foolhardy command from Suetonius. He will not lead his men
against the vastly superior numbers of the British, but explains
that this is not cowardice:

> Honor got out of Flint, and on their heads
> Whose virtues, like the Sun, exhal'd all valours,
> Must not be lost in mists and fogs of people,
> Noteless, and out of name, but rude and naked:
> Nor can *Rome* task us with impossibilities,
> Or bid us fight against a flood: . . .
>
> (II, 1; VI, 95)

Suetonius goes him one better, however, by a demonstration of
selfless valour which is clearly more noble than this caution.
Penius suffers the humiliation of seeing from a distance the
brilliant success of Suetonius against the British, and his comment
is:

> I have lost mine honor, lost my name,
> Lost all that was my light: these are true *Romans*,
> And I a *Britain* coward, a base Coward; . . .
>
> (III, 5; VI, 124)

Penius regains his honour in a strange scene where Petillius first
offers him the forgiveness of Suetonius and then, surprisingly,
urges him towards suicide. When Penius dies upon his sword,
cheered on by Petillius, he has taken 'the way of honor' (IV, 3;
VI, 136).

A fourth contrast is drawn between the two daughters of Bonduca when the British are making their last stand. Bonduca now rises to the nobility expected of great heroes and heroines: rather than surrender to the Romans, she determines that she and her daughters will take poison. Her courage is matched by that of her first daughter, but her second daughter makes a pathetic appeal for life. Stoicism is thus set against human weakness, insults and stirring speeches against pleas for mercy. The second daughter is converted to honour, however, and is followed in suicide by her sister and mother. Suetonius himself says of Bonduca that 'She was truly noble, and a Queen' (IV, 4; VI, 143).

The heroine who gives the tragedy its name comes to her noble end in the fourth act, leaving the last act largely to Caratach (with a diversion, already mentioned, of the disgrace and reinstatement of Petillius). Caratach is the ultimate emblem of honour. His heroism is exalted at the expense of the queen's reputation in the first scene of the act, only a few lines after Suetonius' eulogy of her. This unexpected return to the contrast made at the opening of the play is brought about by the caustic reflections of Caratach on the inept generalship of the queen, responsible for the British defeat. Now Caratach appears in the role of innocent and noble victim, as did Bonduca in the fourth act. So great is Caratach's admiration of honour, wherever it is manifested, that he salutes the corpse of Penius with an eloquent funeral oration. As the Roman army closes in upon him, Caratach is accompanied by his little nephew, Hengo, whose precocious valour furnishes a highly sentimental version of the main theme. Finally Caratach is captured by Suetonius, and the play ends with the embraces and mutual compliments of these two most honourable enemies.

At times victory seems less important than behaving as a noble warrior should. The emphasis is almost that of the courtesy book, and in this regard parallels the emphasis of the fashionable romances of the period. Technically a tragedy, *Bonduca* shows how tragedy may become a celebration of virtue in which human weakness and limitation are dwelt on even less than in *Tamburlaine* or *Bussy D'Ambois*. Fletcher's tragedy is not far removed from the heroic play as Davenant conceived it.

In *The Tragedy of Sir John Van Olden Barnavelt* (1619), based on what were current events in the Netherlands, Fletcher and Massinger portray a hero similar in some respects to Chapman's

Byron—a once-great man who clings obstinately to the illusion that nothing he does can alter that greatness. The play shows clearly that his cause is a poor one. The Netherlands have made great gains in their battle for freedom, but Barnavelt is determined to fight the Prince of Orange, who is getting too much credit for this success. The rebellion costs not only his own life but those of many of his followers, who try to dissuade him from pursuing glory at all cost. A much smaller figure than he imagines himself to be, Barnavelt acts from spite, the meanest of motives:

> No, this ingratefull Cuntry, this base people
> most base to my deserts, shall first with horror
> know he that could defeat the Spanish counsailes,
> and countermyne their dark works, he that made
> the State what 'tis, will change it once againe
> ere fail with such dishonour.
>
> (I, 1, 50–5)[43]

Yet in his public speeches he is a heroic figure. When certain lords urge him to submit to the Prince of Orange, he replies:

> when I am a Sycophant,
> and a base gleaner from an others favor
> as all you are, that halt vpon his crutches
> shame take that smoothnes, and that sleeke subiection.
> I am myself, as great in good, as he is,
> as much a master of my Cuntries fortunes. . . .
>
> *   *   *
>
> I neuer knew to flatter, to kneele basely,
> and beg from him a smile, owes me an honour; . . .
>
> (III, 1095–100, 1123–4)

His refusal to see another man as head of the government becomes the hero's superiority to flattery and all baseness. His personal integrity is invincible, no matter how great the odds against him. He is a man of honour.

To these characteristics of his self-portrait is added one more in the eloquent speech he makes before his execution: in his final moment he becomes a martyr, an innocent and pathetic victim:

> I dye for saving this vnthanckfull Cuntry.
>
> *   *   *

Commend my least breath to his Excellence,
tell him the Sun he shot at, is now setting,
setting this night, that he may rise to morrow,
for ever setting: now let him raigne alone,
and with his rayes, give life, and light to all men,
May he protect with honour, fight with fortune,
and dye with generall love, an old, and good Prince;
my last petition, good Cuntrymen forget me,
your memories wound deeper than your mallice,
and I forgive ye all: a little stay me,—
Honour, and world, I fling ye thus behind me,
and thus a naked poore-man, kneele to heaven;
be gratious to me, heare me, strengthen me,
I come, I come: ô gratious heaven: . . .

(V, 3, 2956, 2981–4)

The discrepancy between the character of the hero and his role
is even more striking than in the case of Byron, about whom there
is nothing petty. Barnavelt's nobility is a garment put on whenever he addresses an audience. In effect, he clothes himself in
rhetoric.

The False One (1620, by Fletcher and Massinger) is a better play
than either *Bonduca* or *Barnavelt*. The contrasts between different
sorts of behaviour are less forced than in *Bonduca*, and the honour
and nobility of the principal characters are more genuine than in
Barnavelt. It is the story of Caesar's meeting with Cleopatra when
he visits Egypt after the defeat of Pompey. Caesar's essential
nobility is established by his contempt of the Egyptians for having
his defeated enemy murdered. To Ptolemy, who thought to win
favour with Caesar by the murder, he says:

            I have heard too much,
And study not with smooth shews to invade
My noble Mind as you have done my Conquest.
Ye are poor and open: I must tell ye roundly,
That Man that could not recompence the Benefits,
The great and bounteous services of *Pompey*,
Can never dote upon the Name of *Caesar*; . . .

(II, 1; III, 320)

'The false one' of the title is Septimius, the renegade Roman who betrays and murders Pompey. He is the exact antithesis of Caesar not only in his willingness to conspire with Egyptians against a Roman but also in his purely materialistic motivation. Gold is the power he worships, by means of which he will make the world say his deeds are pious and brave (II, 2; III, 323). His avarice is a central point of reference; for, as in the romances, contempt of riches is the surest indication of nobility in *The False One*. Even Caesar, who has praised Pompey's 'bounteous services', is shaken by a display of Egyptian gold put on by Ptolemy to tempt him. At this point in the play occurs one of the most surprising developments. Cleopatra has already had herself delivered to Caesar wrapped in a 'packet', and his Roman followers have naturally seen in her the major temptation to betray his ideals. But in the event she uses her power over him to make him scorn her brother's gold. Though she has a motive for this behaviour in her quarrel with Ptolemy, she is even more offended by Caesar's apparent lapse from the heroic greatness she expected of him:

> He is no man:
> The shadow of a Greatness hangs upon him,
> And not the vertue: he is no Conquerour,
> H'as suffer'd under the base dross of Nature:
> Poorly delivered up his power to wealth,
> (The god of bed-rid men) taught his eyes treason
> Against the truth of love: . . .

>   *   *   *

> he is no Souldier,
> (All honourable Souldiers are Loves servants)
> He is a Merchant; . . .
>
>   (IV, 2; III, 346)

Here in small compass are the values of heroic romance, and Cleopatra loses no time in reminding Caesar of them:

> You flung me off, before the Court disgrac'd me,
> When in the pride I appear'd of all my beauty, . . .

>   *   *   *

Gave all your thoughts to gold, that men of glory,
And minds adorn'd with noble love, would kick at:
Souldiers of royal mark, scorn such base purchase:
Beauty and honour are the marks they shoot at; . . .

(IV, 2; III, 349)

Caesar is saved: 'By the gods/The bravery of this womans mind, has
fired me' (IV, 2; III, 349).

The Cleopatra who thus defends unmaterialistic virtue and
noble love is obviously made of sterner stuff than Shakespeare's
heroine, who, for all her courage and all her appreciation of
Antony's heroism, is slippery and 'riggish'. In a later scene of *The
False One*, when Cleopatra's life is in danger and her sister Arsino
asks her whether she can 'stand unmov'd', her reply recalls
Marston's Sophonisba:

Yes, *Arsino*,
And with a Masculine Constancy deride
Fortunes worst malice, as a Servant to
My Vertues, not a Mistress; then we forsake
The strong Fort of our selves, when we once yield,
Or shrink at her assaults; I am still my self,
And though disrob'd of Soveraignty, and ravish'd
Of ceremonious duty, that attends it,
Nay, grant they had slav'd my Body, my free mind
Like to the Palm tree walling fruitful *Nile*,
Shall grow up straighter and enlarge it self
'Spight of the envious weight that loads it with: . . .

(V, 4; III, 365)

With this staunch defence of integrity she is another 'wonder of
women', and a heroine in her own right, fully the equal of her
male counterpart.

The False One is an example of that sub-genre, the tragedy with
a happy ending, which was related to the development of tragicomedy in the Renaissance.[44] At the close of the final act, with the
ignoble characters all defeated and Caesar about to demonstrate
his generosity by giving the crown of Egypt to Cleopatra, nobility
and honour have triumphed at less cost than in *Bonduca*. Such an
ending has an obvious congruence with the premises of heroic
drama.

It is a short step from such a tragedy as this to the tragicomedies in the Beaumont and Fletcher corpus, many of which exalt heroic virtue with an enthusiasm and a rhetoric similar to those in *Bonduca* and *The False One*. Among them *The Loyal Subject* (1618, by Fletcher alone) is notable for its concentration upon honour as exemplified by the hero, a noble, patriotic and put-upon general, and by his almost equally impressive two sons and two daughters—an entire family of honour, who finally triumph over the contriving of an evil counsellor and a susceptible duke. In a series of artfully planned scenes their virtues are contrasted with the greed and lechery of their enemies.[45]

Behaviour of exemplary nobility is to be found even in some of the comedies. In *Monsieur Thomas* (1614, by Fletcher alone) a farcical plot counterpoints a serious one in which Francisco falls in love with Cellide, whom his older friend, Valentine, has adopted and plans to marry. The dilemma of Francisco, caught between love for the girl and gratitude to a generous friend, is the core of the plot. Situation after situation is created by the determination of all three characters to live up to the highest ideals. The delicacy of sensibility and the way Fletcher exploits it can be seen when Cellide is persuaded by Valentine against her will to visit Francisco, whose love, though never admitted, has been guessed by his friend and rival. When Cellide, partly out of pique with Valentine, behaves affectionately to Francisco, he is so shocked that he rebukes her for wantonness. But the integrity thus revealed makes her genuinely in love with him. After a moment of understandable bewilderment on his part, they exchange vows and then, because of their loyalty to Valentine, renounce each other. Their admirable tact and control are rewarded at the end when Francisco is revealed to be Valentine's lost son and, even in his father's eyes, the obvious match for Cellide.

Both the sensitivity and the courtesy of these three noble characters are directly attributable to Fletcher's source, Honoré d'Urfé's pastoral romance, *L'Astrée*, the bible of the French 'précieux'. Neither the romance nor Fletcher's play presents genuinely heroic characters, but it may be said of both works, as Marco Mincoff has said of Tasso's pastoral play, *Aminta*, that they arouse 'admiration not for the hero himself but for his code'.[46] Even in *Bonduca*, among hardened warriors, the eagerness to behave properly is apparent; for the cultivated trio in *Monsieur Thomas* it is the major consideration.

One more example of the importance of a code of behaviour in Beaumont and Fletcher can be found in *Valentinian* (1614, by Fletcher alone), a tragedy also derived from *L'Astrée*. The emperor for whom the play is named is both wicked and proud, but only occasionally displays the breadth of vision which might put him in the category of heroic villainy with Selimus. The victim of his lechery, the virtuous wife, Lucina, is more nearly heroic in her self-defence, but heroic action is smothered in surmise as the emperor's villainy and the plight of his subjects become the topics of debate. Before the rape of Lucina, her husband Maximus discusses with Aecius the duty of the subject when the ruler is vicious,[47] and after the rape they argue whether or not she should commit suicide. After Lucina's death Maximus debates with himself whether honour compels him to kill the emperor and also his friend Aecius, who would never countenance regicide. Whatever elevation the play has is largely due to these solemn considerations of conduct.

The Beaumont and Fletcher plays occupy a crucial position in the history of heroic drama because of the great influence they exerted on their own times and on the Restoration period, when the theory and practice of this form were at their height. Aside from a few characters, such as Bonduca, Barnavelt, Caesar and Cleopatra, their heroes and heroines rarely have the dimensions of the greatest Elizabethan figures. Miranda, for instance, for all his nobility, does not strike one as 'past the size of dreaming', to use Cleopatra's words about Antony, and Miranda is more typical of Beaumont and Fletcher protagonists than the other four characters just mentioned. Nevertheless, almost all the characters in the more serious plays seem to try to live heroically. It is their authors' strategy to put them in exquisite dilemmas where their principles will be tested, and where, as often as not, they must make painful choices between such values as love and religion or friendship and patriotism. Their passionate desire to live up to their ideals creates the tension in these situations, on which the dramatic effect of the plays depends. It is as if the heroic ethos elsewhere associated with the great central characters permeated the texture of entire plays.

If heroism in the Beaumont and Fletcher plays is at once more pervasive and less sharply defined, it is also subtly different in several respects from heroism in earlier heroic plays. The examples discussed have illustrated a shift from ethics toward etiquette. Closely related is a refinement of sensibility such as appears also in the new romances of the period. The theme of love assumes greater importance. The concern with honour, already strong in both classical epic and medieval romance, becomes more obsessive, owing in part, no doubt, to the influence of the Spanish romances on which Beaumont and Fletcher often drew.

With regard to their influence, two formal characteristics are of paramount importance. The preference of these authors for tragicomedy helped to establish on the stage a form which well served the emphasis on human potentiality found in heroic literature, including the romance. And secondly, their taste in rhetoric helped to form the language of the Caroline and Restoration stage. They showed that the speeches of heroes could be both extravagant and elegant, and thus appeal to the increasing numbers in the audiences of both public and private theatres who found Marlowe and even Shakespeare somewhat crude. Dryden was to say that Beaumont and Fletcher 'understood and imitated the conversation of gentlemen',[48] and although he was thinking of their portrayal of witty rakes in their comedies, his comment has some application to the heroic characters as well. Their concern with the proper thing to do extends to the proper way to speak. The resulting difference in heroic style may be suggested by comparing two passages. First Tamburlaine boasting to Bajazeth before their encounter and encouraging Zenocrate to insult Zabina:

> By this my sword that conquer'd *Persea,*
> Thy fall shall make me famous through the world:
> I will not tell thee how Ile handle thee,
> But euery common souldier of my Camp
> Shall smile to see thy miserable state.

> * * *

> *Zenocrate*, the loueliest Maide aliue,
> Fairer than rockes of pearle and pretious stone,
> The onely Paragon of *Tamburlaine,*
> Whose eies are brighter than the Lamps of heauen,
> And speech more pleasant than sweet harmony:
> That with thy lookes canst cleare the darkened Sky:
> And calme the rage of thundring Iupiter:

Sit downe by her: adorned with my Crowne,
As if thou wert the Empresse of the world.
Stir not *Zenocrate* vntill thou see
Me martch victoriously with all my men,
Triumphing ouer him and these his kings,
Which I will bring as Vassals to thy feete.
Til then take thou my crowne, vaunt of my worth,
And manage words with her as we will armes.

(III, 3, 1180–4, 1215–90)

And second, the hero of Fletcher's *A Wife for a Month* describing a sea-fight with the Turks and offering to rescue the heroine, whom an extraordinarily wicked tyrant has condemned to death unless she can find a husband who will give up his own life at the end of a month:

I set into him, entertain'd the *Turk*,
And for an hour gave him so hot a breakfast,
He clapt all linnen up he had to save him,
And like a Lovers thought he fled our fury;
There first I saw the man I lov'd, *Valerio*,
There was acquainted, there my soul grew to him,
And his to me, we were the twins of friendship.

*   *   *

I lov'd my friend, not measur'd out by time,
Nor hired by circumstance of place and honour,
But for his wealthy self and worth I lov'd him,
His mind and noble mold he ever mov'd in,
And wooe his friend because she was worthy of him,
The only relique that he left behind, Sir;
To give his ashes honour, Lady take me,
And in me keep *Valerio*'s love alive still,
When I am gone, take those that shall succeed me,
Heaven must want light, before you want a Husband....

(V, 1; V, 68–9)

The casual humour mixed with the heroic description produces a more complex tone than Tambulaine's plain defiance, and the graceful gesture of self-sacrifice becomes a more courtly compliment to the lady than the lyrical praise of Zenocrate, followed by the demand that she 'manage words' with Zabina. It is entirely characteristic of Fletcher that the speaker of these lines should turn out to be the very 'friend' he is describing—Valerio in disguise. His fine heroic speech is a cover for a successful palace revolution which brings the play to a happy ending. While it lasts, however, the hypothetical situation of these tense moments is heroic in a very Fletcherian way, and its special character is well projected in the language.

By rearranging and modifying the component elements of the pattern of heroic drama Beaumont and Fletcher gave it a shape which their immediate successors did not much alter. In the terms George Kubler uses to describe visual works of art, they found new solutions to the formal problem of heroic drama, and thereby occupied what seem to have been the chief 'available positions' in the sequence of such solutions.[49] Comparable opportunities to affect the development of this form were not given to those who came next.

Another way of explaining their powerful influence is to say that they had the imagination or the good fortune to anticipate the taste of the era which followed Charles I's accession to the throne, when his French queen, Henrietta Maria, brought with her the fashionable 'préciosité' of the salons. Since the chief goals of this movement were refinement of manners and speech, it is not surprising that the relative politeness and the polished rhetoric of Beaumont and Fletcher proved appealing.

Philip Massinger, who had an even larger share in the collaborative plays than Beaumont, created a more traditional hero when he wrote a play by himself, called *The Unnatural Combat* (1626). Malefort, the central character, is one of those monsters of evil who from time to time attracted the writers of heroic plays, though, despite the sensational nature of many of the Beaumont and Fletcher plays, there are no good examples of the type there. The evil characters, of whom there are plenty, are not conceived on a grand scale, or, at most, are given moments of grandeur, as is the wicked queen mother, Brunhalt, in *Thierry and Theodoret*. But Malefort is obviously outstanding at his first appearance, when he is, apparently unjustly, on trial for intelligence with the enemy, to whom his son has defected. His first speech, which William Gifford calls an 'indignant burst of savage ostentation', recalls his former military victories for the state, and elicits the comment, 'He still retains/The greatness of his spirit' (I, 1; I, 138).[50] In the next act he fights and wins 'the unnatural combat' with his son, but not before the latter has hinted very darkly indeed that his father is guilty of a sin too dreadful to name. Not until the end are all the facts revealed, that Malefort, having poisoned his first wife, fell in love with his daughter by the second. By this time the grandeur of the patriotic warrior has gradually been transformed into monumental depravity. The heroic dimensions of the character are assured in a scene where Malefort rages with the storm like King Lear, and is finally killed by a thunderbolt. Energetic villainy, old style, is allowed to run riot here.

In some of his solo productions Massinger adopted the newer heroic style, as in *The Maid of Honour* (1621), a tragicomedy similar in several respects to *The Knight of Malta*. And on one occasion, collaborating with Thomas Dekker, Massinger experimented with a rare type of hero, the saint. Dorothea of *The Virgin Martyr* (1620) is a Christian whose faith is unshaken by the martyrdom inflicted on her by the Roman Theophilus. After her death he is converted, tortured, and, after cheering his tormentors on, rewarded with a dying vision of Dorothea. The basic problem of making a martyr's life not only instructive but dramatically effective is that the fortitude to be admired must be shown by the victim's calm endurance, while the villains occupy most of the audience's attention with their nefarious activities. It is an acute form of the problem faced by Chapman with Clermont D'Ambois and Cato. The solution of Dekker and Massinger is supernatural 'machinery', which makes the play at times more like a medieval miracle play than a seventeenth-century heroic play. When Dryden attempted a play of this sort, he was embarrassed to find that for most of the audience his villain eclipsed his saint. Corneille, in *Polyeucte*, was one of the few who succeeded in creating a dynamic martyr.

During the troublesome reign of Charles I the 'courtier playwrights', sensitive to the taste of Queen Henrietta Maria, followed the paths opened up by Beaumont and Fletcher. These fluent but largely untalented amateurs treated the dilemmas of idealized lovers and warriors in plays to be performed at court, usually by a professional company, but in one notorious instance, by the queen and her ladies-in-waiting. This was Walter Montagu's *The Shepherd's Paradise* (1633), which lasted some seven hours and consisted largely in the conversations of well-bred characters who analysed their extraordinarily tangled love affairs in hair-splitting detail. This unexciting play was made a *cause célèbre* by the publication immediately afterward of *Histriomastix*, in which the Puritan William Prynne attacked dancing and acting by women, and was thought to be aiming directly at the queen. In its own right *The Shepherd's Paradise* is a monument to the untheatrical lengths to which the refined sensibilities of pastoral romance can be carried.

In more viable plays by the courtier playwrights somewhat similar discussions of love were a familiar feature, as in *Aglaura* (1637) by the vastly more gifted Sir John Suckling. There the fashionable topic of Platonic love appeared along with an avowed anti-Platonic lover, whose blasphemies against the religion of love were part of the tradition, just as satire of Petrarchan conventions was part of the tradition of Petrarchan love poetry. Even d'Urfé's *L'Astrée* had its Hylas, a libertine who constantly argued with the more devoted lovers. But in Suckling's play love debates were combined with a rousing action motivated by political ambition as well as love and lust and leading to a bloody finale for idealists and villains alike. The plot was, in fact, reminiscent of Beaumont and Fletcher, and still more so in a second version with a new fifth act, which transformed the play into a tragicomedy. Shortly after the Restoration Richard Flecknoe wrote:

> . . . *Beaumont* and *Fletcher* first writ in the Heroick way, upon whom *Suckling* and others endeavoured to refine agen; one saying wittily of his *Aglaura* that 'twas full of fine flowers, but they seem'd rather stuck then growing there; . . .[51]

For the performance of *Aglaura* Sir John paid for unusually fine costumes, which he then gave to the players (the King's Men), and, according to the undependable John Aubrey, he also had scenery for his play, following the Continental style. If Aubrey is right, this was an unusual occasion, for scenery was rarely used in England at this time except for the court masques. One or two records of its use for plays survive, however—for *The Shepherd's Paradise* (designed by Inigo Jones) and for William Cartwright's *The Royal Slave*, performed for the king and queen at Christ Church, Oxford, and again at Hampton Court.

It is difficult to say how much the London theatres were

affected by the spectacular productions at court. *Aglaura* was given at Blackfriars with the original costumes and conceivably with scenery. We have no certain evidence of the use of scenery until the years just preceding the Restoration, but there was nothing but the high cost and the persistence of the older tradition to prevent scenery from being used in the indoor theatres.[52] It is certain, in any case, that plays written for the court, such as *Aglaura*, *The Royal Slave*, and Lodowick Carlell's *The Deserving Favourite*, were later publicly acted at these theatres. In this way the taste of the court for polite heroics must have become increasingly familiar to London audiences.

For all their mediocrity, the plays of the courtier playwrights and of other amateurs of the town and the university form a vital link as Alfred Harbage has shown[53] between the earlier drama and the heroic drama of the Restoration. Most important of all is their concentration on what he calls 'patterns of perfection in heroic virtue' (p. 56) and their concomitant emphasis on courtesy, so prominent in medieval romance. They helped greatly to create the climate in which both courtiers and professional playwrights of the succeeding era worked.

It is well known that two men in the court circle, Sir William Davenant, a professional playwright who became a courtier, and Thomas Killigrew, a courtier who became a playwright, were to play stellar roles in the re-establishment and refashioning of the theatre after the accession of Charles II. Before the closing of the theatres both of them wrote plays in the fashionable heroic mode, such as Killigrew's *Claracilla* (1636), whose heroine has the revealing line, 'Civilities are always fruitful', or Davenant's *Love and Honour* (1634) with its prophetic title. The nature of the blend in Davenant's tragicomedy can be inferred from one speech by Alvaro, Prince of Savoy, when he finds that a young count in his service has presumed to capture the beautiful daughter of his greatest enemy:

> A cholerick beare or hungry panther would
> Have us'd her with more soft remorce; had I
> Incounterd her in the mad heate of chace,
> In all the fury of the fight, I would
> Have taught my angry steed the easie and
> The peacefull motion of a lambe.

She should have set his back, soft as the ayre,
And in her girdle bridle[d] him, more curb'd
Than in his foaming bitt, whilst I, her slave,
 Walk'd by, marking what hasty flowers sprung up,
Invited by her eye-beames from their cold roots;
And this would each true soldier do, that had
Refin'd his courage with the sober checks
Of sweet philosophy.

(I, 1, 254–67)⁵⁴

A warrior's displeasure with valour insufficiently refined by 'sweet philosophy' is expressed in the language of pastoral romance. The speech is both artificial in its reliance on the conventions of that genre and 'natural' in its seeming attempt to imitate the rhythms of conversation. Above all, the hero presents himself as an accomplished gentleman, to whom courtesy is as important as valour.

James Shirley, one of the ablest professional playwrights of the period, concentrated with less fierce intensity than his courtly rivals upon 'patterns of perfection in heroic virtue'. He, too, was an admirer of Beaumont and Fletcher, whose dramatic skill he praised astutely in an address 'To the Reader' published with the First Folio (1647) of their works. Largely from them he seems to have learned what the courtier playwrights never did—how to write effective plays. His tragicomedies are especially Fletcherian, and bear on the development of heroic drama in a similar way. *The Young Admiral* (1633), for instance, presents a patriotic warrior-hero plotted against by a wicked prince and placed in a series of dilemmas in which he must choose between his country and the woman he loves, or between her and his father. Though each test provokes noble flights of rhetoric, the resolution of the plot is brought about not by any action of the hero's but by the strategems of the two heroines. The 'young admiral's' situation is somewhat similar to that of Admiral Chabot in Chapman's play, which Shirley apparently revised soon after writing his *Young Admiral*, but the Chapman-Shirley play cuts much deeper into the problem of unrewarded virtue. *The Young Admiral* was not only a commercial success but was liked by the king and queen when it was performed at court, and received an unusual commendation from Sir Henry Herbert, Master of the Revels, who praised the play, when he licensed it, as a 'patterne to other poetts, not only for the bettring of maners and language, but for the improvement of the quality . . .'.[55]

None of Shirley's four tragedies is so heroic as *Chabot* or as certain tragedies in the Beaumont and Fletcher canon, such as *Bonduca* or *The False One*. The most interesting of them, *Love's Cruelty* (1631), retains some of the dramatic effectiveness of Beaumont and Fletcher while reflecting the taste of the Caroline court as truly as any of the courtiers' plays. The hero's name, Bellamente, hints at his pursuit of honour, love and friendship, the ideals that underlie heroic romance, though in this play they inspire very little action that could be called heroic. The core of the play is the testing of these ideals in situations that seem to mirror contemporary life in polite society. Thus the curiosity aroused in Clariana by Bellamente's praise of his friend Hippolito leads to a libertine affair in which Shirley's chief concerns appear to be the progressive emotional involvement of the heroine and the response of the hero when he discovers the infidelity. Bellamente's efforts to suppress the evidence and to behave to the world as if nothing had happened constitute, in a sense, a heroic effort to live up to a courteous and civilized standard, but they also seem to represent a sacrifice of ethical standards to etiquette.

The best Caroline dramatist, John Ford, seems at first glance to have been the least interested in the qualities celebrated in heroic drama. For, diverse as they are, the most heroic plays have certain things in common. Their principal characters pursue energetically some ideal which stretches human capacities to the utmost, whether the ideal is impossibly remote and therefore self-destructive, like that of Coriolanus, or attainable, like that of Caesar in *The False One*; whether self-centred, like that of Tamburlaine, or beneficial to all, like that of Henry V; perverted, like those of the villain heroes, or thoroughly noble, like those of the *chevaliers sans peur et sans reproche* who, early and late, appear in the most romantic plays. The energy of their quest is an affirmation of the ideal, finding its natural dramatic expression in an elevated and extravagant rhetoric which we call heroic rant. What Ford's characters most obviously lack is this sort of energetic utterance. An exception might be made for Giovanni in certain scenes of *'Tis Pity She's a Whore*, when, for instance, he says to his sister, 'I hold fate/Clasp'd in my fist' (V, 5, 11–12),[56] but even this proud boast is made to seem ironic if not almost pathetic by our knowledge at the time of its utterance that Giovanni is in the power of his enemy. His sister, aware that such boasting is idle, reminds him that he should be preparing for death. Giovanni's scepticism not only makes a Christian preparation seem irrelevant but also isolates him from his sister, whom he loves more than anyone. His loneliness and bewilderment are moving in this scene, but they are not the marks of a great hero.

More typical of Ford is Calantha in *The Broken Heart*, of whose death scene Charles Lamb wrote, 'I do not know where to find in any Play a catastrophe so grand, so solemn, and so surprising as this'.[57] As reports of the deaths of her father, her friend Penthea, and her lover, Ithocles, are brought to her, this princess remains outwardly unmoved, continuing to play her part in the revels celebrating a court marriage. Later, just before her death, which these shocks have caused, she explains her extraordinary conduct:

> Oh, my lords,
> I but deceived your eyes with antic gesture,
> When one news straight came huddling on another
> Of death, and death, and death. Still I danced forward;
> But it struck home, and here, and in an instant.
> Be such mere women, who with shrieks and outcries
> Can vow a present end to all their sorrows,
> Yet live to vow new pleasures, and outlive them.
> They are the silent griefs which cut the heart-strings;
> Let me die smiling.
>
> (V, 3, 67–76)[58]

The moment is 'grand' and 'solemn', as Lamb said. It is also very quiet: one imagines Calantha's voice as hardly raised above a whisper. She is a Stoic like Sophonisba, but her death of a broken heart is far from the heroic gesture of swallowing poison to avoid captivity. In only one respect, but an important one, does this quiet scene resemble those in more obviously heroic plays: it is clearly calculated to arouse the wonder of the spectators at the greatness of the heroine's spirit.

Calantha's concern for decorum is shared by many of Ford's characters. Though they seem in this respect similar to the polite ladies and gentlemen who paid court to Queen Henrietta Maria, the atmosphere of Ford's plays is not that of 'préciosité'. Even in *The*

Lover's Melancholy, which at moments seems rather like a pastoral romance, the ideal for which the characters are striving is something more than courtesy and yet something other than heroic virtue as it is usually understood. One character says:

> O, lady, in the turmoils of our lives,
> Men are like politic states, or troubled seas,
> Tossed up and down with several storms and tempests,
> Change and variety of wrecks and fortunes;
> Till, labouring to the havens of our homes,
> We struggle for the calm that crowns our ends.
>
> (V, 1)[59]

The struggle for calm, typical of Ford's heroes, differentiates them from their more active and spectacular confrères in heroic drama. Understatement is as characteristic of Ford as hyperbole of Marlowe.

The hero of Ford's *Perkin Warbeck* differs in certain respects from all his others, and might be taken as Ford's comment on such self-deluded heroes as Chapman's Byron. Alone among Ford's plays, this is a history play, in which the author, always keenly aware of the work of his predecessors, has deliberately set out to revive a genre long neglected. The language is frequently reminiscent of Shakespeare's histories. Warbeck, the impostor who claimed the throne in the reign of Henry VII, is given a dashing elegance of speech which immediately impresses James IV of Scotland as 'The language of a king' (II, 1, 104).[60] Though never so inflammatory as the eloquence of Henry V nor so rhapsodic as Byron's, the language of Perkin Warbeck is elevated above the quiet norm of Ford's drama. Like Giovanni in *'Tis Pity*, he is in this respect exceptional. He has even more claim than Giovanni to being considered truly heroic, for Giovanni's assurance is corroded by scepticism, while Perkin Warbeck remains confident to the very end. It is, of course, supremely ironic that this most assured of Ford's heroes is a sham, but he is not shown recanting, as he does in the historical sources from which Ford drew. Instead, he 'bears it out even to the edge of doom', either self-deluded to the point of madness or an actor more in love with his role than with life. As he is led off to the gallows he says to his followers:

> Be men of spirit,
> Spurn coward passion! So illustrious mention
> Shall blaze our names, and style us Kings o'er Death.
> (V, 3, 205–8)

This has the ring of genuine heroic rhetoric, but in Ford's drama this kind of heroism is at best a dream.

Although none of his plays is in the main stream of heroic drama, Ford makes his contribution to the genre by showing what is strange and wonderful in a style much simpler than was conventionally expected. In most of his plays the characters strive for goals determined by the ideals of chivalry, only to find their efforts frustrated, or to find, alternatively, that the struggle to attain them has cost 'not less than everything'. Their somewhat eccentric heroism, often tempered by pathos, opens a vista towards the drama of Otway.

Notes

1 See Nicholas Brooke's introduction to the Revels Plays edition of *Bussy D'Ambois* (London and Cambridge, Mass., 1964), liv–lvii. The prologue printed in the 1641 quarto describes the success of various actors in the title-role.

2 Quotations from the comedies are taken from *The Plays of George Chapman*, ed. T. M. Parrott, *The Comedies* (New York, 1961; orig. 1914).

3 The sexual emphasis of these episodes is evident in his name, which is a slang term for penis.

4 *The Poems of George Chapman*, ed. Phyllis B. Bartlett (New York, 1941), 49. The shortness and sketchiness of the play as we have it has led most commentators to suppose that this is a considerably altered acting version. Ennis Rees argues plausibly that it may be rather close to what Chapman wrote: 'Chapman's *Blind Beggar* and the Marlovian Hero', *Journal of English and Germanic Philology*, LVII (1958), 60–3. See Millar MacLure's discussion in *George Chapman* (Toronto, 1966), 84–6.

5 I include myself in this eager but unfortunate group: *The Herculean Hero*, 88–111. The quantity of *Bussy* criticism precludes referring to all of it; Robert P. Adams discusses and dissents from a great deal of it in 'Critical Myths and Chapman's Original *Bussy D'Ambois*', *Renaissance Drama*, IX (1966), 141–61. Some of the important treatments are: Ennis Rees, *The Tragedies of George Chapman* (Cambridge, Mass., 1954), 29–50; Edwin Muir, *Essays on Literature and Society*, revised ed. (Cambridge, Mass., 1965), 22–32; Roy Battenhouse, 'Chapman and the Nature of Man', *English Literary*

History, XII (1945), 87–107; Peter Ure, 'Chapman's Tragedies', *Jacobean Theatre* (London, 1960), 227–47; Jean Jacquot, intro. to *Bussy d'Amboise* (Paris, 1960), v–cxli; MacLure, *Chapman*, 108–25. T. B. Tomlinson takes Chapman up only to put him down as decadent and hollow in *A Study of Elizabethan and Jacobean Tragedy* (Cambridge and Melbourne, 1964), 256–65.

6 Cf. T. S. Eliot on 'The Metaphysical Poets' and on wit (in 'Andrew Marvell'); *Selected Essays* (New York, 1932), 241–63.

7 See Ure's discussion of this speech, *Jacobean Theatre*, 227 ff., and MacLure's treatment of the 'inward'/'outward' antithesis in all the tragedies, 108–57.

8 I quote from Nicholas Brooke's edition, the only modern one to follow the text of the First Quarto (1607–8), the superiority of which he defends persuasively (pp. lx–lxxiv). The Second Quarto (1641) is a version revised, as Brooke believes, not only by Chapman but by someone else, possibly Nathan Field, who starred in a revival of the play in about 1610.

9 Address 'To the Reader' prefixed to *The White Devil* (1612).

10 See Brooke's introduction, pp. xl–xlii.

11 For example, 'The Shadow of Night' (1594). I discuss the relation of Tamyra and the conjuring scenes to this tradition at greater length in *The Herculean Hero*, 96–102. See also MacLure, 35–45, 123 n.; and Jacquot, lxx–lxxxi.

12 The only suggestion that Behemoth has a corrupting effect on Bussy is the latter's decision to adopt 'policy' (i.e. craft) as a principle of conduct (IV, 2, 155–60). I agree with MacLure (p. 123) that 'surely this is an outburst of desperate naïveté from the despiser of "the witch Policy" '.

13 See *The Herculean Hero*, 104–8; Jacquot, xciv–xcvii; Brooke, l–liv.

14 Brooke shows (lxix) how the effect achieved by depersonalizing Monsieur and the Guise is blurred by the rearrangement of material in the 1641 quarto, in which they re-enter the story after their choric conversation.

15 In the 1641 quarto this speech is much less effectively placed seventy-five lines earlier.

16 See Alfred Harbage's comments on 'Theatre of a Coterie', *Shakespeare and the Rival Traditions*, 29–57; and *The Herculean Hero*, 98–101, 110–11.

17 Jacquot devotes a most interesting section of his introduction (pp. xxiv, xlvi–l) to judgments of Bussy published after Chapman's play but remarkably similar to his presentation of faults and heroic qualities. Jacquot's suggestion is that Chapman may have been familiar with an oral tradition which also lay behind the publications cited.

18 *Jacobean Theatre*, 245.

19 Thelma Herring shows that he is 'a sophisticated development' of the *eiron* of Old Comedy: 'Chapman and an aspect of Modern Criticism', *Renaissance Drama*, VIII (1965), 158. See also MacLure, 103–7.

20 Quotations from *The Conspiracy* and from the remaining Chapman plays are taken from *The Plays of George Chapman*, ed. T. M. Parrott, *The Tragedies* (New York, 1961; orig. 1910).

21 *Hercules Furens*, l. 1138.

22 See the discussion of 'learning' in Chapman by Rees, 2–13.

23 See MacLure, 133.

24 *Chapman's Homer*, ed. Allardyce Nicoll, 2 vols. (New York, 1956), II, 4; I have changed italic to roman type. Rees (pp. 8, 29 ff.) makes this distinction central to his interpretation of all the tragedies. His discussion is illuminating, though so rigid an application of this dedication to the earlier *Bussy D'Ambois* distorts the meaning of that tragedy.

25 See MacLure, 151.

26 See Thelma Herring (*Renaissance Drama*, VIII, 168–70), for the date.

27 Ben Jonson, *Sejanus*, ed. Jonas A. Barish (New Haven and London, 1965), 28; all quotations from the play are taken from this edition.

28 *Jacobean Theatre*, 244.

29 See Anthony Caputi, *John Marston, Satirist* (Ithaca, N.Y., 1961), 240.

30 *The Plays of John Marston*, ed. H. Harvey Wood, 3 vols. (London, 1934–9), II, 7. Since lines are unnumbered in this edition, from which all quotations are taken, volume and page will be indicated after act and scene. Philip J. Finkelpearl's description of the play is apt: '*The Wonder of Women* is an attempt to embody in a character and an action Marston's vision of perfection' (*John Marston of the Middle Temple* [Cambridge, Mass., 1969], 241).

31 Caputi (p. 245) points out the special appropriateness of this masque-like ceremony for the boy actors.

32 The romantic nature of the action is implicit in Peter Ure's account of it in an important article, 'John Marton's *Sophonisba*: A Reconsideration', *Durham Univ. Journal*, n.s. X (1948–9), 89–90. Although he is right that the testing of love is not so important as the celebration of Stoic virtue, his enumeration of the trials of the lovers shows how readily Roman and romantic elements could be combined in the portrayal of heroism.

33 All quotations from Webster's plays are taken from John Russell Brown's editions of *The White Devil* and *The Duchess of Malfi* for The Revels Plays (London and Cambridge, Mass., 1960 and 1964).

34 All quotations from the play are taken from *The Dramatic Works of Thomas Dekker*, ed. Fredson Bowers, IV (Cambridge, 1961).

35 The plays published as Beaumont and Fletcher's, and usually so called, included one or two by Beaumont alone, some by Fletcher alone, some in which he collaborated with Massinger and others, and one or two in which neither Beaumont nor Fletcher had a hand. Cyrus Hoy, in the most recent study of the authorship of these plays, summarizes his results in *Studies in Bibliography*, XV (1962), 85–6.

36 The one chivalric episode in Book IV was inserted by the printer of the 1561 edition.

37 See Maurice Magendie, *Du Nouveau sur L'Astrée* (Paris, 1927), 252–3.

38 'An Essay of Dramatic Poesy', in Ker, I, 81.

39 In *The Pattern of Tragicomedy in Beaumont and Fletcher* (New Haven, 1952) I showed that the special development of rhetoric in these plays was in part an outgrowth of the oratorical tradition of declamation (pp. 86–98). For discussion of the Beaumont and Fletcher 'pattern' see pp. 1–42.

40 Felix E. Schelling cites *The Knight of Malta* and *The Laws of Candy* as Fletcherian tragicomedies which were sources of the heroic play (*Elizabethan Drama*, 2 vols. [Boston and New York, 1908], II, 350).

41 Unless otherwise indicated, all quotations from Beaumont and Fletcher are taken from *The Works of Francis Beaumont and John Fletcher*, 10 vols. (Cambridge, 1905–12). Since lines are unnumbered in this edition, volume and page are indicated following act and scene.

42 All quotations from *A King and No King* are taken from Robert K. Turner's edition (Lincoln, Neb., 1963), which presents a text superior to that of Glover and Waller.

43 All quotations from *Barnavelt*, which was not printed in the seventeenth century, are taken from Wilhelmina P. Frijlinck's edition of the manuscript (Amsterdam, 1922). In quoting I have expanded contractions.

44 See Marvin Herrick, *Tragicomedy* (Urbana, Ill., 1955), 63–124.

45 See my discussion of the play as variations on the theme of honour in *Pattern of Tragicomedy*, 143–51.

46 '*The Faithfull Shepherdess*: A Fletcherian Experiment', *Renaissance Drama*, IX (1966), 174. See B. J. Pendlebury's discussion of *L'Astrée* as the source of heroic sentiment in *Dryden's Heroic Plays* (New York, 1967; orig. 1923), 24 ff.

47 See Clifford Leech's discussion of this aspect of the play in *The John Fletcher Plays* (London, 1962), 114-20.

48 'An Essay of Dramatic Poesy', in Ker, I, 81.

49 *The Shape of Time* (New Haven, 1962), 33 ff., 89.

50 *The Plays of Philip Massinger*, ed. William Gifford, 4 vols. (London, 1805). Since lines are unnumbered in this edition, volume and page are indicated following act and scene.

51 'A Short Discourse of the English Stage' (1664), in *Critical Essays of the Seventeenth Century*, ed. J. E. Spingarn, 3 vols. (Bloomington, Ind., 1957; orig. Oxford, 1908), II, 92; hereafter referred to as 'Spingarn'.

52 Some of the most recent opinion on this subject can be found in three articles: John Freehafer, '*The Italian Night Piece* and Suckling's *Aglaura*', *Journal of English and Germanic Philology*, LXVII (1968), 249-65; K. R. Richards, 'Changeable Scenery for Plays on the Caroline Stage', *Theatre Notebook*, XXIII (1968-9), 6-20, and again pp. 114-5. Also consult G. E. Bentley, *The Jacobean and Caroline Stage*, 7 vols. (Oxford, 1941-68).

53 *Cavalier Drama* (New York, 1964; orig 1936), 7-71. Harbage emphasizes the difference between Fletcher's professionally theatrical work and the amateur efforts of the courtiers, but he also acknowledges that 'Fletcher showed the way for Cavalier drama' (p. 41). His discussion should be read in its entirety for details which cannot be included here and for his judicious conclusions.

54 *Love and Honour and The Siege of Rhodes*, ed. James W. Tupper (Boston and London, 1909).

55 *The Dramatic Records of Sir Henry Herbert*, ed. J. Q. Adams (New Haven, 1917), 19. See Albert Wertheim's discussion of the play in his unpublished dissertation, 'The Dramatic Art of James Shirley' (Yale University, 1966), 209-16.

56 '*Tis Pity She's a Whore*, ed. N. W. Bawcutt (Lincoln, Neb., 1966).

57 *Specimens of English Dramatic Poets*, 2 vols. (London, 1893), II, 199. The work was originally published in 1808.
58 *The Broken Heart*, ed. Brian Morris (New York, 1966).
59 *John Ford (Five Plays)*, ed. Havelock Ellis (New York, 1957), 68-9.
60 All quotations from *Perkin Warbeck* are taken from Perer Ure's edition (London, 1968).

Interchapter: Corneille

No account of heroic drama in England would be complete
without a discussion of Pierre Corneille, whose relationship to
English drama is unique. By the time of his first major success
with *Le Cid* in 1636 the great Elizabethan plays had long been
written and the theatres would soon be closed by the Puritans,
while the great period of French drama was just beginning.
Corneille's career as a dramatist did not end until 1674, fourteen
years after the reopening of the theatres in England, thus over-
lapping the pre-Commonwealth and Restoration periods and
covering the intermission between the acts. Not only was his
influence on Dryden and other Restoration dramatists openly
acknowledged, so that recognition of it has become a cliché of
dramatic history, but also, though less well known, the similarity
of some of his plays to certain English plays of the first quarter of
the century is striking. On occasion he turned to the same episodes
in Roman history that his English predecessors had dramatized,
and even altered history in somewhat similar ways, as can be
seen by comparing his treatment of Cleopatra in *La Mort de
Pompée* with Fletcher and Massinger's in *The False One*. The
prominence of the dilemma in his plays also recalls Fletcher, as
does the ethos of romance—especially of Spanish romance in *Le
Cid* and *Don Sanche d'Aragon*. When he pays tribute to the courage
and constancy of Sophonisba he reminds the English reader of
Marston. Doubtless these coincidences of theme and treatment
can be explained by Continental influences to which both the
English playwrights and Corneille responded, for whether or not
he had heard of Shakespeare, as one recent critic supposes,[1] it is
unlikely that he knew the lesser luminaries at a period when
English culture was hardly a beacon to the French. Nevertheless,
the clarity with which these common characteristics appear in
Cornelian drama makes it an illuminating commentary on the
plays treated in the last two chapters as well as a source of
influence on those in the following chapter.

Both practice and theory contribute to the light Corneille throws on English heroic drama. His long array of heroes, eminently interesting in their own right, can also serve as points of reference in describing the chief types of English hero. And the criticism contained in the 'Discours' of 1660 and the 'Examens' prepared in the same year for the collected edition of his plays makes explicit much of what might be inferred about the rationale of the English plays. Passionately interested in theory and also in defending his own practice, Corneille relates the special features of heroic drama to the assumptions of Aristotelian poetics.

In a brief chapter not even the major plays of Corneille can be discussed in detail. It will be possible only to indicate the characteristic themes of the plays and the various manifestations of the Cornelian hero. Since categories are more important than chronology in such a discussion, some of the plays will be taken out of the sequence in which they were written.

Like Chapman, Corneille anticipated some of his heroic themes in the comedies he wrote at the outset of his career. Alidor of *La Place royale* (1634) is a remarkable case in point, as Serge Doubrovsky has demonstrated,[2] for his efforts to free himself from the fetters of love—to master his emotions and to impose his will on the woman who threatens to make him dependent—prefigure the struggles of many heroes. Alidor has the misfortune to love and to be loved by the well-named Angélique, whom he considers perfect. Misfortune, in that he considers himself an extraordinary spirit (Corneille in his dedicatory epistle calls him 'extravagant')[3] who should not be constrained by his passion:

> Il ne faut point servir d'objet qui nous possède;
> Il ne faut point nourrir d'amour qui ne nous cède:
> (I, 4, 205–6)

This conviction of his superiority commits him to what Doubrovsky calls the 'projet aristocratique', characteristic of the Cornelian hero and derived in large measure, as Paul Bénichou has suggested, from a rejuvenation of chivalric ideals through contact with classical heroism in Plutarch and Seneca.[4] Alidor sees his love of liberty menaced by the tyranny of Angélique and, as he later says, by the god of love, 'petit insolent'. The stance of Alidor, the proto-hero, constitutes both an amusing comment on the extravagance of the cult of love in chivalric romance and a comic assertion of individual freedom. In these respects he is the Gallic equivalent of Chapman's Irus and Tharsalio or of Mirabel in Fletcher's *The Wild-Goose Chase*.

Doubrovsky mentions, in order to dismiss, the suggestion that Alidor is a Don Juan (p. 69), but some connection with the libertine tradition is hard to deny. Though it is true that he almost puritanically proclaims his aversion to affairs with married women, he refers in the same speech to the 'mille qu'autrefois tu m'as vu caresser' (I, 4, 283)—something short of Don Juan's *mille e tre* (in Spain alone), but still impressive. The liberty Alidor seeks is, after all, the chief goal of the libertine. There is a further connection between Alidor and libertinage in a passage of the dedicatory epistle, where Corneille claims to have learnt from the dedicatee that the love of an 'honnête homme' should always be voluntary, and that one should never continue an affair beyond the point where one has the power to break it off (II, 220). The 'honnête homme', suave practitioner of 'la politesse mondaine', paradoxically owed something to the high ideals of courtly romance, as promulgated by 'les précieux', and something to the scepticism and license of the libertines. Thus Alidor, though much less debauched than the rakes of Restoration drama (here Doubrovsky is clearly in the right), nevertheless anticipates them in exemplifying the link between heroism and libertinage.

The ending of *La Place royale* is, in one sense, not at all what one expects in comedy, for Angélique, after two abortive schemes on the part of Alidor to give her to his friend Cléandre, resolves to enter a convent. For her, still in love with Alidor but now aware of his perfidy, there is no happy resolution. In another, somewhat ironic sense, the dénouement is typically comic in that the hero has achieved his main goal—independence of Angélique—even though he has done so largely through a series of accidents over which he could not exercise his control. When he congratulates himself on being both free of Angélique and not obliged to see her the wife of someone else, we may see him as in fact the victim of his mistaken doctrines, and feel that his heartlessness appears here in the worst possible light. Though the tone is far from tragic, a question is raised which will be treated in much greater depth in *Horace*: what price is paid for the total suppression of sentiment in the interest of self-mastery?

Corneille was keenly interested in the relationship between comedy and tragedy. Too great an admirer of Aristotle to ignore the *Poetics*, and too close an observer of what worked in the theatre to follow slavishly in the master's footsteps, he decided that the distinction could not be made solely on the basis of the rank of the characters. Though the ancients allowed only characters 'd'une condition très médiocre' in comedy, he writes in the 'Discours du poème dramatique', this is not the case in our time, 'when even kings may appear there' (I, 23). And conversely, the presence of kings will not make the play a tragedy, for a simple love story in which kings are involved, with no threat to their lives or their kingdoms, is not sufficiently elevated for tragedy. There must be some 'grand intérêt d'état' (loosely, 'important affairs of state'), some passion 'more noble and more male' than love, and danger of losing more than a mistress (I, 24). Not that love is unsuitable for tragedy, but it must take second place, as it does in *Le Cid*, where the obligations of high birth and the concern for honour win out over it. When a play such as *Don Sanche d'Aragon* has royal personages whose story is indeed complicated by affairs of state, but who are never in serious danger of banishment or of the loss of their lives or kingdoms, Corneille calls it a 'comédie héroïque'. Thus in his criticism he erects a sort of generic ladder on which one climbs, rung by rung, from comedy to tragedy, from the least to the most serious, and from unheroic to heroic.

The tragedies are all, in one way or another, heroic. It is possible to divide them, as Robert J. Nelson[5] and Serge Doubrovsky have done, according to the different characteristics of the protagonists—to find some heroes more truly heroic than others, and even to recognize with Doubrovsky a major strain of self-destruction in many of them (p. 469), but each one has a largeness of spirit (what Corneille calls 'grandeur d'âme'), a firmness of purpose and an energy which merit the term heroic.[6]

The first and best known of them is Rodrigue of *Le Cid* (1636). The cruel dilemma which forces him to duel with Chimène's father in order to avenge an insult to his own father creates the tension which is never relaxed. In the famous 'stances' the opposing demands on him are lined up in the neat balance of the verses, and then reduced to oxymoron:

Père, maîtresse, honneur, amour,
Noble et dure contrainte, aimable tyrannie,
Tous mes plaisirs sont morts, ou ma gloire ternie.
L'un me rend malheureux, l'autre indigne du jour.

(I, 6, 311–14)

It is a far more acute version of the dilemma of Erec or Yvain,
caught between the demands of love and prowess (with the concomitant thirst for glory). As Corneille says in a passage already
alluded to, family honour wins out in both Rodrigue and
Chimène: he is impelled to kill her father, and she to demand his
death.

Rodrigue's decision to fight marks him as 'généreux', a term
much used in seventeenth-century France and difficult to translate into English. Derived from the Latin *generosus*, it means
primarily well or nobly born, and thus implies an aristocratic
code of behaviour, closely related to the chivalric code. 'Generosity' in its standard English sense would be only one of the
traits of the 'généreux', but an important one, since it, like
courage, was a sign of a great heart.

A subtle but important distinction must be made between the
'générosité' of the Cornelian hero and that described by Descartes
in a famous passage of his treatise on *Les Passions de l'âme* (1649).
In Article 153 he defines it as consisting partly in a man's knowledge that the one thing he can call his own is his free use of the
power of will ('libre disposition de ses volontés'), and partly in his
resolution to use it well, that is to undertake and perform whatever he judges to be best. So far the definition might seem to
apply well to Rodrigue and many later heroes in Corneille, but
Descartes goes on to explain (Art. 155) that those who are
'généreux' are ordinarily so aware of their shortcomings that they
are the most humble of people, and that the great actions they
perform are above all for the benefit of others (Art. 156). They
are always masters of their passions, and their self-esteem differs
from pride in that it comes solely from the awareness of using free
will properly. The desire for other goods such as 'l'esprit, la
beauté, les richesses, les honneurs', more esteemed because they
belong to few people, leads to a very culpable pride and to hate,
envy, jealousy and anger (Art. 158).[7] There is no getting around
the jealous guarding of family honour in *Le Cid*, and this is not

exactly what Descartes seems to mean by acting for the benefit of others, while his list of values cherished because they are rare approaches dangerously close (with the exception of 'richesses') to what Rodrigue desires.

The 'générosité' of Rodrigue is therefore somewhat more individual and more aristocratic than Cartesian 'générosité', but the heroism it fosters is less fiercely egotistic than that of a Tamburlaine. Corneille is at some pains to show that it is the Count, Chimène's father, whose family pride threatens the harmony of the court and kingdom, so that Rodrigue's offence in killing him is more pardonable (II, 1 and 6). Furthermore, Rodrigue's heroic defence of the city against the Moors, undertaken on his own initiative, is a gratuitous act which benefits the entire kingdom. When the Théâtre National Populaire staged the play with Gérard Philippe as Rodrigue, his great narration of the fight was made to symbolize the importance of this hero to his country as he stood in the centre of the stage before the king, with the rest of the court in a semi-circle around him. His energetic declamation—the verbal equivalent of his heroic exploit—was clearly the animating force of the kingdom and at the same time the point which determined its circular order.

The intrinsic value of Rodrigue's ideals is further suggested in at least two ways. At his first meeting with Chimène after the duel, she shows her respect for his code by explaining that it must be her code too:

> De quoi qu'en ta faveur notre amour m'entretienne,
> Ma générosité doit répondre a la tienne:
> Tu t'es, en m'offensant, montré digne de moi;
> Je me dois, par ta mort, montrer digne de toi.
>
> (III, 4, 929–32)

Then at the end of the play the king, by urging her to give up her pursuit of vengeance, and finally tricking her into doing so, makes it appear that her 'générosité' is tainted by excess, and that only Rodrigue's is compatible with the good of the state (IV, 5; V, 6). Thus, in the interest of the larger order, the lovers' dilemma is abolished: family honour no longer opposes desire; 'prouesse' is joined with 'fine amor'.

Horace (1640) constitutes in one respect a curious commentary on *Le Cid*. Here the conflict of individual feeling and public obligation appears in the most extreme form. Horace is forced to settle the war between Rome and Alba by fighting the Alban Curiace, his wife's brother, who is engaged to his sister Camille. Firmly subordinating his friendship to his patriotic duty, Horace glories in the constancy which enables him to control his passions (and thereby shows himself a more Cartesian 'généreux'). When he has killed not only Curiace but also the two brothers of Curiace, and has thus made Rome the master of Alba, he is reproached by Camille, who even dares to speak against Rome for having pushed him to this act of inhumanity. This is too much for Horace, who then plunges his sword into his sister. Though he is pardoned by the king, as was Rodrigue, the play raises, as *Le Cid* never does, the question of what has been sacrificed for heroic constancy. Instead of a reconciliation between private and public happiness, the last acts present a bleak picture of the total victory of the patriotic ideal over personal affection. Magnanimity of a sort has produced heartlessness. When Horace draws his sword against his sister, it is as shocking as if Coriolanus had refused Volumnia and ordered the attack. The ideals of the two heroes are almost diametrically opposed, but equally important is the difference between sacrificing the ideal to nature, as Coriolanus does, though it is 'most mortal' to him, and sacrificing nature to constancy. Together, even more than separately, the two plays suggest how absolute a dilemma may be posed by the logical requirements of a heroic ideal.

In the tragedy of Polyeucte, the Christian martyr (1642–3), Corneille again presents the sacrifice of personal feeling to an ideal, but here the sacrifice has his unequivocal approval. Polyeucte, in fact, is always right, whether in his original decision to overturn the pagan idols at the sacrifice, or in his later refusal to give up his religion even when urged by his wife and her father. Not only does Corneille in his 'Examen' defend the portrayal of a character whose goodness exceeds the Aristotelian mean (III, 479–81), but he also uses the play in his second 'Discours' ('De la tragédie') as one example of tragedy which succeeds by arousing pity alone rather than pity and fear (I, 59–64). The danger in presenting a wholly good man who suffers at the hands of a bad man, according to Corneille, is that our anger at the oppressor, an improper response to tragedy, will eclipse our pity for the victim (I, 56). The reason this does not happen in *Polyeucte* is said to be that Félix, the Roman governor who orders the execution of the Christians, is not so much a fierce persecutor as a timid politician, who fears the consequences of any laxity. This explanation reveals the importance of the great soul in Corneille's conception of tragic character. If Félix were not pusillanimous we should resent him even more than we pity Polyeucte. Merely despising him, we can concentrate our attention on the 'grandeur d'âme' of the hero, mentioned in the second line of the play, and even come to think well of the weakling at the end, when he is converted to Christianity by the example of the greater spirit.

Nicomède (1651) is another unexceptionable hero, and is also a prince who devotes himself in the most trying circumstances to the good of his father's kingdom of Bythinia. Not even the machinations of Arsinoé, an ambitious step-mother, one of the century's favourite stereotypes, can undermine his filial and patriotic loyalty. His exemplary virtue aside, Nicomède is a more conventional hero than Polyeucte. A great warrior, who has added whole kingdoms to the domain of his father, Prusias, he is also in love with a captive queen, Laodice. But with his step-mother poisoning his father's mind against him and trying to engineer a marriage between her own son and Laodice, there is little he can do for himself short of revolt. His situation is made even more frustrating by the presence at court of Flaminius, the envoy of Rome, who is abetting the efforts of Arsinoé to have her son declared the successor of Prusias, for the Romans fear the strength of Nicomède. Thus the great conqueror and lover is forced by his loyalty to play a strictly defensive game—to react, but never to act.

Corneille succeeds, as Chapman in *The Revenge of Bussy D'Ambois* never does, in projecting an image of contained energy. Unawed by the Roman threats, Nicomède speaks his mind to Flaminius, and seeks constantly to make his father act like a true king rather than a petitioner of Rome. The attempt is fruitless, but as Prusias sinks deeper into his weakness, Nicomède emerges more and more clearly as the most powerful character in the play. At the end comes a scene which dramatizes his dynamic calm as perfectly as the scene of Rodrigue's narration renders his vital energy. The schemes of Nicomède's enemies have at last been frustrated by an uprising of the people, and he has been rescued from the guards who were about to take him prisoner to Rome.

Prusias and even Arsinoé, who is made of much sterner stuff, are nervously awaiting the end, when Nicomède enters:

> Tout est calme, Seigneur: un moment de ma vue
> A soudain apaisé la populace émue.

(V, 9, 1779–80)

It is the great moment of the play and one of the splendours of Corneille. Not revenge but rescue, not rebellion but the restitution of order. To Prusias he says, 'Je viens en bon sujet vous rendre le repos', and instead of insulting over his enemies, he assures Flaminius with polite irony that he sees the tactics of Rome as part of the fine art of governing. Since he understands that Arsinoé's hatred is grounded in her maternal love, he offers to make her son a king of some Asian country which yet remains for him to conquer. This last Tamburlaine-like glimpse of the future completes the picture of Nicomède, quietly poised between conquests, able to calm multitudes by his mere appearance, his infinite capability expressed in polite and compassionate gestures.

Corneille is well aware that his hero is unusual—that he is not conceived according to the rules of tragedy—for not only is he entirely virtuous (I, 59), but he arouses 'admiration' rather than pity (V, 507–8).[8] The success of the play on the stage seems to Corneille to show that admiration for the 'fermeté des grands cœurs' is as agreeable [and as legitimate] a response to tragedy as compassion. He believes that it may be a means of purgation unthought of by Aristotle,[9] in that admiration for great courage leads to hate of pusillanimity. Thus Corneille takes his place with Minturno and Sidney as one of the chief apologists for 'admiration'.

The last scene of *Nicomède* is one of the purest examples of Cornelian greatness of spirit. Nicomède's character has already inspired the emulation of his step-brother, who has rescued the hero from his guards. In this scene the hardened Machiavellian, Arsinoé, admits that she cannot defend her heart 'contre tant de vertu'; Prusias is won over, and even the Roman Flaminius applies to Nicomède the terms 'magnanime' and 'généreux'. The last speeches are a polyphonic celebration of greatheartedness.

A comparison of this play with Rotrou's *Cosroès* of two years before brings out the significance of Corneille's phrase, 'la *fermeté* des grands cœurs' (my emphasis) and of his insistence in the

'Examen' on admiration rather than pity. Siroès, the hero of
Rotrou's play, is in a situation remarkably similar to Nicomède's,
the victim of a step-mother who is trying to have him disinherited
in favour of her son. Siroès is magnanimous and loyal like Nicomède—he even admires his step-mother's 'grand cœur' when she
has treated him to an abusive tirade (V, 2, 1395) [10]—but his heart
is anything but firm. On the verge of victory he is so contrite when
reproached by Cosroès, his father, that he gives orders to release
his wicked brother and step-mother. As it happens, the orders
arrive only after they have both committed suicide, followed by
Cosroès. As one of the characters accurately says to Siroès in the
last scene:

> Hà Sire! malgré vous, le destin de la Perse
> Vous protège, et destruit tout ce qui vous traverse.
>
> (V, 7, 1719–20)

He admits that his is a 'cœur irrésolu' (V, 6, 1681), and of such
stuff the great Cornelian heroes are not made. Siroès is indeed
pitiable if not exasperating, but neither his virtuous vacillation nor
his good luck are calculated to arouse the admiration commanded
by Nicomède's 'Tout est calme, Seigneur'.

Corneille's lasting concern with largeness of spirit appears in a
section of the first 'Discours', where he is discussing Aristotle's
requirement (*Poetics*, xv) that the characters should be good.
Corneille thinks Aristotle cannot have meant 'virtuous', but may
have meant good in the sense of brilliant and heightened in a way
suitable to that particular person. Thus his own Cléopâtre, the
extraordinarily wicked mother in *Rodogune* (1644) shows such a
'grandeur d'âme' in all her crimes that one can admire her mind
even while detesting her actions (I, 31–2). By such a theory one
might justify the villain-heroes of the English stage, though
Cléopâtre is clearly the antagonist rather than the heroine of
Rodogune. When Corneille for once made a villain the protagonist
of a tragedy in *Attila* (1667), he portrayed him more as a politician
subject to insane rages than as a great hero, but the remarks on
Cléopâtre make it easier to grasp the distinction in Corneille's
work between greatness and goodness. He has, to be sure, given
most of his heroes a far larger than average portion of virtue, but
that is not what really matters. 'Grandeur d'âme' is the badge of

their heroism, and like so many of the Cornelian values, as Bénichou and others have reminded us, it is closely related to a characteristic universally praised in medieval romance. There *largesse* can mean anything from liberality in rewarding a faithful vassal to magnificence and magnanimity, and in these extensions of its meaning it stands, like 'grandeur d'âme', for the opposite of all meanness and pusillanimity—a natural concomitant of 'prouesse'.

The *Sophonisbe* of 1663 is a formidable example of this sort of 'grandeur', and of the patriotic fervour to which it is so often intimately allied in Corneille. At the beginning of the play, when the heroine receives a message from her husband Syphax, who is hoping that an honourable peace with Rome will allow him to return to her, she sends the somewhat cool reply that he should think of glory even more than of love (I, 1, 34).[11] This is exactly what she has done, as she goes on to explain to the inevitable lady in waiting: when she accepted Syphax as a husband despite her love for Massinisse, she 'immolated her tenderness for the good of her country'. She can boast that 'contre Carthage et contre ma grandeur' she has never listened to her heart (I, 2, 43, 53). It will be remembered that Marston's Sophonisba was also the 'wonder of women', whose constancy and love of her country triumph over desire; but even she appears more susceptible to the attraction of a lover than does Corneille's superwoman.

Though Corneille had presumably never heard of Marston, he knew well *La Sophonisbe* of Jean de Mairet, a play which differed from his even more. One of the earliest 'regular' (i.e. 'classical') tragedies, it was performed in 1634 and became very popular. Corneille testifies to his own admiration for it almost thirty years later in the prefatory address to the reader published with his version, but explains the necessity of treating the story differently. Though he speaks mainly about his way of dealing with the sources, the greatest difference between the plays lies in the conception of the heroine. Mairet's Sophonisbe is a woman desperately in love. Knowing that her infatuation for Massinisse is opposed to the interests of Carthage, she speaks of herself as

> Moy qui trahis mon nom, ma gloire, & ma patrie,
> Pour aymer Massinisse avec idolatrie.

(II, 1, 391-2)

She has the strength, however, to make Massinisse send her poison when his Roman superiors have ordered him to send her to Rome. She swallows the poison, and Massinisse kills himself over the corpse.

The Sophonisbe of Corneille puts her 'gloire' above her feelings for Massinisse or Syphax:

> Je sais ce que je suis et ce que je dois faire,
> Et prends pour seul objet ma gloire à satisfaire.

> (III, 5, 993–4)

Neither of the two men quite lives up to her expectations: Syphax thinks of love a little too much, and Massinisse disappoints her keenly by not taking poison himself when he sends some to her. Her dying speech, as reported in the last scene, contains the strange statement that although her slavery in Rome would have been an appropriate punishment for the cowardice of both men, she owed it to herself, as the daughter of Asdrubal, to choose death rather than ignominy (V, 7, 1787–90).

Mairet had sought pity for his heroine, believing, as he said in his address to the reader, that the proper end of tragedy was 'commisération' (p. 9). Though Corneille does not say so, the response he hoped for was surely admiration, as in *Nicomède*.[12] Here, too, he might have spoken of 'la fermeté des grands cœurs', for the heart of Sophonisbe is both great and firm but not tender. Corneille says that he gave her 'un peu d'amour', but that she masters it completely (VI, 464). Self-mastery and courage force even her rival Eryxe (a character of Corneille's invention) to admire her at the end, but Massinisse is not moved, as in Mairet, to kill himself. Instead, we are left with the ironic but instructive prospect that his inconstant affections will turn back to Eryxe. There is nothing to wonder at in Massinisse.

Another form of 'grandeur d'âme' is the magnanimity which enables the emperor Auguste in *Cinna, ou la clémence d'Auguste* (1640) to rise above his justified anger and to pardon those who were conspiring against him. Still another, in the midst of the improbable confusions of identity in *Héraclius* (1646), is the generosity which makes two men vie for the honour of being the prince whom the tyrant plans to execute. One more species of heroic largeness of spirit appears in *Agésilas* (1666), where a king surrenders the woman he loves to another man, and overcomes his long-seated resentment of a noble subject. He is pushed to this height by a counsellor who says:

> Qu'il serait magnanime
> De vaincre et la vengeance et l'amour a la fois!

$$(V, 5, 1951-2)$$

The last important action of the play is the reconciliation of king and subject, paving the way to three marriages which will confirm the harmony based on 'La magnanimité de ce cœur généreux' (V, 7, 2046).

All three of these tragedies end with a widening of horizons, an opening of perspectives characteristic of romance. Since the central concern of the heroic is with the great deeds, the noble aspirations and the exalted feelings of which man might be capable, the typical romance ending is the one which is most obviously appropriate, though as we have seen, many plays with a markedly heroic emphasis end with the recognition of tragic limitation—failure to attain the ideal. Corneille follows out the logic of the heroic hypothesis in a large percentage of his serious plays by giving them more or less happy endings (clearly that of *Horace* is much less so than that of *Agésilas*). He originally called *Le Cid* a tragicomedy, changing the designation later to tragedy, and some editors have felt that he should have called *Agésilas* a tragicomedy or heroic comedy rather than a tragedy. But the generic label is of relatively little significance in comparison to the fact of these numerous happy endings in which the principal characters have risen to the height of their potentialities.

Though Corneille's last play, *Suréna* (1674) ends tragically, it is a remarkable dramatization of a heroic ideal. The chief concern, as in most of the final plays of Corneille, is love, the theme made fashionable by the long seventeenth-century romances read by the 'précieux'. The hero is a warrior whose spectacular success in restoring Orode to the throne of Parthia has, by an irony of fate, made it more, rather than less, difficult for him to obtain what he wants most—the hand of the Princess Eurydice, who loves him but has been promised to the king's son, Pacorus. When the king, by way of paying off his indebtedness, offers Suréna his daughter, Mandane, the hero is unable to speak frankly of his love for Eurydice for fear of offending further the monarch whose dependence on him is already gallingly offensive. In depicting the relationships of all the characters caught in this situation Corneille shows the psychological delicacy usually associated with Racine, several of whose plays had been performed by this time; but Corneille uses this analysis to define the heroic character of his protagonist. Although almost nothing happens before the assassination which ends the play, and although Suréna is frustrated from first to last, Corneille manages to reveal his strength with increasing clarity. As his royal enemies appear more and more mean-spirited in their devious scheming against him, Suréna seems to grow in stature and self-assurance to the point where he asserts truly, but also in the form of a heroic brag:

> Mon crime véritable est d'avoir aujourd'hui
> Plus de nom que mon roi, plus de vertu que lui.
>
> (V, 2, 1511–12)

When Palmis, his sister, urges him to give in to the king's wishes if only in consideration of her and of Eurydice, he refuses, explaining, 'Un peu de dureté sied bien aux grandes âmes' (V, 3, 1678). This is our last view of him before he is felled by an arrow from an unknown hand. His 'hardness' is beautifully contrasted with the sensibility of Eurydice, who, when Palmis reproaches her for not weeping at the news of Suréna's death, says simply, 'Non, je ne pleure point, Madame, mais je meurs' (V, 5, 1732).

Obliged by circumstances to be even less active than Nicomède, Suréna is, by the end of the play, a commanding figure, hard, firm, courageous—one who has been forced to move from dedicating his energies to the service of the state to the assertion of his integrity in opposition to his king. In this final stage he is one of the most individual of Corneille's heroes.

Of the plays discussed here only four (*Sophonisbe*, *Agésilas*, *Attila* and *Suréna*) had not yet been performed in 1660, when Charles II came to the English throne, and three of these appeared in the next seven years. At the very beginning of the Restoration, then, the great majority of Corneille's plays had been presented, and in this year he brought out the edition with his 'Examens' and the theoretical 'Discours'. In these volumes, if not on the stage, the generation of playwrights who were about to revive the English theatre would have found the heroic exemplars we have been examining and also models of verse and structure unlike any that prevailed in the English theatre before 1642.[13] For the Restoration plays with which we shall be most concerned the well advertised 'three unities' are relatively unimportant, though they mattered to Corneille, were debated in England as well and occasionally were even respected there. Very important were Corneille's regular use of carefully balanced, rhyming alexandrines and his occasional use of lyrical stanzas, as in Rodrigue's soliloquy in Act I, Scene 6 of *Le Cid.* The formality of these verse forms, so different from English blank verse, removes the plays a step further from everyday reality, and is therefore, according to Dryden, the more appropriate for 'a serious play', which is 'indeed the representation of Nature, but 'tis Nature wrought up to a higher pitch'. He goes on to say that in tragedy, which deals with noble persons, 'heroic rhyme is nearest Nature, as being the noblest kind of modern verse'.[14] Furthermore, the balance of line against line or half line against half line points up the dialectic of choice between competing values:

> Noble et dure contrainte, aimable tyrannie . . .
> (I, 6, 312)
> Tu t'es, en m'offensant, montré digne de moi;
> Je me dois, par ta mort, montrer digne de toi.
> (III, 4, 931–2)

Finally, to limit ourselves to the most obvious qualities of his style, a courtly formality of manner, matching the formality of metre and syntax, characterizes the speeches of even those who are on intimate terms. Here is Laodice, agreeably surprised by the return of Nicomède:

> Après tant de hauts faits, il m'est bien doux, Seigneur,
> De voir encor mes yeux régner sur votre cœur; . . .
> (I, 1, 1–2)

And here is one of the princes in *Rodogune* addressing his mother, Cléopâtre:

> Jusques ici, Madame, aucun ne met en doute
> Les longs et grands travaux que notre amour vous coûte, . . .
> (II, 3, 583–4)

These gentlemen and ladies never forget their position, though they are capable of passionate utterance. In certain scenes, indeed, one has the impression that the control exercised by the formality of verse and etiquette allows the poet to indulge in more daring hyperbole than would be tolerable in a less formal situation. Which is perhaps to return to Dryden's point that this sort of verse is appropriate when nature is 'wrought up to a higher pitch'.

The precise effects of Corneille's style were, of course, inimitable in England, where there was, in any case, a vigorous native tradition to be continued. Nevertheless, no one would deny that Davenant, Orrery, Dryden and others were profoundly affected by the example of Corneille. In the following chapter there will be no effort to argue just how much of Restoration heroic drama was due to French and how much to native influence, for this topic has been canvassed in great detail by many scholars. Instead, Corneille, as well as the earlier English dramatists, will be used as points of reference in describing the nature of English heroic drama in the last forty years of the seventeenth century.

Notes

1 Louis Herland, 'L'imprévisible et l'inexplicable dans la conduite du héros. . . ', *Le Théâtre tragique*, ed. J. Jacquot (Paris, 1962), 239-49.
2 *Corneille et la dialectique du héros* (Paris, 1963), 59-83.
3 *Œuvres de P. Corneille*, ed. Ch. Marty-Laveaux, 12 vols. (Paris, 1862), II, 220. All references to Corneille are to this edition; act, scene, and line number are given for the plays, volume and page for the critical essays.
4 *Morales du grand siècle* (Paris, 1967; orig. 1948), 21.
5 *Corneille: His Heroes and their Worlds* (Philadelphia, 1963).
6 Doubrovsky insists on the 'secret weakness' of each hero (p. 475), and entitles the last three sections of his book 'Le Déclin du Héros', 'La mort du Héros', and 'L'Echec du Héros', but this seems to me to overstate the case.
7 *Œuvres de Descartes*, ed. Charles Adam & Paul Tannery, 11 vols. (Paris, 1964-), XI, 445-9. See Doubrovsky's excellent discussion (pp. 65-8), to which I am indebted. On this point Bénichou ((pp. 35-8) is, I believe, somewhat misleading. See Jean Boorsch, 'Remarques sur la Technique Dramatique de Corneille', *Studies by Members of the French Department of Yale University*, ed. Albert Feuillerat (New Haven, Conn., 1941), 101-62; and Arthur Kirsch, *Dryden's Heroic Drama* (Princeton, N.J., 1965), 52.
8 Thus the 'Examen'. In the second 'Discours' (I, 59) he is included with Polyeucte and Héraclius among those who arouse only pity. The contradiction is less serious than it appears, for in the 'Discours' Corneille is discussing characters who arouse pity rather than fear, whereas in the Examen he is proposing a response which is neither pity nor fear. Nicomède's plight is obviously more apt to inspire pity than fear, as Corneille understood the

Aristotelian requirements, but the point is that one may look up to Nicomède and not merely feel sorry for him.

9 On Corneille's 'poétique d'admiration' see Georges May, *Tragédie Cornélienne, tragédie Racinienne*, Illinois Studies in Language and Literature, XXXII
(Urbana, Ill., 1948), 23-5; also Boorsch, 'Remarques', esp. 140-1.

10 All references to *Cosroès* are to the edition by Jacques Scherer (Paris, 1950).

11 *La Sophonisbe*, ed. C. Dédéyan (Paris, 1945). All references are to this
edition.

12 Jacques Guicharnaud makes the point in his valuable comparison of the
plays, 'Beware of happiness: Mairet's *Sophonisbe*', *The Classical Line*, Yale
French Studies, XXXVIII (1967), 207.

13 Many English playwrights were also familiar with the plays of Corneille's
contemporaries in France, and could have found there some of the same
characteristics of style and heroic conception, but Corneille's reputation
in England as a writer of tragedy was such that it is reasonable to use his
plays as examples of the models to which the English turned.

14 'Essay of Dramatic Poesy', Ker, I, 100-1.

Four

The Restoration

1 Davenant and Orrery

In the dedication of the third edition of *The Siege of Rhodes* in 1663 Davenant contrasted the opposition of those who would 'deny *heroique plays* to the gentry' in England with the protection afforded by 'two wise *cardinals*' (Richelieu and Mazarin) to 'the great images represented in tragedy by *Monsieur Corneille*'.[1] By this time he and Sir Thomas Killigrew held patents granted by Charles II to the two theatrical companies, the Duke's Company and the King's Company, which were vying for favour with the elegance of their productions. With the drama once more established, Davenant was free to present the gentry with his '*ideas* of greatness and vertue'. During the theatrical hiatus of the Commonwealth he had expressed his concern with these ideas by composing an epic, *Gondibert*, and, just four years before the Restoration, by staging the first version of *The Siege of Rhodes*. In the Preface to *Gondibert*, written in Paris in 1650 and addressed to Thomas Hobbes, he reviewed heroic poetry from Homer through Virgil, Lucan and Statius to Tasso and Spenser, and then revealed the surprising fact that the form of his poem was modelled on English drama, because

> I cannot discerne by any help from reading or learned men, who have been to me the best and briefest Indexes of Books, that any Nation hath in representment of great actions, either by *Heroicks* or *Dramaticks*, digested Story into so pleasant and instructive a method as the English by their *Drama*; . . .
>
> (Spingarn, II, 17)

194

Though it is specifically the *form* of English drama to which he
acknowledges a debt, equating the books and cantos of his poem
with acts and scenes, he has noted the 'representment of great
actions' in these plays and has seen drama and heroic poetry as
similar enterprises. Like other authors of exemplary literature, he
hopes his poem will inspire the world's 'Chiefs', despairing of
'Common men', to whom he will not even try to appeal (p. 14).
His aristocratic view is set forth in words that precisely define virtue
as it is exemplified in innumerable heroic plays:

> I may now beleeve I have usefully taken from Courts and
> Camps the patterns of such as will be fit to be imitated
> by the most necessary men; and the most necessary men
> are those who become principall by prerogative of
> blood, which is seldom unassisted with education, or by
> greatnesse of minde, which in exact definition is Vertue.
>
> (p. 14)

'Greatnesse of minde' (compare Corneille's 'grandeur d'âme')
is the quality most obviously celebrated in *The Siege of Rhodes*,
performed in 1656 at Davenant's residence, Rutland House.
Familiar as are the circumstances of this dramatic venture, they
cannot be passed over, since, as Dryden was to write a few years
later:

> For Heroic Plays (in which only I have used it without
> the mixture of prose), the first light we had of them, on
> the English theatre, was from the late Sir William
> D'Avenant.[2]

To get around the law prohibiting plays Davenant, always an
energetic and ingenious entrepreneur, devised a series of 'entertainments', the first of which was a dramatized debate, on 23 May
1656, about the value of opera as a 'moral representation', in
which virtue would appear 'in the bright images of the heroes'.[3]
Diogenes, the cynic, argues that this will cost too much and that
virtue is not to be acquired by watching such shows, but opera is
vindicated by Aristophanes. These 'declamations' are interspersed
with songs and instrumental music, and the entertainment is
rounded off, with splendid irrelevance, by a debate about the
relative advantages of London and Paris.

This *First Day's Entertainment at Rutland House* was succeeded after a few months by *The Siege of Rhodes. Made a Representation by the Art of Prospective in Scenes, and the Story sung in Recitative Musick.* It was at once a heroic play and an opera, was similar in some ways to a masque, and offered the novelties of actresses and movable scenery. Though the action was minimal and the verse undistinguished, *The Siege of Rhodes* secured for itself a unique place in dramatic and theatrical history. Dryden again helps us to situate it in those traditions:

> The original of this music, and of the scenes which adorned his work, he had from the Italian operas; but he heightened his characters (as I may probably imagine) from the example of Corneille and some French poets.
>
> (Ker, I, 149)

That the music was more than a dodge to avoid prosecution can be inferred from Diogenes' disparagement of music ('a deceitful art') in the *First Day's Entertainment*:

> Does not the extasy of music transport us beyond the regions of reason? Changing the sober designs of discretion into the very wildness of dreams; urging softer minds to aim at the impossible successes of love; and enkindling in the active the destructive ambitions of war?[4]

It is clear from the arguments of this unfriendly critic that the standard view of music made it a natural auxiliary in appealing to admiration, and specifically in arousing sympathy for the aims of heroic lovers and warriors. The power of music to achieve these results had been recognized for many years and had led to extensive use of incidental music on the Elizabethan stage. Fully aware of this tradition, Dryden defended his use of drums and trumpets 'to raise the imagination of the audience' (Ker, I, 154). Thus opera was in a sense one logical extension of heroic drama.

Similarly, the scenery of *The Siege of Rhodes* was designed to astound, its splendour unfortunately diminished, as Davenant explains in an address 'To the Reader', by the narrowness of the stage at Rutland House. Nevertheless, since the use of such scenery in England had been restricted, with a few exceptions, to the court masque, the staging of Davenant's opera was a major novelty. He had entrusted the designing of it to Inigo Jones's pupil, John Webb. The detailed description of the sets in the editions of *The Siege of Rhodes*, comparable with those usually given in the editions of masques, show in some detail how great a contribution the scenery made to the total effect.[5]

'The story represented . . . is heroical,' Davenant writes in the address 'To the Reader', 'and notwithstanding the continual hurry and busie agitations of a hot siege, is (I hope) intelligibly convey'd to advance the characters of vertue in the shapes of valour and conjugal love.' (p. 184). Heroical it is, but not in the way one might be led to suppose. Alphonso, the conjugal lover of Ianthe, does not greatly affect the course of the Turkish siege, though he fights bravely and is wounded. Heroism in *The Siege of Rhodes* is shown less by valour than by magnificent gestures such as Ianthe's in sailing to the besieged city to be with her husband, or Solyman's in releasing her after her capture, and offering the couple the chance to sail home to Sicily. By refusing the offer Alphonso shows that he belongs with these generous spirits, though for a considerable portion of the opera he is afflicted by an unworthy jealousy of Ianthe. At the end she pardons him, and the lovers are reconciled. When Davenant put his opera on after the Restoration, he slightly enlarged the original drama and added Part II, in which Roxolana, the 'tempestuous wife' of Solyman, becomes jealous of Ianthe, who has come on behalf of Rhodes to beg for mercy. But even this fierce woman is conquered by Ianthe's beauty and virtue; Alphonso's jealousy, aroused again, is again allayed, and Ianthe is empowered by Solyman to arrange the terms of the surrender. Generosity is all.

As a spectacularly staged and musically accompanied dramatic poem in which relatively little happens in the course of glorifying a form of heroic behaviour, Davenant's opera shows its indebtedness to the masque, a form in which he had written for the court of Charles I. Though there is no dancing in *The Siege of Rhodes* (possibly because of the smallness of the stage) its five divisions are called 'entries', a term often used for the various sections of a masque. The development of opera from masque through Davenant to Dryden and Purcell is plain and well known, but the masque tradition exercised more influence on the heroic plays of Davenant's successors than is generally recognized. Reinforcing certain characteristics of romance, such as formality and remoteness, it also counteracted, in some measure, the thrust of that tradition towards action unlimited. The ceremonial character of many scenes in Restoration heroic drama is closely allied to the techniques of the masque.

One of the most striking innovations of *The Siege of Rhodes* was its rhyming lines. In order to accommodate the verse to the demands of recitative and aria, Davenant used lines of varying length, rhyming them sometimes alternately, sometimes in pairs. Certain passages consisted of the pentameter couplets which were already becoming fashionable, thanks to the work of Waller and Denham, and were soon to be adopted in heroic plays. In the Epistle Dedicatory of *The Rival Ladies* (1664) Dryden paid tribute to Waller and Denham, but said, 'if we owe the invention of it to Mr Waller, we are acknowledging for the noblest use of it to Sir William D'Avenant, who at once brought it upon the stage, and made it perfect, in the *Siege of Rhodes*' (Ker, I, 7). 'Perfect' is a lavish compliment, but Dryden's testimony shows what weight Davenant's example had.

There is no saying (and no need of saying) who was most responsible for the vogue of rhyme in the heroic play. Roger Boyle, the first Earl of Orrery, wrote one of the first (non-operatic) heroic plays in rhyming couplets, *Altemira* or *The General* (at various times both titles were used), in 1661.[6] According to Orrery's chaplain, 'King Charles was the first, who put my lord upon writing plays', and the earl himself says that he then wrote 'a Trage-Comedi, All in Ten Feet verse, & Ryme. I writt it, in that manner . . . because I found his maj[ty] Relish'd rather, the French Fassion of Playes, then the English . . .' (I, 23). For reasons which are not clear, the play was not performed in England until September 1664, though the king had presumably seen it in manuscript shortly after it was written, and it had been performed in Dublin in 1662. In the months preceding the English performance of *The General* two other rhymed heroic plays had been put on in London, *The Indian Queen* by Sir Robert Howard and his brother-in-law, John Dryden (in January) and another of Orrery's plays, *Henry V* (in August). When Dryden dedicated his tragicomedy, *The Rival Ladies*, to Orrery in the summer of that year he was apparently familiar with more than one of his lordship's plays, which he praised highly, observing that Orrery had done more for rhymed plays by writing them than Dryden could hope to do by advocating rhyme (Ker, I, 9). By the time he published his essay 'Of Heroic Plays' with *The Conquest of Granada* (1672) he was able to say 'Whether Heroic Verse ought to be admitted into serious plays, is not now to be disputed: 'tis already in possession of the stage; and I dare confidently affirm, that very few tragedies, in this age, shall be received without it' (Ker, I, 148).

The importance of Lord Orrery's plays to dramatic history is out of proportion to their intrinsic worth. In the first place, even though written avowedly in 'the French Fassion' of rhyming couplets, they are in themselves all the proof we need of the continuity of English dramatic tradition, about which Alfred Harbage writes persuasively in his *Cavalier Drama*.[7] *The General*, a tragi-comedy of wildly improbable love tangles, is so reminiscent at times of Fletcher, at times of Suckling, Cartwright and other Caroline dramatists, that Harbage's phrase, 'one of the last of the Cavaliers', seems thoroughly justified. Bits of the situation and several names recall *Philaster*; Clorimun, the general, is, like Fletcher's 'loyal subject', a noble and patriotic warrior forced into retirement by a wicked usurper; a highly refined, at times Platonic, love animates some of the principal characters, as in the 'précieux' romances and in those English plays written to gratify the taste of Queen Henrietta Maria. The code of behaviour exemplified by Clorimun, Lucidor, his rival and Altemira, the heroine, is the very highest, as we see when she persuades Clorimun to save Lucidor's life in Act III against the orders of the tyrant, or when Clorimun, unurged, protects Lucidor from the attack of the tyrant's nefarious son in the last act. The masterpiece of courtesy and rigour is Altemira's demand, when all the wicked characters have been disposed of, that Clorimun give his consent to her marriage with Lucidor.

From time to time there is some satiric wit at the expense of such nobility, as in a scene (II, 2) where some army officers discuss their mistresses, or even in this exchange between Clorimun and his difficult lady:

> *Alt.* Hee who his Mistrisse favour cannot gett
> Ought to be pleas'd that hee does meritt itt.
> *Clor.* To misse the purchace and yet pay the price
> Makes virtue more unfortunate than vice.
>
> (III, 2, 53–6)

In one instance the vulnerability of the dialogue to satire is attested by a comment of Sir Charles Sedley, recorded by Pepys. Clorimun, pressed by Altemira, has finally said:

> I'le save my Rivall and make her confesse
> 'Tis I deserve what hee does but possesse.
>
> (III, 2, 143–4)

'Why, what, pox,' says Sir Charles Sedley, 'would he have him have more, or what is there more to be had of a woman than the possessing her?'[8]

The full blast of anti-Platonic sentiment seldom gets into Orrery's heroic plays, which differ in this respect from those of many of his successors and also from such earlier plays as Suckling's *Aglaura*. Orrery is closer to a Gallic purity of genres, to which Davenant also adheres in *The Siege of Rhodes*.

To see what Orrery took from the Cavaliers and their *cavalleria anglicana* it is useful to compare *The General* with Sir Samuel Tuke's *The Adventures of Five Hours* (1663), an enormously successful play which also owed much to the earlier drama. Based, like several of the Beaumont and Fletcher plays, on Spanish romance, this tragicomedy depends heavily for its effect on an exciting plot, full of surprising turns. The main theme is love, as in *The General* and the hero, Don Antonio de Mendoza, is a paragon, designed, as Sir Samuel wrote in his dedication to Henry Howard, 'as a Copy of Your Stedy Virtue';[9] yet neither Don Antonio nor the almost-as-virtuous Don Octavio is ever tested so strenuously as Clorimun, nor asked to rise to a superhuman standard of excellence. Although *The Adventures of Five Hours* is in what Harbage calls 'the Cavalier mode', the extremes of elevation found in some Cavalier plays are missing, whereas these are exactly what Orrery took and gave a further boost. Furthermore, Tuke chose an intrigue in which there is no 'intérêt d'état'—for Corneille one of the distinguishing features of the serious play—while in *The General* the restoration of the legitimate monarch is a secondary theme closely related to the love theme. Though there are a few passages in rhyme, Tuke, unlike Orrery, did not push further along this line of Caroline experimentation. Perhaps equally indebted to the Cavaliers, Orrery and Tuke wrote very different sorts of drama.

Two other plays performed in 1664 indicate the range of

experimentation with heroic elements in the drama. Dryden's
The Rival Ladies (1664) is more like *The Adventures of Five Hours* in
the complications of its romantic plot and in its concentration
on love affairs on which affairs of state do not impinge; but
Dryden uses rhyme more extensively,[10] and the nobility which
moves one lover at the end of the play to surrender his lady to his
rival sounds a heroic note largely absent from Tuke's play. Though
The Rival Ladies is considerably less elevated than *The General*, it
shows occasionally the heroic sensibility which was to characterize so many of Dryden's later plays.[11]

Sir George Etherege's *The Comical Revenge, or Love in a Tub*, far
more of a comedy than either *The Adventures of Five Hours* or *The
Rival Ladies* (as the title itself makes clear enough), has nevertheless a heroic love plot, in which the noble characters readily fall
into rhymed couplets in their discussions of 'excess of Virtue' or
'some extream of Honour, or of Love' (II, 2).[12] The juxtaposition
of rakes and their low-comedy adventures with the tragicomedy
of romantic lovers produces a piquant combination later used by
Dryden in two of his best comedies, *Secret Love, or The Maiden
Queen* (1667) and *Marriage à la Mode* (1671). The fact that such
plays succeeded on the stage is one of several indications that
Restoration audiences could both respond with admiration to
heroic behaviour and laugh at it, as Sir Charles Sedley did at
The General.

Clorimun's magnanimous gesture of surrendering Altemira to
Lucidor has its analogues in earlier romantic fiction and drama,[13]
but also recalls forcibly certain moments in Cornelian drama in
which a generosity of spirit is demonstrated. Orrery's serious concern with 'grandeur d'âme' is, in fact, very similar to Corneille's.
Henry V (1664) provides several examples of it within the standard
romance framework found in so many plays by both playwrights.
Orrery chooses to show his king more as the suitor of Princess
Katherine than as the victor of Agincourt, though he is every inch
a king, and even explains that

> Those, who from Royal veins derive their blood,
> Find only in a Throne what's great and good; . . .
>
> (II, 1, 96–7)

To show the king as a lover, however, Orrery invents a rivalry
between him and Owen Tudor who, in history, did indeed marry

Katherine after Henry's death. In Orrery's play he is already in love with her when the king asks him to act as the royal emissary to secure her hand. As Tudor thinks over his dilemma, the popular Renaissance theme of love and friendship is given a characteristically heroic transformation:

> But stay! why should not I, even I alone,
> Raise Love and Honour to a height unknown?
> If, for his sake, my passion I forego,
> In that great Act I pay him all I owe:
> Who for his King against his Love does act
> Pays Debts much greater than he can contract.
>
> (II, 1, 144–9)

And when, in the fourth act, he reluctantly reveals his secret to the king, the big scene of the play is based on their vying to outdo each other in generosity and renunciation.[14]

Greatness of spirit is conspicuous again in *Mustapha* (1665) as well as Orrery's predilection for the well nigh perfect hero, another respect in which he resembles Corneille. Mustapha is the elder son of the Solyman who besieged Rhodes, but this play concentrates on the tensions within the royal family caused by Roxolana's ambition for her son Zanger. Solyman is now besieging Budapest, where his two sons are charmed by the Hungarian queen. For a moment love threatens the undying friendship the brothers have sworn to each other in defiance of a barbarous custom by which Mustapha would be expected, upon his accession, to have Zanger assassinated. But after an argument, in the manner of Chaucer's Palamon and Arcite, about whose love is greater, Mustapha makes the magnanimous gesture of speaking in favour of Zanger, who then says to the queen:

> That which he beg'd for me I beg for him.
> Tracing his steps how can I surer tread?
> I'le follow Vertue which I should have led.
>
> (III, 3, 420–3)

In the bloody dénouement Zanger makes the grander gesture of the two by committing suicide when Mustapha has been assassinated as a result of Roxolana's plotting.

Even Roxolana has a great spirit, or what the wicked pashas, the only true villains of the play, call 'Her heightn'd mind and nature' (II, 2, 99). It is they who push her motherly ambition towards crime, encouraging her to believe it is the only way to preserve her son. Her nature appears more truly in her first appearances in the play when she takes pity on the infant son of the Queen of Hungary and intercedes with Solyman to save his life. Later she also shows her compassion to the queen herself, a pathetic suppliant at Solyman's court. Thus, instead of making her greatly villainous, Orrery chooses to make her greatly capable of pity and sadly misled by ambitious underlings. In the last scene of the play, overwhelmed by remorse and punished by permanent exile, she becomes an object of pity along with both Zanger and Mustapha, but all three characters have been so consistently elevated that the pity felt for them is blended with admiration. In *Mustapha*, as in his first two plays, Orrery emphasizes magnanimity even more than valour—largesse more than 'prouesse'. Dramatically superior to the earlier plays, and performed with settings by John Webb, the designer of *The Siege of Rhodes*, *Mustapha* became a great success.

2 *Dryden's Plays to 1677*

The Indian Queen by Howard and Dryden,[15] performed in January 1664, before any of Orrery's plays had been seen in London, differs from them considerably while sharing their explicit concern with the essential heroic ingredient, greatness of spirit. In the first scene of the play the hero, Montezuma, is contrasted with his prisoner, Acacis, a man of unexceptionable virtue, who would be perfectly at home in an Orrery play. Montezuma, an invincible warrior, unaware of his true identity as the heir to the Mexican throne, has brought victory to the Inca of Peru, only to be denied the hand of the Inca's daughter, Orazia. In a rage he thinks of attacking the Inca, but he is restrained by Acacis, the son of the usurping Queen of Mexico, whose armies have been defeated:

> No, I must your Rage prevent,
> From doing what your Reason wou'd repent;
> Like the vast Seas, your Mind no limits knows,
> Like them lies open to each Wind that blows.
>
> (I, 1, 59–62)[16]

When Montezuma decides to fight for the Mexicans and offers to release Acacis to join him, Acacis is too honourable to accept, and despite his admiration for Montezuma, issues another reproof:

> When choller such unbridled power can have,
> Thy vertue seems but thy revenges slave.
>
> (I, 1, 106–7)

Where Acacis is firmly controlled by virtuous principles, Montezuma, without being wicked, is 'unbridled', 'open to each Wind' and, like the sea, ignorant of limits. In the next act Orazia, another model of virtue, sounds the same note when she says:

> O *Montezuma*, cou'd thy love engage
> Thy soul so little, or make banks so low
> About thy heart, that thy revenge and rage,
> Like suddain floods, so soon shou'd over-flow!
>
> (II, 1, 37–40)

and Montezuma, comparing himself to Acacis, says 'Vertue is calm in him, but rough in me.' (II, 1, 103).

Montezuma's excuse is that, being of unknown origin, he is free to serve whatever monarch he chooses. He is referred to as a 'God-like Stranger' (I, 2, 76), a term which immediately suggests the romantic sources of the plot.[17] Artaban, in one of these—La Calprenède's *Cléopâtre*, to which Dryden turned again in *The Conquest of Granada*—is also a noble and invincible stranger. Montezuma further resembles Artaban, and Achilles before him, in having been trained in the forest before taking up his career in a more civilized milieu (V, 1, 230–53). There, in the midst of uncorrupted nature, he first learned 'the noble thirst of fame'. Yet, however thoroughly sanctioned by a long tradition of epics, romances and epic-romances, Montezuma does not escape the moral criticism levelled at him by the more strictly virtuous Acacis and Orazia. Montezuma is, in other words, one of those Herculean heroes who appealed to Marlowe, Shakespeare and Chapman, and who were to appear in several of Dryden's plays. The excesses which cause Montezuma to be described in metaphors of overflow are what make him, though less virtuous, more wonderful than the noble Acacis.

Balancing Acacis and Orazia on one side of Montezuma is the passionate and ruthless Zempoalla on the other, the 'Indian

Queen' herself. Her only principle is the gratification of her ambition and her love, and a moment when one drive comes in conflict with the other leads to her defeat and suicide. Davenant cites 'the distempers of Love or Ambition' in the Preface to *Gondibert* as 'too often the raging Feavers of great minds',[18] and yet not totally repulsive, because they are the excesses of desirable characteristics. On the basis of this observation, Zempoalla, like the Roxolanas of Davenant and Orrery, is not totally unsympathetic. She is made to appear more attractive by comparison with her general and lover, Traxalla, in whom the 'distempers' of both love and ambition are combined with a thoroughly mean spirit. Zempoalla at least commits her considerable energy to planning on a large scale, and is capable of splendid scorn for the hypocrisy of legitimate monarchs:

> Nor will I at the name of cruel stay:
> Let dull successive Monarchs mildly sway:
> Their conquering Fathers did the Laws forsake,
> And broke the old e're they the new cou'd make.
>
> (III, 1, 112–15)

If she always spoke as well as this, she might rob Montezuma of some of his lustre. Unfortunately, the conflicts in her vast soul are sometimes rendered in such flat and obvious asides and self-debates that awareness of mechanics interferes with one's response to heroic greatness (e.g. III, 1, 31–43; IV, 1, 89–97). At the last, with her son dead, her ambition thwarted, and her love for Montezuma proved hopeless, Zempoalla becomes a pathetic figure. Though the transition is clumsily, and hence unconvincingly, handled, her last speech before committing suicide combines pathos with dignity and courage. Her 'Yes, I will cease to grieve, and cease to be' (V, 1, 286, in response to Montezuma's generous concern) does not rise to the height of Eurydice's 'Non, je ne pleure point, Madame, mais je meurs' in *Suréna*, ten years later, but it is not ineffective. Her last lines are more obviously heroic:

> The greatest proof of courage we can give,
> Is then to dye when we have power to live.
>
> (V, 1, 295–6)

In this last scene the thoroughly wicked Traxalla is killed by Montezuma, and the thoroughly good Acacis kills himself in despair of winning anything but pity from Orazia. The choice of Montezuma by this mild heroine is a triumph for 'rough' virtue, which she prefers to 'calm'. A hint of the excitement of Dryden's later plays appears in the handling of this alignment of characters. Like Davenant and Orrery, Dryden and Howard adopt a dialectical structure such as they could have found in Caroline drama and also (in an infinitely more subtle and finished form) in Corneille, but *The Indian Queen* shows some of the vigour which distinguishes Dryden from the other English playwrights in the prosecution of his dialectic.

The considerable success enjoyed by *The Indian Queen* was due at least in part to its being splendidly mounted at the Theatre Royal in Bridges Street, which had opened the previous May, permitting the King's Company to compete in spectacular effects with the Duke's in Lincoln's Inn Fields. On 5 February John Evelyn recorded in his diary:

> I saw acted the *Indian Queene* a Tragedie well written, but so beautified with rich Scenes as the like had never ben seene here as happly (except rarely any where else) on a mercenarie Theater.[19]

Zempoalla's costume was enhanced by 'wreaths' of feathers from Surinam, contributed by Aphra Behn[20] (for who was to say that the fashions of Surinam differed from those of pre-conquest Mexico?), and is probably represented in Vincent's later mezzotint, entitled 'The Indian Queen'. It was natural to exploit this success and at the same time save money by writing another play for which some of the same sets and costumes could be used, and this Dryden did with *The Indian Emperor* in April 1665, when it competed with Orrery's *Mustapha*, also elaborately mounted.[21] *The Indian Emperor* became one of the most successful Restoration plays.

By the time Dryden dedicated the first edition to the Duchess of Monmouth in October 1667, he was able to comment upon the favour that heroic plays were finding in the theatres, wholly attributable, he believed, to the approbation of the court,

> the most eminent persons for Wit and Honour in the Royal Circle having so far own'd them, that they have judg'd no way so fit as Verse to entertain a Noble Audience, or to express a noble passion.

(Calif. Dryden, IX, 23)

Since this 'Noble Audience' had been particularly 'indulgent to this Poem', Dryden begged the duchess to favour it, as she did to the extent of acting in it the next year in an amateur performance at court, where she was said to be one of only three actors who performed well.[22]

The relationship between heroic drama and its noble audience has a great importance in the history of the genre. It is well known that the audience which came to the new and more expensive theatres built after the Restoration was in general more of a coterie audience than that which filled the theatres in the earlier part of the century. The king himself often came to these theatres, besides seeing plays performed at court. But it is easy to exaggerate the aristocratic nature of the audience. Servants were seated in the cheapest seats, and citizens attended in increasing numbers as the century drew towards its close. So far as heroic drama is concerned, the essential point may be that it appealed to the aristocratic leanings of an audience, many of whom were not nobly born.[23] Heroic drama encouraged its audience to feel capable of refined perceptions and high aspirations, as had the poetry of the troubadours, chivalric romances and, *a fortiori*, the vast romances which succeeded *L'Astrée* in the 'précieux' campaign to improve manners and language. That a noble audience for heroic drama existed we know; that its boundaries did not exactly coincide with the peerage is a reasonable supposition.

Such dedications as this one to the Duchess of Monmouth may be seen, as I have suggested elsewhere,[24] as part of a grand strategy to appeal to what was noble in the audience (including patrons, spectators and readers) if not, in a sense, to create an audience of heroes. Looked at from this point of view, the heroic compliments of these dedications serve not only a practical purpose (for Dryden's financial need was real) but also a rhetorical one, so closely related to the plays for which they seek favour that the dedication frequently reveals something of the nature of the play. In this instance the duchess is praised for her beauty, virtue, honour and quasi-divine goodness:

> 'Tis so much your inclination to do good that you stay
> not to be ask'd; which is an approach so nigh the Deity,
> that Humane Nature is not capable of a nearer.
>
> (Calif. Dryden, IX, 24)

That is, she becomes one with the magnanimous characters of
Corneille, Orrery, Davenant or Dryden, and the ideal patroness
of a great character such as Montezuma (who is imagined as
kneeling before her) or a great enterprise such as the writing of
this play. For the play and its author share some of the characteristics of its great-minded but imperfect hero:

> 'Tis an irregular piece if compar'd with many of Cor-
> neilles, and, if I may make a judgement of it, written
> with more Flame then Art; in which it represents the
> mind and intentions of the Author, who is with much
> more Zeal and Integrity, then Design and Artifice,
> MADAM, *Your Graces most Obedient And most Obliged
> Servant*, JOHN DRYDEN.
>
> (*Ibid.*, IX, 25–6)

To the readers of *The Indian Emperor* the author explains how
the play is connected to *The Indian Queen*, 'part of which Poem
was writ by me'.[25] We are to suppose that Montezuma and
Orazia have had two sons, Odmar and Guyomar, and a daughter,
Cydaria; and that Zempoalla and Traxalla left behind them two
daughters, Almeria and Alibech, and a son, Orbellan. It is now
twenty years since Montezuma's coronation; Orazia is dead, and
Cortez is about to conquer Mexico. The symmetrical children
and the opposed conquerors suggest the patterning of the play.
The schematization which contrasts Montezuma with Acacis on
the one hand and Zempoalla on the other in *The Indian Queen*,
while at the same time contrasting Zempoalla with Traxalla, is
carried to extraordinary lengths in the later play. The love
relationships provide the opportunity to make many of the
obligatory comparisons: Guyomar and Odmar love Alibech,
Montezuma loves Almeria, Cortez loves Cydaria in competition
with Orbellan. Lady can be compared with lady and lover with
lover in the purity of their love and also in their ability to weigh
love against patriotic duty. The prosecution of the war inevitably
leads to further comparisons of the courage and honour of the
combatants and their ladies. And finally another comparison
complicates still further what is already an elaborate pattern: the
religion of the Spanish conquerors is set over against the natural,
primitive religion of the Mexicans. This mighty maze is not
without a plan, but the plan does not lead to what one can

certainly call the centre. One set of contrasts partly cancels out another, while certain developments of the situation appear to contradict basic assumptions about the characters.

Given the portrayal of Montezuma in *The Indian Queen*, his actions in this play are most surprising, and hence illustrate some of the difficulties of interpreting *The Indian Emperor*. We see first the effect of Montezuma's infatuation for Almeria, the daughter of his enemy: 'My Lyon-heart is with Loves toyls beset' (I, 2, 182). He is a Hercules tamed by Omphale. A moment later he is almost slaughtered by rebellious Indians, when Cortez arrives to save his life but demand that Montezuma pledge fealty to Charles V and renounce his gods. Montezuma refuses firmly but politely, nicely balancing his personal debt to Cortez against his integrity and his duty to his people, and managing to make some trenchant comments on Spanish royalty, guaranteed to appeal to an English audience. Cortez, though very noble at his first appearance, leaves most of the discussion of terms to his under-lings when he spies Cydaria, and gives his attention to Montezuma only long enough to agree that they must fight.

During the next three acts there are many opportunities to compare the two men as lovers. Montezuma succumbs increasingly to his passion for Almeria, who is a somewhat feebler version of her mother, Zempoalla. Under her influence Montezuma condemns the captured Cortez to death over the objections of his son Guyomar (III, 4), who at this point resembles the Montezuma that was but is no longer. By the end of the scene the old emperor, though prevented from killing Cortez by Guyomar, and from killing Guyomar by Odmar, promises Almeria that in two days' time he will complete the conquest 'Of these few Sparks of Vertue which remain' (l. 130). What a falling off is here! This is not the irregular greatness of a Herculean hero, but something approaching the monumental villainy of Maximin, the tyrant of Dryden's next heroic play. In contrast to him Cortez behaves with exemplary nobility except at the moment (II, 2) when he almost gives up the fight in order to please Cydaria. In the scene of his capture he offers himself to Montezuma to save Guyomar and Odmar; in prison he resists both the threats and the lures of Almeria, who has conceived an overwhelming passion for him. As Arthur Kirsch says, 'Every choice which Montezuma makes between his love and his obligations to himself and to his country is resolved at a sacrifice of personal integrity; every decision which Cortez makes demonstrates his worthiness'.[26] As parallels to Montezuma's degeneration and Cortez's nobility we see Odmar agree to murder Cortez in his tent and later to compound with the Spaniards, while Guyomar thwarts the plan to murder Cortez and refuses to make any deal with the enemy.

The fifth act is full of surprising turns. Here Montezuma, finally in the power of the Spaniards, is put on the rack by a Christian priest without the knowledge of Cortez. Totally disregarding his pain, the Indian emperor defends his religion with wit, while the Christian priest displays bigotry and ferocity. There is not the slightest doubt where Dryden's sympathies lie, as he makes clear enough in referring to his sources in 'The Connexion':

> The difference of their Religion from ours, I have taken from the Story it self; and that which you find of it in the first and fifth Acts, touching the sufferings and constancy of *Montezuma* in his Opinions, I have only illustrated, not alter'd from those who have written of it.
>
> (Calif. Dryden, IX, 28)[27]

In the nick of time the suffering and constant hero is once more rescued by Cortez, and their reunion is a tearful one, marked by mutual forgiveness. Further developments of the situation lead at last to the point at which Almeria has Montezuma and Cydaria locked in a tower besieged by Cortez. Rather than be captured, Montezuma commits suicide, and Almeria follows suit after wounding her rival Cydaria. Cortez at the end has his love and Mexico, but Guyomar, the one absolutely unsullied character, leaves with Alibech for a snowy retreat where they can enjoy love and freedom in peace, untroubled by the Spaniards.

Neither Montezuma nor Cortez is always the great hero in this play. If Cortez seems to be so for more of the time, he nevertheless suffers whenever the comparison is made in terms of primitive versus European. As a lover, though dangerously swayed by passion, he never sinks to the depths reached by Montezuma. As a warrior he never rises to Montezuma's height in courage and endurance. Among the women Cydaria is constantly virtuous and Almeria constantly wicked, but Alibech, like Montezuma and Cortez, has her ups and downs. At her worst she tempts her rival lovers to betray Montezuma. These manipulations of character, rather than serving the purposes of the play's dialectic, help to confuse it. As in a Fletcherian tragicomedy, the ideals remain the same but the characters supporting them change in accordance with the demands of the situation.

The last act is notable not only for the many turns taken by the plot but for the prominence given to pathos. The tears of Montezuma and Cortez have already been mentioned, but the pathetic behaviour of Cydaria also merits attention. Pepys considered hers 'a great and serious part', and twice complained of how badly Nell Gwynn interpreted it[28] (one would hardly expect it to have been the ideal vehicle for Nell's talent). After being a demanding mistress throughout the play, if not quite so difficult as Orrery's Altemira, Cydaria in the last act falls into the power of a more formidable woman. The fury of Almeria scorned brings out by contrast the softness and weakness of her rival, left by her father's suicide defenceless and alone. With Cortez at the gate of the tower where Almeria has locked her, and Almeria threatening to kill her if he enters. Cydaria pleads for her life and confesses her unheroic fear of death:

> I yet am Tender, Young, and full of Fear,
> And dare not Dye, but fain would tarry here.
>
> (V, 2, 277–8)

The two examples of pathos in Act V differ from each other in one important respect. The tears shed by Cortez and Montezuma (which may also draw tears from the audience) are evidence of their capacity for forgiveness and compassion—of a largeness of mind which goes beyond all personal ambition. Davenant's Roxolana displays these characteristics when she takes pity on Ianthe, and Orrery's Roxolana when she saves the infant king of Hungary. In all these characters pity is a badge of heroism. But in the case of Cydaria an appeal is made (all too obviously, by twentieth-century standards) to the pity of the audience for one whose goodness is no match for the power of her enemy. A few years later, in his Preface to *Troilus and Cressida* (1679), Dryden wrote:

> But when we see that the most virtuous, as well as the greatest, are not exempt from such misfortunes, that consideration moves pity in us, and insensibly works us to be

helpful to, and tender over, the distressed; which is the noblest and most god-like of moral virtues.

(Ker, I, 210)

In such cases it is the audience, not one of the characters, who display 'the noblest and most god-like of virtues', but a further distinction must be made. This sentiment may be elicited, as Dryden's formula suggests, by strong characters, such as Nicomède, Suréna or Mustapha, as well as by a timid character such as Cydaria. The characters in the first category are much more heroic, and command more admiration mixed with the pity they inspire. Those in the second category, though frequently present in heroic drama, are not heroic in the fullest sense, and clearly adumbrate the protagonists of sentimental drama.

Since the 'first heroic play' of this period was also an opera, and since several Restoration dramatists, including Dryden, wrote opera libretti, it should be remarked that both *The Indian Queen* and *The Indian Emperor* have features suggestive of opera, and that the former play was made into an opera in the last years of the century. *The Indian Queen* has an unusual sung prologue as the curtain rises to reveal a Mexican landscape, and one scene (III, 2) is devoted to Zempoalla's visit to a prophet, who conjures up the God of Dreams and some Aerial-Spirits, who sing a song. The supernatural material of this scene is what Dryden meant by 'the enthusiastic parts of poetry', whose place in heroic drama he defended in the essay 'Of Heroic Plays' (Ker, I, 152–3). Almost certainly this kind of scene would have been accompanied by instrumental music even in a play, and obviously lent itself to operatic treatment, as the musical version shows. *The Indian Emperor* has a comparable scene in '*A pleasant Grotto*', where the Spaniards are entertained by songs and dances (IV, 3), as well as a love scene in quatrains (I, 2, 349–72) which the editors of the California Dryden very properly call a 'lyrical interlude' (IX, 318), and a 'poetic' soliloquy by Cortez (III, 2, 1–10), which could easily be imagined as a song. Many Restoration plays represent, as these do, a kind of borderland between what we think of as 'straight plays' and operas. The distinction was less clear then, and the fact that this was so reveals something about both Restoration opera and the heroic play.

Dryden's next heroic play, *Tyrannic Love* (1669), was a not entirely successful experiment with a bolder contrast between good and evil characters than any he had yet portrayed—the contrast between St Catherine of Alexandria and Maximin, the Roman tyrant who ordered her martyrdom. It is possible that the subject was suggested to Dryden by the successful revival of Massinger and Dekker's *The Virgin Martyr*,[29] which Pepys attended three times in 1667–8, largely to hear 'the wind musique when the angel comes down', which pleased him 'beyond anything in the whole world'.[30] Whether or not this was the original impetus, Dryden's avowed intention in the Preface to the first edition was to write an exemplary play, which might conduce to holiness and not just to good manners. To distinguish his heroine clearly from her pagan captors Dryden relies on two devices. One is the use of supernatural spirits, including the saint's guardian angel, Amariel, to convey the transcendent nature of her virtue. Spectacle plays an important part in these scenes, especially in Act V, where Amariel '*descends swiftly with a flaming sword, and strikes at the Wheel* [prepared for the torture of St Catherine], *which breaks in pieces; then he ascends again*' (V, 1; III, 454).[31]

With the miraculous side of Christianity handled in this fashion, Dryden uses argumentation to show the rational superiority of his heroine's religion. If one comes to these scenes directly from the arguments about religion in *The Indian Emperor*, it is somewhat surprising to see the scales loaded in just the opposite way. Mere Roman ethics are shown here (by arguments often borrowed from the Anglican Archbishop Tillotson, as Bruce King has pointed out)[32] to be inferior to Christian faith. St Catherine also reveals her courage in scenes of argument, explaining why she cannot flee from her martyrdom (IV, 2), or reproaching her mother for her fear of death (V, 1). She is altogether a different sort of victim from Cydaria—one whose heroism is beyond doubt.

Yet, to Dryden's dismay, it was not St Catherine but her oppressor who always commanded attention, even to the point of seeming to be the protagonist. Attacked for the impiety of his hero, he replied in the Preface:

> The part of *Maximin*, against which these holy critics so much declaim, was designed by me to set off the character of *S. Catherine*.

(p. 377)

If this was the intention, as there is no reason to doubt, Dryden's conception of his foil was a serious miscalculation. When a martyr like Polyeucte or a perfect warrior like Nicomède or Suréna is opposed by meaner spirits, there is no danger that his glory will be eclipsed. But Maximin, far from being mean-spirited, is the great Elizabethan villain-hero *redivivus*. He plumes up his will by planning crime upon crime with the gusto of a Selimus or an Eleazar; when he falls in love with the saint, he displays the prodigious lust of a Fletcherian tyrant such as Arbaces; when his plans are finally thwarted, he declares war against the gods like Hercules Furens or Tamburlaine:

> What had the Gods to do with me or mine?
> Did I molest your heaven?
> Why should you then make Maximin your foe
> Who paid you tribute, which he need not do?
>
> * * *
>
> But by the Gods (by Maximin, I meant),
> Henceforth I, and my world,
> Hostility with you, and yours, declare.
> Look to it, Gods; for you the aggressors are.
> Keep you your rain and sun-shine in your skies,
> And I'll keep back my flame and sacrifice.
> Your trade of heaven shall soon be at a stand,
> And all your goods lie dead upon your hand.
>
> (V, 1; III, 463–4)

In sheer vitality this goes far beyond the effective but quiet reasoning of St Catherine, and makes Maximin easily the most exciting figure in the play.

None of Dryden's earlier heroes—nor those of Davenant or Orrery—speak with such verve, though rant was to become, as it had been before, one of the hall-marks of the heroic play. It is as if Dryden had re-invented the extravagance of those proto-heroes, the ranting tyrants, Herod and Cambises. With a difference, however. The final image in Maximin's defiance—the shopkeeper gods, stuck with unsaleable goods on their hands—betrays Dryden's humourous awareness of the extravagance, as does a Horatian comment in the Prologue:

Poets, like lovers, should be bold and dare,
They spoil their business with an over-care;
And he, who servilely creeps after sense,
Is safe, but ne'er will reach an excellence.
Hence 'tis, our poet, in his conjuring,
Allowed his fancy the full scope and swing.
But when a tyrant for his theme he had,
He loosed the reins, and bid his muse run mad:
And though he stumbles in a full career,
Yet rashness is a better fault than fear.

(p. 383)

Such hints of satirical laughter became characteristic features of Dryden's heroic plays, and were noted from the first. Colley Cibber, for instance, believed that some of the extravagances of Morat in *Aureng-Zebe* were ludicrous: 'and doubtless the Poet intended those to make his Spectators laugh, while they admir'd them; . . .'[33] The observation could be applied with justice to Maximin's lines; for while he never becomes a figure of fun, he is occasionally distanced for a moment, as he is here, by a humorous touch which exposes all that he has been saying to laughter. Earl Miner, noting the line in *MacFlecknoe*, 'And little Maximins the gods defy', comments, 'It is the joke of an exceedingly capacious mind upon itself'.[34] Maximin, then, may be smiled at but not discounted. His very extravagance makes him the forerunner of Dryden's most perfectly achieved heroes.

The Epilogue to *Tyrannic Love* offers another indication that the Restoration audience (surely not unique in this respect) could laugh at what it had taken seriously a moment before. Nell Gwyn, who played the tragic part of Maximin's daughter, a suicide in the last scene, leapt up as she was being borne off the stage to say:

Hold; are you mad? You damn'd confounded dog!
I am to rise, and speak the epilogue.
I come, kind gentlemen, strange news to tell ye;
I am the ghost of poor departed Nelly.

*   *   *

To tell you true, I walk, because I die
Out of my calling, in a tragedy.

(pp. 467–8)

215

The vogue of comic epilogues to serious plays was as great as that of the jig following Elizabethan tragedies, and no more difficult to explain. It is worth mentioning only to dissipate what has sometimes been considered the mystery that the audience for heroic drama was also the audience for licentious comedy. In 1671 this same audience was applauding a hilarious burlesque of heroic drama, *The Rehearsal*, by the Duke of Buckingham and others, in which Dryden was represented as the author, Mr Bayes, but applause for Dryden's heroic plays did not cease.

Although *Tyrannic Love* is not a wholly successful play, partly because of the imbalance between protagonist and antagonist, it does not suffer, as does *The Indian Emperor*, from a bewildering elaboration of design. The subsidiary action—based on a typically romantic situation in which Placidius loves Valeria, who loves Porphyrius, who loves Berenice, the wife of Maximin—is tied firmly to the main plot not only by Maximin's involvement in both but also by presenting four others characters who suffer from the tyranny of love and yet show, as Placidius says, that 'Love various minds does variously inspire' (II, 1; III, 407). Great variety within the confines of thematic unity is characteristic of what L. A. Beaurline has well called the 'impassioned design' of Dryden's serious plays.[35] In the best of them the dramatization of heroic passions carries with it an intellectual excitement which is also a passion.

The Conquest of Granada is one of the best.[36] The first part seems to have been acted at the very end of 1670, and the second early in January 1671, achieving an immediate success. That spectacle was again a contributory factor we can see from John Evelyn's comment in his diary for 9 February: 'next day was acted there the famous Play, cald the Siege of Granada [a happy error] two days acted successively: there were indeede very glorious scenes & perspectives, the work of Mr. Streeter.' In a letter of somewhat earlier date his wife made a longer comment which touches on so many central issues that it deserves quotation in full:

> Since my last to you I have seen 'The Siege of Grenada',
> a play so full of ideas that the most refined romance I
> ever read is not to compare with it; love is made so pure,
> and valour so nice, that one would image it designed for
> an Utopia rather than our stage. I do not quarrel with

the poet, but admire one born in the decline of morality should be able to feign such exact virtue; and as poetic fiction has been instructive in former ages, I wish this the same event in ours. As to the strict law of comedy I dare not pretend to judge: some think the division of the story is not so well if it could all have been comprehended in the day's actions.[37]

Unlike most earlier two-part plays, this one was initially planned in ten acts (the 'conquest' does not occur until the end of Part II), and both the range and the complexity of the design stem from romance, with which Mrs Evelyn compared it. It was precisely the proliferation of major characters and episodes which distinguished romantic epic from classical epic in the eyes of the Italians who attacked Ariosto in the sixteenth-century quarrel over the legitimacy of romance as a literary form,[38] though even Tasso's *Gerusalemme Liberata*, favoured by the opponents of Ariosto, had a complexity of plot not to be found in Homer and Virgil. The design of *The Conquest of Granada*, then, belongs squarely in a tradition of heroic poem which has been importantly modified by romance.

Further evidence of the impact of romance on this play (and on seventeenth-century theories of heroic poetry) appears in Dryden's famous 'reflexion' in the essay 'Of Heroic Plays', prefixed to *The Conquest of Granada*, 'that an heroic play ought to be an imitation, in little, of an heroic poem; and consequently, that Love and Valour ought to be the subject of it' (Ker, I, 150). If any doubt remained about the importance of the romance tradition in *The Conquest of Granada*, it would be dispelled by the tournament at the end of Part II, in which the hero vindicates the heroine's honour, playing Lancelot to her Guenever.

The management of the plot represents a major advance over *The Indian Emperor*. Again intersecting love stories complicate and are complicated by the political situation. The Moors in Granada, besieged by the forces of Ferdinand and Isabella, are themselves divided by a feud between the Zegrys and the Abencerrages. The Abencerrago chief competes with the king's brother for the favours of an ambitious Zegry lady; the Zegry chief has conceived a passion for the queen; an ideal love is shared by a young Zegry and an Abencerrago; and into this tangled web a noble stranger enters, the hero of the play, to give his victorious arm first to one side, then to the other, and to give his heart to the queen. Yet, unlike the symmetrical complications of *The Indian Emperor*, these are perfectly controlled so as to work to one end, the showing forth of true heroic greatness.

Dryden's often-quoted account of the ancestry of Almanzor was mentioned in the opening pages of this book. His hero was modelled, it seems, on Achilles, Tasso's Rinaldo and the Artaban of La Calprenède (who had also inspired the Montezuma of *The Indian Queen*). Dryden makes much of the French exaggeration of the 'point of honour' and of his preference for imperfect heroes, praising Homer and Tasso especially because: 'they contented themselves to show you, what men of great spirits would certainly do when they were provoked, not what they were obliged to do by the strict rules of moral virtue' (Ker, I, 157). A description early in the play of Almanzor's recent exploits reveals him as just such a character:

> Then to the vanquish'd part his fate he led;
> The vanquish'd triumph'd, and the victor fled.
> Vast is his courage, boundless is his mind,
> Rough as a storm, and humorous as wind:
> Honor's the only idol of his eyes;
> The charms of beauty like a pest he flies;
> And, rais'd by valor from a birth unknown,
> Acknowledges no pow'r above his own.
>
> (I, 251–8)[39]

Not only is he 'boundless', 'rough' and 'humorous' like his Indian predecessor; he is also a reincarnation of man in the lost age of innocence. Again the lines are familiar:

> Obey'd as sovereign by thy subjects be,
> But know that I alone am king of me.
> I am as free as nature first made man,
> Ere the base laws of servitude began,
> When wild in woods the noble savage ran.
>
> (I, 205–9)

To bring this wild creature within the bounds of civilized society and political order is the task of love, whose 'charms . . . he flies' until he meets Almahide, the queen. He first describes her effect upon him with some of Dryden's half-humorous extravagances:

> I'm pleas'd and pain'd, since first her eyes I saw,
> As I were stung with some tarantula.

> *   *   *

> I'm bound; but I will rouse my rage again;
> And, tho' no hope of liberty remain,
> I'll fright my keeper when I shake my chain.
>
> (III, 328–9, 342–4)

But soon, far from being poisoned, he is being educated by Almahide as is the knight of romance by his lady. He learns to curb his desire for her, to save the king at her request, and to fight for her 'Not now for love, but for my honor's sake' (Part II, V, 1, 10).

He never matches the score of the noble Ozmyn, who responds to each agonizing turn of his affair with Benzayda, the daughter of his father's enemy, with a combination of the greatest courage and the most refined sensibility. Only Benzayda and Almahide achieve the same uniformly high marks. Dryden refers to them as 'patterns of exact virtues' (Ker, I, 157), with whom he compares his great-spirited hero. Yet Almanzor has an energy which none of them has. It appears in his many ranting speeches, in which he is a successor to Maximin, and it appears in the way he affects Almahide. Though never for a moment letting down her virtuous guard as the betrothed, and then the queen, of the Moorish King Boabdelin, she is moved by Almanzor towards a more dynamic conception of virtue and love than the mere obedience for which she was trained. Now, 'aiming higher', she has lost her 'rest' (V, 3, 206). In her very efforts to persuade Almanzor to forget her, she pays tribute to the force of love in a figure of speech which must have gripped the imaginations of the survivors of the great fire of London:

> But 'tis, at worst, but so consum'd by fire,
> As cities are, that by their falls rise high'r.
> Build love a nobler temple in my place;
> You'll find the fire has but inlarg'd your space.
>
> (V, 3, 271–4)

Thus Almahide and Almanzor exert upon each other a reciprocal effect. If their relationship is a considerable distance away from D. H. Lawrence's twin stars, it is comparable in that neither male nor female completely dominates the other.

With this love affair we are to compare not only the idealized static love of Ozmyn and Benzayda, but the brutal lust of Zulema for Almahide, culminating in an attempted rape, and the triangular love of Abdalla, the king's brother, and Abdelmelech, the Abencerrago chief, for Lyndaraxa. In these characters a debased form of love is characterized not only as the opposite of reason but also as the concomitant, and sometimes the cause, of political disorder. Both Zulema and Lyndaraxa are power-mad, and in her case 'love', so called, is nothing more than the means to a throne. Like many other characters in heroic drama, she analyses herself explicitly, almost as an observer might:

> As in some weatherglass my love I hold;
> Which falls or rises with the heat or cold.
> I will be constant yet, if fortune can;
> I love the King;—let her but name the man.
>
> (IV, 2, 5–8)

Whoever can rule will be her lover. She and Zulema are both Tamburlaines (she makes the comparison herself in the last act of Part II) stripped of any dreams of order which might make their fixation on earthly crowns seem like a noble aspiration.

More puzzling at first is the comparison of Lyndaraxa to Almanzor, for she, too, is boundlessly energetic and equally unwilling to acknowledge any power above her own. Dryden delays a confrontation between them until the third act of Part II, when she tries to lure him away from Almahide. In this scene the constancy of Almanzor's hopeless love and the solidity of his faith in himself expose the emptiness which underlies Lyndaraxa's endless vacillation and explains the insecurity which she covers over with brazen assurance.

Lyndaraxa is, of course, another tempestuous soul like Zempoalla, but she is also a perverse form of the demanding mistress of romance, whose lover must win innumerable fights to gain her hand. Going beyond these prototypes, she is also the embodiment of an idea. Capricious as Fortune, and wanting nothing more than the power Fortune might give her, she seeks to identify herself with the goddess, and becomes, instead, her abject slave. When the collapse of her ambition is imminent and she decides to involve as many of her enemies as possible in her fall, she portrays herself in a simile which is ludicrous if taken as physical description, but singularly appropriate as expressing the disproportion between her hopes and the reality:

> But, like some falling tow'r
> Whose seeming firmness does the sight beguile,
> So hold I up my nodding head awhile,
> Till they come under; and reserve my fall,
> That with my ruins I may reach 'em all.
>
> (IV, 2, 136–40)

The love affairs of this *femme fatale* become a means of depicting a Hobbesian state of nature, 'where every man is enemy to every man',[40] and the result is political chaos, whereas the love of Almanzor and Almahide conduces to ideal political harmony. The goal for both love and politics is presented by King Ferdinand and Queen Isabella, who do not appear until the first scene of Part II. Though they are too shadowy to be called embodiments of the ideals which inform the play, they are effective in invoking those ideals. When Isabella saves the captured Ozmyn from execution, for instance, she defends him as a lover and gives a definition of love which ties the play firmly to the chivalric tradition:

> Love's a heroic passion which can find
> No room in any base degenerate mind:
> It kindles all the soul with honor's fire,
> To make the lover worthy his desire.
> Against such heroes I success should fear,
> Had we not too an host of lovers here.
> An army of bright beauties come with me;
> Each lady shall her servant's actions see:
> The fair and brave on each side shall contest;
> And they shall overcome, who love the best.
>
> (Part II, I, 1, 145–54)

And at the end Almanzor sees Ferdinand as the one monarch he can revere:

I bring a heart which homage never knew;
Yet it finds something of itself in you:
Something so kingly that my haughty mind
Is drawn to yours, because 'tis of a kind.

(Part II, V, 4, 153–6)

This statement precisely balances Almanzor's brag to Boabdelin
in the first scene of Part I:

Obey'd as sovereign by thy subjects be,
But know that I alone am king of me.

(I, 205–6)

Boabdelin is a weak monarch, unable to control the warring
factions in his disordered kingdom and finally slain by one of his
own subjects. Against this representation of corrupt civilization
Almanzor at first upholds the nostalgic ideal of a golden age, 'Ere
the base laws of servitude began'; but as he develops with the
guidance of Almahide, he comes to recognize the superior kingship represented by Ferdinand. Primitive liberty is reconciled with
civilized authority in this final image of royalty.

The final affirmation of love and political order, which is, in a
way, the end of the hero's quest, is firmly supported by the theme
of reconciliation. In the sub-plot the star-crossed lovers, Ozmyn
and Benzayda, bring about the reconciliation of their fathers,
which foreshadows the end of the feud between the Zegrys and
the Abencerrages. A more remarkable reconciliation leads to the
conquest of the city by the Christians. As Almanzor defends the
Moors against Ferdinand's chief general, the Duke of Arcos, a
voice tells him that this is his father, and the fighting stops as
father and son embrace. The Moors now accept their Spanish
conquerors; the three 'patterns of exact virtues' are converted to
Christianity, and Almanzor, who has in reality been Spanish and
Christian all along, without knowing it, is united with the
widowed Almahide under the special protection of the united
thrones of Aragon and Castile.

In *The Conquest of Granada* Dryden put together the pieces of a
distinctive form of heroic play, towards which he had been moving
since his collaboration with Howard on *The Indian Queen*. He
succeeded in using the complications of a romantic plot to define
his idea of heroic greatness, and adapted to the character of his

222

hero the rant of the tyrant Maximin. This sort of linguistic energy, once sacrificed to Caroline refinement, was not only restored to the heroic play but made to serve as one means of projecting a wild but noble nature. At the same time the language of dialectic, at which Dryden singularly excelled, was effectively used to point up the contrasts in his elegant design. For those who did not respond to this intellectual appeal there was the excitement of a story with many unexpected turns (of which Buckingham made fun in *The Rehearsal*) and, once again, of an exotic and semi-operatic spectacle in the 'zambra dance' at Boabdelin's court. The combination of obvious and recondite, theatrical and literary, is reminiscent of *Bussy D'Ambois*.

Dryden might be accused of having his cake and eating it too in the treatment of Almanzor, for on the one hand his brilliant pattern of contrasts shows off to advantage the rough virtue of his hero, while on the other hand the movement of the play depicts the civilizing of that hero's instincts and the channelling of his energy. Martin Price states the situation admirably when he says of Almanzor, 'His rebelliousness is the necessary criticism of a mock-order, and his energy is the very pulse of life that should animate a true order'. And yet, as he says later, unresolved questions remain: 'The natural man is capable of true greatness, and he can ascend to the highest level of neo-Stoic moral discipline. But is he truly natural, or does he seem natural only because he carries within him a higher order of being?'[41] A similar dilemma is posed in *Aureng-Zebe* (1675), and though the emphasis differs considerably there, the same questions remain unresolved again. They are, after all, basic questions of the heroic mode, growing out of the opposition of energy and order.

In his dedication of *Aureng-Zebe* to the Earl of Mulgrave, Dryden called it 'a Tragedy; the Characters of which are the nearest to those of an Heroick Poem'.[42] In support of the implied distinction between *The Conquest of Granada* and this play it can be said that the ending is indeed more shocking, with the violent death of Morat, the delirium and death of the Empress Nour-mahal and the self-immolation of Melesinda upon Morat's funeral pyre. But the difference is one of degree. Lyndaraxa, Boabdelin and several others die in the last act of *The Conquest of Granada*, and in both plays a hero, reconciled with his father, is about to marry the woman he loves.

223

As to the characters being 'nearest to those of an Heroick Poem', Nourmahal is Dryden's grandest version of the passionate and ambitious woman—a worthy lineal descendant of Zempoalla. While she schemes, with a cruder ferocity than Arsinoé in *Nicomède*, to put her son Morat on the throne, Aureng-Zebe, the older brother, displays the noble loyalty of Corneille's hero in defending his father, even though, in Dryden's play, the tension between these two is greatly increased by the infatuation of the old Emperor for Indamora, the captive queen promised to his son. Only in his love is Aureng-Zebe immoderate like Almanzor. When Indamora comes to him in the first act, he imagines her as a 'calm Harbour' for his 'Tempest-beaten Soul', and tells her:

> If Love be Vision, mine has all the fire
> Which, in first Dreams, young Prophets does inspire:
> I dream, in you, our promis'd Paradice:
> An Age's tumult of continu'd bliss.
>
> (I, 378–81)

Her revelations of the Emperor's importunities, however, bring anything but calm, and she is obliged to bring Aureng-Zebe back to the recognition of his filial duty by telling him to 'stand the blameless pattern of a Son' (I, 456). Later in the action he displays a less justifiable passion when he wrongly suspects Indamora of loving his brother.

If Aureng-Zebe deviates from strict virtue in only this one respect, his half-brother, Morat, approaches Maximin in his self-centred drive for power. His are the greatest brags:

> I'm in Fate's place, and dictate her Decrees.
>
> (IV, 179)

or (referring to the gods):

> Crimes let them pay, and punish as they please:
> What Pow'r makes mine, by Pow'r I mean to seize.
> Since 'tis to that they their own greatness owe
> Above, why should they question mine below?
>
> (IV, 375–8)

And he defies both his brother and his father in his attempt to seize the throne and Indamora. In Aureng-Zebe and Morat appear the opposed heroic impulses to generous self-sacrifice and untrammelled self-assertion.

The tragedy of *Aureng-Zebe* is as compact in comparison to *The Conquest of Granada* as is *Tyrannic Love* in comparison to *The Indian Emperor*, though the design is again an intricate set of contrasts. Aureng-Zebe differs not only from his brother but also from his father, the source of the divergent inclinations of his sons, as was the old Montezuma, the father of Guyomar and Odmar. The old Emperor's passion for Indamora is an exaggerated form of Aureng-Zebe's fiery love. Fully aware of the injustice he is doing to his loyal son, he is so blinded by the desire to supplant him that he plays his wife's game of favouring Morat until the moment he discovers that his younger son plans to rob him of everything. Foolish and reprehensible as he is, the Emperor is an understandable character and at certain moments—mainly those in which he is warding off the attacks of Nourmahal—almost appealing. He is splendidly sarcastic when she reproaches him for his new love and vaunts her 'known virtue':

> Such virtue is the plague of humane life:
> A virtuous Woman, but a cursed Wife.
>
> (II, 257–8)

> *   *   *

> What can be sweeter than our native home!
> Thither for ease, and soft repose, we come:
> Home is the sacred refuge of our life:
> Secur'd from all approaches, but a Wife.
>
> (II, 272–5)

Though the plot opposes Aureng-Zebe to his father as noble victim to unjust oppressor, the speeches of the two men are occasionally rather similar. When the jealous fit is on Aureng-Zebe, he treats Indamora to anti-feminist remarks very similar to his father's (though inspired in this instance by Milton's Samson):

> Ah Sex, invented first to damn Mankind!
> Nature took care to dress you up for sin:
> Adorn'd, without; unfinish'd left within.
>
> (IV, 490–2)

In both father and son a vein of cynicism is tapped when they encounter misfortune, and the passages in which they express it are among the poetic high points of the play. Aureng-Zebe varies invective with philosophical contemplation, some of which was once very familiar. A few examples will illustrate the satirical tone which relates these speeches to the passages of invective:

> How vain is Virtue which directs our ways
> Through certain danger to uncertain praise!
>
> (II, 502–3)

> This is the Ceremony of my Fate:
> A parting treat; and I'm to die in State.
> They lodge me, as I were the *Persian* King:
> And with luxurious Pomp my death they bring.
>
> (IV, 5–8)

> When I consider Life, 'tis all a cheat;
> Yet, fool'd with hope, men favour the deceit;
> Trust on, and think to morrow will repay:
> To morrow's falser than the former day;
> Lies worse; and while it says, We shall be blest
> With some new joys, cuts off what we possest.
>
> (IV, 33–8)

In the pointedness of such lines Dryden found a style of dialogue in which he excelled and which proved to be a suitable expression of heroic vigour. Deliberately different as his language is from Chapman's, *Bussy D'Ambois* and *Aureng-Zebe* have in common a certain density of linguistic texture which is unusual in heroic drama, and yet fully in keeping with the serious commitment of both authors to heroic poetry. The aphorisms and sallies of *Aureng-Zebe* are manifestations of wit, which Dryden associates with a great mind, as he explains in the dedicatory epistle to this play, where the malice of self-seeking courtiers is attributed to their dullness.[43] The witty fashion in which the Emperor and his son express themselves helps to confirm the heroic greatness of the young man and to suggest that even in the old reprobate it is not quite extinct.

The three principal women are also to be compared and contrasted. Dryden wrote in the dedicatory epistle that he had made Melesinda, Morat's wife, 'in opposition to *Nourmahal*' (p. 107), but in fact Indamora is also 'in opposition to *Nourmahal*', and is in certain respects unlike Melesinda. Dryden referred to Melesinda's utter devotion to her husband as opposed to Nourmahal's hostile scheming, and here one could add Melesinda's pitiful docility as opposed to Nourmahal's furious aggressiveness. However, when Nourmahal seems to be gaining the upper hand and Indamora's life is in danger, it is Melesinda who tries to give courage to Indamora. Melesinda, having long since resigned herself to death, has lost her fear, while Indamora, at other times firm and strong in her serenity (as when Aureng-Zebe wrongly accuses her), is now terrified and helpless. When Melesinda leaves to seek aid from her husband, Nourmahal arrives, and in her insulting words establishes the contrast between her and Indamora:

> Why dost thou shake?
> Dishonor not the vengeance I design'd:
> A Queen, and own a base Plebeian mind!
>
> (V, 305-7)

Apparently some 'fair ladies' were displeased with the unheroic behaviour of both Indamora and Melesinda, whom Dryden defended in the dedicatory epistle by saying that their behaviour was 'natural, and not unbecoming of their Characters'. Rather than follow the pattern of romance on this occasion, he had 'onely represented a practicable Virtue, mix'd with the frailties and imperfections of humane life' (p. 107).

As their fortunes vary, Indamora and Melesinda reveal in turn their frailty and their noble natures, each showing compassion to the other in her moments of distress. Each one is thus a foil for the other, and both are foils for the more continuously heroic characters such as Nourmahal and the two brothers.

Dryden's statement about mixing 'practicable Virtue' with the 'frailties and imperfections of humane life' should not be construed as an indication that he was abandoning the heroic enterprise, for his other statement that the characters of this play 'are the nearest to those of an Heroick Poem' precedes it by only a few sentences. Furthermore, the defence of imperfect characters is very similar to his justification of Almanzor's irregularity in the essay 'Of Heroic Plays', where he claims the precedent of Homer and Tasso. No basic shift of direction is indicated either by the

portrayal of frailty or by the pathos of the scenes involving Indamora and Melesinda. While revealing an increased emphasis on
emotion, which will be discussed at a later point, they are no
more out of place in a heroic play than were the comparable
scenes of pathos in *The Indian Emperor*. Here too the capacity for
pity is depicted as a characteristic of nobility. Pleading with Morat
for mercy to Aureng-Zebe, Indamora says:

> Had Heav'n the Crown for *Aureng-Zebe* design'd,
> Pity, for you, had pierc'd his generous mind.
> Pity does with a Noble Nature suit: . . .
>
> (III, 475–7)

Both the dramatic effectiveness of the play and its range of
tone can be seen in a series of dramatic moments which lead up
to the conclusion. The first is the reconciliation of the old Emperor
with Aureng-Zebe, a scene somewhat comparable to the report of
Almanzor's recognition of his father, but presented here directly
and hence more forcibly. The Emperor, having been betrayed by
Morat, sees at last the consequences of his cruelty to his oldest
son, whose affection he thinks he has alienated. When Aureng-
Zebe assures him that his loyalty is unchanged, though he is now
powerless to offer anything but pity, the Emperor says:

> Can you forgive me? 'tis not fit you shou'd.
> Why will you be so excellently good?
>
> (IV, 580–1)

At the same time, Indamora forgives the hero for his jealousy, and
he is moved by the double reconciliation to make a final attack
on his enemies. This scene ends the fourth act.

The fifth act begins with an extraordinary scene in which
Indamora persuades Morat that true greatness must be guided by
virtue. She asks him what 'great spirits' aim at, and what he
desires. He replies:

> Renown, and Fame,
> And Pow'r, as uncontrol'd as is my will.
> *Indamora.* How you confound desires of good and ill!
> For true renown is still with Virtue joyn'd;
> But lust of Pow'r lets loose th'unbridl'd mind.
> Yours is a Soul irregularly great,

Which wanting temper, yet abounds with heat:
So strong, yet so unequal pulses beat.

(V, 86–93)

Morat is converted, and allows his energies to be redirected by Indamora, as were those of the less irregular Almanzor by an earlier 'pattern of exact virtues'.

The full effect of the change in Morat does not appear until the scene of his death, but before that comes the violent scene in which Nourmahal insults over a cowering Indamora, totally devoid of the strength she has just shown with Morat. Here the focus of attention is the horrifying rage of Nourmahal, who is bent on destroying her rival; for she has conceived an incestuous passion for Aureng-Zebe, and has been rejected by him. It is Almeria and Cydaria in a far more exciting version.

As Nourmahal is about to kill her victim (Dryden's stagecraft owes something to the contrivance of Fletcher here), her son Morat staggers onstage, fatally wounded. He falls towards Indamora as he delivers some lines which point up the significance of the stage business:

> . . . ev'n in death, I find
> My fainting body byass'd by my mind:
> I fall toward you; still my contending Soul
> Points to your breast, and trembles to its Pole.

(ll. 332–5)

When Melesinda arrives, Morat is surrounded by the three women, who now appear in a new configuration. On this occasion Melesinda can only lament, Nourmahal's revenge is frustrated by the intervention of her dying son, and Indamora, ready for death, seems the strongest of them all—'My Soul grows hardy, and can death endure' (l. 360). Morat asks forgiveness of his wife, but nevertheless addresses his last words to Indamora:

> I leave you not; for my expanded mind
> Grows up to Heav'n, while it to you is joyn'd:
> Not quitting, but enlarg'd! A blazing Fire,
> Fed from the Brand.

(ll. 433–6)

Compared with this moving and emotionally complex episode, the one which follows is somewhat disappointing, though it provides a sudden turn and helps to complete the pattern of the play. Aureng-Zebe, having witnessed the death of his brother in Indamora's arms, falls immediately into his old jealousy. The ensuing quarrel seems about to end with Indamora's decision to leave so unreasonable a lover, when the Emperor, now fully on the side of the angels, brings about a reconciliation.

In the presence of these three reconciled (and re-reconciled) characters is now enacted a final pageant of ordered and disordered love. First comes the funeral procession of Morat, in which Melesinda walks, on her way to cast herself on the pyre, 'kindling by his side,/Adorn'd with flames' (ll. 633–4). Then Nourmahal rushes in, distracted by the poison she has taken, and imagining herself 'all fire'. She dies, obsessed by her passion for Aureng-Zebe. The fire of self-destruction and the fire of self-sacrifice are both related to the 'blazing Fire' of Morat's 'expanded mind', fed by the 'brand' of Indamora's heroic virtue. Out of this general conflagration rises the old Emperor's plea for the rest which (understandably) he never had with Nourmahal, and which he now wishes for Aureng-Zebe and Indamora. *The Conquest of Granada* ends with Almanzor's hurrah for 'Great Ferdinand and Isabel of Spain!' accompanied, no doubt, by a flourish of trumpets. The last words of *Aureng-Zebe* come from the Emperor, and they are more sombre and more serene:

> Take you the Reins, while I from cares remove,
> And sleep within the Chariot which I drove.

There is no doubt that *Aureng-Zebe* is a more emotional play than *The Conquest of Granada*, nor that certain scenes are what we consider sentimental. The heightened emotional appeal of this play and of several others in the mid-seventies is no doubt related to a changing critical climate to which Eric Rothstein has drawn attention; critics were increasingly emphasizing the importance of arousing the emotions of the audience in order to secure the proper effects of tragedy.[44] But the sequence of scenes just described does not support the contention that the exploitation of sentiment has resulted in a 'subversion of the heroic ethos'.[45] This would be the case only if the increased importance of pathos were accompanied by a considerable reduction of the stature of the principal characters, as it was in some plays of this period. Here, however, the characters are pushed to the limits of their capacities, enlarging these capacities in the movement towards extraordinary forgiveness, an 'expanded mind' or the fire of absolute passion. The chief personages of *Aureng-Zebe* are thus the legitimate heirs of the heroic figures of Dryden's earlier plays, whom they resemble in so many respects, though for the first time Dryden moves his titular hero several steps away from the irregular greatness of the earlier heroes and in the direction of the perfect virtue usually depicted in the secondary characters. In so doing he approaches somewhat closer to Corneille and to Lord Orrery.

In *All for Love* (1677) as in *The Conquest of Granada* and *Aureng-Zebe* Dryden is at the top of his dramatic form. It was the play which pleased him most as he looked back over his career late in life: '. . . I never writ anything for myself but *Antony and Cleopatra*' (Ker, II, 152). Though this refashioning of Shakespeare belongs in a different category from his original heroic plays, and is famous as the occasion on which, after defending rhyme so ardently, he abandoned it, both the characterization and the style are closely related to his earlier practice.

The Prologue to *Aureng-Zebe* has already announced that the poet

> Grows weary of his long-lov'd Mistris, Rhyme.
> Passion's too fierce to be in Fetters bound,
> And Nature flies him like Enchanted Ground.
>
> (ll. 8–10)

As the couplets of that play are loosened by enjambment, thus preparing the way for blank verse, so the unrhymed lines of *All for Love* sometimes have a formal antithetical structure which recalls the heroic couplet:

> He first possess'd my Person; you my Love:
> *Caesar* lov'd me; but I lov'd *Antony*.
>
> (II, 354–55)

Freed of the 'fetters' of rhyme, the passions are indeed allowed even greater scope than in *Aureng-Zebe*, and the interaction of the characters is correspondingly more 'natural', in Dryden's terms, though an intellectual scheme continues to dominate the structure and extend the meaning of each encounter.

The extent of the freedom Dryden took in this play can be measured in relation to three models which he discusses in the Preface: French tragedy, Shakespeare and 'the Ancients'. In French tragedy, specifically in Racine's *Phèdre*, Dryden objects to a too great refinement of manners, which has 'transform'd the *Hippolitus* of *Euripides* into Monsieur *Hippolite*' (ll. 119–20). Along with this objection, which is not essentially different from that in the essay 'Of Heroic Plays' to the French exaggeration of the 'point of honour', Dryden once more states his preference for heroes who are imperfect, and not so civil as to be foolish or dull. His praise for 'the Genius which animates our Stage' (ll. 86–7) is by implication praise for a more irregular wit, such as that which he and his contemporaries ascribed to Shakespeare. It is no surprise, then, when he says, 'In my Stile I have profess'd to imitate the Divine *Shakespeare*' (ll. 305–6),[46] but this statement follows another in which he professes to have followed 'the practise of the Ancients' (l. 295), by which he means the Greek tragedians. Thus, if the English model is preferred to the French for the greater freedom it gives to portray an imperfect and irregular hero, it is to be modified in the direction of a regular structure by reference to the Greeks. As usual, Dryden's position is determined by a set of delicate balances.

His concern for a compact, classical structure has the ironic consequence that his imitation of Shakespeare has less of the epic sweep of *Antony and Cleopatra* than his earlier play, *The Conquest of Granada*. The neat organization of *All for Love* has been analysed so often that very little need be said about it here. The opening act in which Ventidius raises Antony's spirit to a determination to leave Cleopatra and regain his lost valour is succeeded by an act in which Cleopatra reasserts her influence without, however, discouraging his plan to fight with Caesar. In the third act Ventidius brings up heavier artillery in the persons of Antony's Roman wife and children, who nullify the effect of his momentary victory over Caesar and his reunion with Cleopatra. By the end of Act IV however, Antony has so offended his wife that she has left him; and though he has quarrelled with Cleopatra, he is trembling on the verge of reconciliation with her. The fifth act, bringing his final military reverse and the triumph of Caesar, restores the lovers to each other, and ends in their double suicide. The opposition of Rome and Egypt, which underlies Shakespeare's play as well, becomes the structural framework of Dryden's.

Of the two famous protagonists it is Cleopatra whose character is most altered. Shakespeare's 'riggish' heroine becomes a dignified enchantress, whose love for Antony is 'a noble madness' and a 'transcendent passion' (II, 17, 20), excessive, to be sure, but heroic from the start. Though she vaunts the superiority of her love to the dutiful affection of 'dull Octavia', his legal wife, Cleopatra would also like to be thought Octavia's superior in constancy, and hence, in the realm of romantic ideals, his true wife, 'For 'tis to that high Title I aspire' (V, 414). Shakespeare's heroine rises to the same claim in her last moments, but the majestic and courageous Cleopatra of Fletcher and Massinger's *The False One* or of Corneille's *La Mort de Pompée* comes closer to Dryden's conception.

On the one occasion when Cleopatra uses guile to achieve her end she does so with the greatest reluctance. Alexas urges her to feign a passion for Dolabella, in order to rouse Antony's jealousy, but she protests that such deceit would be contrary to her nature. Her famous self-comparison to 'a silly harmless household Dove' (IV, 92), which has not struck most modern critics as very apt, is one of several phrases which emphasize her heroic simplicity, a quality she shares with Antony and with Almanzor, who compares his heart to a 'crystal brook' (IV, 1, 45). Antony complains of his 'plain honest heart', in which everyone can see as in 'a shallow-forded Stream' (IV, 434-41), and Dolabella finds Cleopatra's breast 'Transparent as a Rock of solid Crystal;/Seen through, but never pierc'd' (IV, 202-3).

In characterizing Antony Dryden makes a great deal of the bounty which Shakespeare also stresses. Ventidius dilates on it before Antony has appeared:

> O, *Antony*!
> Thou bravest Soldier, and thou best of Friends!
> Bounteous as Nature; next to Nature's God!
> Could'st thou but make new Worlds, so wouldst thou
>   give 'em,
> As bounty were thy being.
>
> (I, 180-4)

Closely related to this characteristic is his largeness of soul, in
which he resembles many of Dryden's heroes:

> Virtue's his path; but sometimes 'tis too narrow
> For his vast Soul; . . .
>
> (I, 124–5)

And in the scene of Octavia's appeal Antony reveals two other
related characteristics, generosity and pity. Octavia is portrayed
as very Roman not only in her advocacy of moral obligation but
also in a stern and dignified pride, not devoid of grandeur. Thus,
although she is in a sense a foil for the portrayal of Cleopatra's
heroic love, Dryden does not demean her by evoking the stereo-
type of the neglected wife. Even Antony recognizes the 'greatness
of [her] Soul' (III, 314), and the conflict between these two
great souls seems to Ventidius a 'strife of sullen Honour' (l. 306).
Though Antony is naturally loath to give in, he begins to show
signs of weakening as Ventidius and Dolabella observe the
struggle. Dolabella says:

> O, she has toucht him in the tender'st part;
> See how he reddens with despight and shame
> To be out-done in Generosity!
>
> (ll. 308–10)

Ventidius catches him blinking back a tear.

It is the children who turn the trick for Octavia, however,
'vanquishing' Antony as they throw their little arms around him.
Ventidius is deeply moved, and so, obviously, the audience is
expected to be. The emotional appeal is even greater than any in
Aureng-Zebe, but precisely what sort of response does this scene
demand? Pity for neglected Octavia and her children? Pity for
Antony, because he has to give in? If such feelings are aroused,
they are secondary to the admiration aroused by Antony's pity
for his family and by sympathy for the dilemma he has recognized
a few lines earlier by saying:

> Pity pleads for *Octavia*;
> But does it not plead more for *Cleopatra*?
>
> (III, 339–40)

A sentimental scene according to our lights, it is not in any way
inconsistent with the premises of heroic drama. It testifies to

another sort of greatness than valour, but a sort already celebrated in many a magnanimous hero.[47]

Antony is again tempted by pity at the end of the fourth act when, after rousing his jealousy all too successfully, Cleopatra and Dolabella plead with him to believe there was nothing culpable in their relationship. For the time being he resists:

> Good Heav'n, they weep at parting.
> Must I weep too? that calls 'em innocent.
> I must not weep; and yet I must, to think
> That I must not forgive.
>
> (IV, 588–91)

The false news of Cleopatra's suicide in the last act, however, makes him repent of his hardness of heart, and his grief is the greatest testimony of his love. The suicide and the death-bed reconciliation with Cleopatra follow, as in Shakespeare, and then the suicide of the queen, where Dryden borrows from Samuel Daniel's *Cleopatra* as well as from Shakespeare.[48] That the hero and heroine are to be pitied in these final scenes would be taken for granted by any Aristotelian critic, and Dryden, in his Preface, regrets that the nature of his protagonists' crime made it impossible 'to work up the pity to a greater heighth' (ll. 18–19), but the final emphasis is on regal transcendence, as the dead lovers, seated on their thrones, command the stage:

> See, see how the Lovers sit in State together,
> As they were giving Laws to half Mankind.
>
> (V, 508–9)

3 Lee and Otway

The more emotional scenes in *All for Love* were probably due not only to the emphasis on the passions in the poetics of the day but also, as Arthur Kirsch says (p. 134), to the examples of Dryden's young contemporaries, Nathaniel Lee and Thomas Otway, both in their twenties in the 1670s. Lee, who was to become a collaborator with Dryden, was already a friend by 1677, when *The Rival Queens* was published with a most commendatory epistle by Dryden:

Such praise is yours, while you the Passions move,
That 'tis no longer feign'd; 'tis real Love:
Where Nature Triumphs over wretched Art;
We only warm the Head, but you the Heart,
Always you warm!

(ll. 33–7)⁴⁹

Nero, Lee's first play, displayed some of the uninhibited rant for which he was to be famous. The character of Rome's degenerate emperor, long famous as a stage tyrant in the pseudo-Senecan *Octavia*, is well suited to the demands of heroic drama, and Lee makes the most of the heartless immorality and the insane egotism:

I ransack Nature; all its treasures view;
Beings annihilate, and make a new:
All this can I, your God-like Nero do.

(I, 2, 40–2)

'How rarely this KING talks!' Poppea comments on another occasion (III, 3, 39), and we may be reminded that Elizabethan tyrants, not to mention Maximin, were known for the same capacity. Nero is also, like his predecessors, an explicit definer of his villainy, who conveniently labels the virtues to which he is opposed:

Shall I be branded with the name of good?
Begone, thou soft invader of my blood;
Mercy and I, no correspondence have;
Pity's a whining tender-hearted slave:
Fury I love, because she's bold and brave.

(IV, 1, 75–9)

In the plays that follow, either pity or fury is often the most conspicuous trait of the hero.

Two of Lee's greatest successes, *Sophonisba* and *The Rival Queens*, illustrate the distinctive character of his drama. In *Sophonisba* (1675), performed a few months before Dryden's *Aureng-Zebe*, Lee brought to the stage once more a heroine who had already proved her worth several times. For Lee she is considerably more than the pattern of constancy which made Marston's 'wonder of women' admired. She is the passionately

loving woman of Mairet's play, who also has the courage and
pride which give Corneille's Sophonisbe her stature. Lee manages
this combination of characteristics with some skill, presenting his
heroine first through the feelings of Massinissa, who is shown at
the opening of the play unmanned by disappointed love and
reduced to a famous sigh: 'O Sophonisba, oh!' (I, 1, 152; the turn
of phrase was not Lee's invention—Coriolanus long before said
'Oh my mother, mother, oh'—and it was Thomson, not Lee, who
doubled the Sophonisbas to provide the butt for Fielding's satirical
line, 'Oh! *Huncamunca, Huncamunca,* oh' in *The Tragedy of Tragedies,*
II, 5). Having secretly married Sophonisba, he believes she has
betrayed him by marrying Syphax, unaware that she was forced
into this alliance by her father. Thus Massinissa appears in the
familiar guise of the warrior whose valour has been destroyed, while
she, the woman responsible for this disaster, seems to be the epitome of love, and fickle love at that. By the end of the first act
Massinissa has roused himself from his lethargy, determined to kill
his love and reassert himself as a warrior. The contrast between
love and valour is made explicit in the concluding lines:

> Love like a Monarch, merciful and young,
> Shedding no blood, effeminates the strong.
> But War do's like a Tyrant vex us more,
> And breaks those hearts, which Love did melt before.
>
> I, 1, 319–22)

The other side of Sophonisba's character appears when Mass
nissa, fighting with the Romans, has defeated the Carthaginians
and killed Syphax. As Massinissa enters, still bitter about her
second marriage, she is prepared to commit suicide rather than
suffer captivity. The ensuing scene of misunderstanding, explanation and reconciliation is more psychologically persuasive, and
hence more gripping, than such scenes in Dryden's plays usually
are. When it ends, Massinissa is once more committed to Sophonisba, and is also determined to defy Rome if Scipio should insist
on making Sophonisba a prisoner. Under her influence love and
valour have been reunited.

In Lee's version of the story both lovers take poison when
Scipio refuses to grant their plea for Sophonisba's liberty. The
last scene is a love-death suggestive of Antony and Cleopatra if
not of Tristan and Isolde. The lovers die in an embrace, asserting

their freedom from Roman power and the superiority of love to empire. Scipio's lieutenant asks, 'What cruel eyes could pity here refrain . . .?' (V, 1, 424), and Scipio is so moved that he vows to give up war, retire to the country, and 'study not to live, but how to die' (l. 434). In the minds of these beholders pity and admiration seem to be mixed in about equal proportions.

That this combination of effects was deliberate, and that Lee attributed them in part to imitation of his great predecessors, can be inferred from what he said a few years later about his *Mithridates* (1678) in the dedication:

> I have endeavour'd in this Tragedy to mix Shakespear with Fletcher; the thoughts of the former, for Majesty and true Roman Greatness, and the softness and passionate expressions of the latter, which makes up half the Beauties, are never to be match'd: How have I then endeavour'd to be like 'em? O faint Resemblance!
>
> (ll. 50–4)

A few lines later his humility is complemented by an attitude more characteristic of the Restoration—Lee desires to be found

> a Refiner on those admirable Writers; the Ground is theirs, and all that serves to make a rich Embroidery! I hope the World will do me the Justice to think, I have disguiz'd it into another fashion more suitable to the Age we live in; . . .
>
> (ll. 66–9)

Love and Valour, which Dryden considered the proper subject of a heroic poem, are also presented in the second plot of *Sophonisba*, based on a story in the Earl of Orrery's romance, *Parthenissa*. Massinissa's nephew, Massina, falls in love with Hannibal's mistress, Rosalinda, who even troubles the composure of Scipio, the Roman soldier *par excellence*. Rosalinda is quite aware of the effect she has on men, commenting on it with the seeming detachment of many characters in heroic drama:

> My charmes, the cold and temp'rate Consul felt,
> Whilst beauties beams did fiercely on him play; . . .
>
> (III, 2, 89–90)

She also feels pity, but no love, for young Massina, and thereby arouses the jealousy of Hannibal. Though the situations in this plot correspond closely to those in the main plot, they are, if anything, still more romantic. Massina commits suicide when he sees his love is hopeless; Rosalinda, masquerading as a warrior, is mortally wounded on the battlefield of Zama; and Hannibal, in whose arms she dies, determines, even though defeated, to revenge her on Rome.

The success of these rousing scenes was undoubtedly heightened by the spectacular staging. The first Roman victory is accompanied by meteorological phenomena which are first described in Lee's most extravagant vein:

> Two Suns their gawdy Charriots Curtains furl,
> And at each other brandish'd lightning hurl, . . .
>
> *   *   *
>
> Through the void place swift Darts obliquely fly;
> Black swarthy Demons hold a hollow Cloud,
> And with long Thunder-bolts they drum aloud; . . .
>
> (II, 2, 58–9, 69–71)

and then presented scenically:

> The SCENE drawn, discovers a Heaven of blood, two
> Suns, Spirits in Battle, Arrows shot to and fro in the Air:
> Cryes of yielding Persons, &c. Cryes of Carthage is
> fal'n, Carthage, &c.
>
> (II, 2, 86 ff.)

In a later scene Hannibal visits Bellona's Temple to consult the priestesses about the future. Songs and incantations reminiscent of *Macbeth* are followed by 'A Dance of Spirits' and a symbolic apparition foretelling Rosalinda's death (IV, 1).

The Rival Queens (1677) deals with Alexander the Great, one of the favourite heroes of romance, but unconventionally diverts attention from him to his queens, Roxana and Statira. In comparison with the fierce rivalry of these two women, the conspiracy which leads ultimately to the poisoning of the emperor seems rather tame. Statira has made Alexander promise never to sleep with Roxana again; he has broken his promise, and Statira has vowed to retire to a lonely cell; but now, repentant, he is eager to be reconciled with Statira, and Roxana is outraged. Her entrance in the third act relates her instantly to some of the other great-souled Amazons of heroic drama:

> Away, be gone, and give a whirlwind room,
> Or I will blow you up like dust; avaunt:
> Madness but meanly represents my toyl.
>
> (III, 1, 45-7)

Lee has abandoned the couplet here, but not the fury of his heroic verse.

In contrast with Roxana, Statira is at first tearful and resigned, sending word to the emperor that with her 'departing breath' she did not rail at him, but 'sobbing sent a last forgiveness to him' (III, 1, 145–8). Roxana, who observes this scene at a distance, is reluctantly impressed by Statira's 'bravery of Soul' (l. 165), though at heart she despises her rival as a 'puny Girl . . . That cry'd for milk, when I was nurs'd in bloud!' (ll. 119–20). She commits a serious tactical error when she lets her fierce spirit goad her into a confrontation with Statira. Starting with polite sympathy, which her rival instantly sees to be false, Roxana soon begins to indulge herself in irony and then outright vituperation ('No, sickly Virtue, no'), rising finally to a cruel bit of sexual boasting, where her hatred is close to madness:

> When you retire to your Romantick Cell,
> I'le make thy solitary Mansion Hell;
> Thou shalt not rest by day, nor sleep by night,
> But still Roxana shall thy Spirit fright:
> Wanton, in Dreams, if thou dar'st dream of bliss,
> Thy roving Ghost may think to steal a kiss;
> But when to his sought Bed, thy wand'ring air
> Shall for the happiness it wish'd repair,
> How will it groan to find thy Rival there?
> How ghastly wilt thou look, when thou shalt see,
> Through the drawn Curtains, that Great man and me,
> Wearied with laughing joys, shot to the Soul,
> While thou shalt grinning stand, and gnash thy teeth, and houl.
>
> (III, 1, 22–37)

Her barbarity makes Statira decide to fight for Alexander, thus giving the action a dramatic turn.

This scene and the one which follows, in which Alexander banishes Roxana and is pardoned by Statira, are among the most effective in the play, providing two actresses with ample opportunity to display their virtuosity. In the first performance Rebecca Marshall, who had played Lyndaraxa and Nourmahal, was Roxana, while Elizabeth Boutell, who had played Benzayda and was to play Cleopatra, was Statira.

The last scene of the play, though it offers nothing comparable to this interplay of character against character, is highly theatrical. As Statira waits for Alexander, she is visited by the ghosts of her father and mother, who warn her in a sung dialogue that she is about to die. Roxana now enters, dagger in hand, and, resisting Statira's pleas for delay, murders her just as Alexander arrives. Her reward is the confirmation of her banishment, but she makes her exit in character, crying for revenge. The emperor's death of poison given him by the conspirators brings the tragedy to a grisly finish.

Bonamy Dobrée, noting the operatic quality of the scene with the singing ghosts, wondered if Lee 'might not, in fact, have been an operatic genius who mistook his medium'.[50] He was not the first critic of Lee to be reminded of opera, for Colley Cibber, writing in the first half of the eighteenth century, made the same comparison. It was prompted in this case by the resemblance of some of Alexander's speeches to arias:

> When these flowing Numbers came from the Mouth of a *Betterton*, the Multitude no more desired Sense to them, than our musical *Connoisseurs* think it essential in the celebrate Airs of an *Italian* Opera.[51]

The triumph of sound over sense in certain speeches is of a piece with the prominence of spectacle and song, and though all these characteristics can be found in Dryden as well, the extent to which Lee relies upon them marks a difference between the two playwrights. Dryden's best plays have a dialectical structure which constantly aims at a definition of heroic values, while Lee's best plays are less schematic and less concerned with fine distinctions. They are lyrical celebrations of a kind of greatness which is frequently manifested in states of extreme emotion, whether pity, fury, fear or exaltation.

Since Lee became insane at the end of his life, both friendly and unfriendly critics have been tempted to relate his extravagant style to the incipient disease. Langbaine, who thought Lee's best work entitled him to be put in 'the First Rank of Poets', quoted the Senecan aphorism which Dryden rendered in his description of Achitophel: 'Great wits are sure to madness near allied.'[52] But when full allowance has been made for the effect of Lee's rhetorical and scenic extravagance, one is obliged to admit that something else in the plays is even more important. Lee's most impressive talent is his way of making such emotional scenes as Massinissa's misunderstanding with Sophonisba or the quarrel of Statira and Roxana seem genuine. Often there is a softness which Langbaine noted in his comment:

> . . . his Muse indeed seem'd destin'd for the Diversion of the Fair Sex; so soft and passionately moving, are his Scenes of Love written.

(p. 321)

Though there is no diminution of heroic stature, the capacity to respond to tender feeling marks Lee's men as well as his women, and in some cases the extent of this capacity seems to be a measure of their greatness. The deaths of Rosalinda, Massinissa, Sophonisba and Statira, though indubitably heroic, are also moments of great tenderness. We know from Langbaine and from Dryden that audiences responded to such scenes; it is a reasonable guess that Dryden began to aim for a similar response in *Aureng-Zebe* and *All for Love*.

Otway's drama is characterized by less rant and less spectacle than Lee's but by a similar concern with the passions and an even greater emphasis on tenderness. In the eighteenth century he became known as 'the tender Otway',[53] and Coleridge, listening to the wind, thought of him when the violence momentarily abated:

> It tells another tale, with sounds less deep and loud!
> A tale of less affright,
> And tempered with delight,
> As Otway's self had framed the tender lay . . .

('Dejection', ll. 117–20)

His first play, *Alcibiades* (1675), is not entirely characteristic, though as Roswell Ham points out (pp. 43–5), many features of the later plays are foreshadowed. A description of the hero's feats on the battlefield shows his close kinship to Almanzor and others:

> Brave *Alcibiades* has wonders done.
> Ne're greater Courage was in *Sparta* shown.
> Troops were not able to withstand his shock,
> Like thunder from a Cloud his fury broke
> On all his Enemies, and like that too,
> Death and Amazement did attend each blow.
>
> (III, 43–8)[54]

Besides valour he has the almost standard virtues of generosity and magnanimity.

More prophetic of the later plays is the pathos which appears at the opening of the second act, where Timandra, 'A noble *Athenian* Lady, betrothed to *Alcibiades*', follows him into exile and seeks consolation from his sister Draxilla in '*A Grove adjoyning to the* Spartan *Camp*'. Both ladies are miserable, but nobly miserable. Timandra says:

> But how grows Gratitude to that degree,
> To be afflicted thus, and weep for me?
>
> *   *   *
>
> What vast and boundless flights does Friendship take!
>
> (II, 25–6, 37)

The young actress in the Duke's Company who played the part of Draxilla was Elizabeth Barry, who became one of the outstanding actresses of the period. The object of Otway's unrequited passion, she took the principal female role in both *The Orphan* and *Venice Preserved*. Alcibiades was played by the greatest of all Restoration actors, Thomas Betterton. Aline Taylor has shown how important good actors were to the success of Otway's plays, for while his dramatic language lacked the pointedness of Dryden and the sheer verve of Lee, his characters and situations offered great opportunities to the interpreter on the stage.[55]

Don Carlos (1676), a better play than *Alcibiades*, scored a resounding success, to which Otway alludes in his Preface, where he modestly refuses to accept the judgment offered him 'That it is the

best Heroick Play that has been written of late' (ll. 49–50). The
arrangement of characters provides for comparisons somewhat
like those to be made in Dryden's plays. Don Carlos, the son of
Philip II of Spain, is both similar to his uncle, Don John of
Austria, and different from him. Each one has a reason for resent-
ing the king, Carlos because his father has married the woman
originally promised to him, and John because he is an illegitimate
brother. Don Carlos has 'A Will unruly, and a Spirit wild' (I,
166), though, like other impetuous and irregular heroes, he
prides himself on transparent honesty: 'I never yet learnt the
dissembling Art' (I, 131). Don John's irregularity takes the form
of defiance of society. In a soliloquy reminiscent of Shakespeare's
Edmund he presents a philosophy of libertinage based on
primitivism:

> Why should dull Law rule Nature, who first made
> That Law, by which her self is now betray'd?
> E're Man's Corruptions made him wretched, he
> Was born most noble that was born most free: . . .
>
> *   *   *
>
> My Glorious Father got me in his heat,
> When all he did was eminently great:
> When Warlike *Belgia* felt his Conquering power,
> And the proud *Germans* Own'd him Emperour.
> Why should it be A Stain upon my Blood
> Because I came not in the Common Road,
> But Born obscure and so more like a God?
>
> (II, 1–4, 10–16)

But Don Carlos is also prepared to defy the law. He reacts to his
father's cruelty by planning to join the rebels in Flanders, and
persists in the scheme even after his arrest by Philip's order—
'These Limbs were never made to suffer Chains' (IV, 369). Only
the queen has power to bring him back to obedience, playing
Almahide to his Almanzor.

The queen is similar to Almahide not only in placing loyalty
to her husband above love for the hero, but also in being paired
with a Lyndaraxa in the person of the Duchess of Eboli, a violent,
scheming woman, whose ambition is to be a queen or, failing that,
to have a royal lover. Don John is the logical choice. Her husband,

Ruy Gomez, is also a schemer, inciting the king to jealousy of his son by means similar to Iago's, and thereby precipitating the tragedy.

The catastrophe to which all this scheming leads is remarkable for the piling up of unexpected deaths and the contrivance of pathos. Eboli, whose liaison with Don John has been discovered, poisons the queen on orders from the king, is murdered by her husband, and makes a dying confession of both her crimes and his. Don Carlos commits suicide and the king kills Ruy Gomez. But in the midst of all this violence the attention of the spectator is directed to the repentance of the king and his reconciliation with Don Carlos. Eboli's confession reduces the king to abject contrition towards his dying queen, whom he has been chastising bitterly a few moments before. The arrival of his son, mortally wounded, plunges him still lower, and his grief becomes unendurable when Don Carlos blames himself for his rebellious thoughts. Echoing the old Emperor in *Aureng-Zebe*, the king asks Don Carlos:

> Why wert thou made so excellently good;
> And why was it no sooner Understood?
>
> (V, 415–16)

The prince and the queen die kneeling side by side, the innocence of their love finally vindicated, and the king, overcome by his guilt, '*Runs off raving*'. Don John is left to take up the heroic quest of his nephew. Increasingly in the latter part of the play he has shown sympathy for Don Carlos. Now, determining to give over his libertinage, he plans to go off to war, 'Where Thirst of Fame the Active Hero warms' (V, 503).

In his Preface Otway, while denying that it was 'the best Heroick Play that has been written of late', wrote:[56]

> . . . this I may modestly boast of, which the Author of the *French Berenice* has done before me in his Preface to that Play, that it never fail'd to draw Tears from the Eyes of the Auditors, I mean those whose Souls were capable of so Noble a pleasure. . . .
>
> (ll. 51–5)

Racine's first great success, *Andromaque* (1667), heralded a series of remarkable tragedies which departed, some more, some less, from the model of Corneille. In *Phèdre* (1677) the brutal power of uncontrollable passion overwhelms the protagonist and leaves an impression of inglorious obsession rather than of power or 'grandeur d'âme'. In *Bérénice* (1670), which Otway had been reading, the departure from Corneille is more subtle, more a matter of changed emphasis. Speaking of Racine's achievement in general, Paul Bénichou remarks, 'il a humanisé l'héroïsme, affiné l'orgueil, attendri le bel amour'.[57] Otway's familiarity with Racine helps to explain a comparable difference in emphasis between *Don Carlos* and Dryden's plays, to which it is much indebted.

Racine makes a general point about tragedy in his Préface to *Bérénice*, the wording of which is directly relevant to *Don Carlos*. Before speaking of the tears with which the public have 'honoured' his play, he explains that the action of tragedy should be great and the characters heroic; that the passions should be aroused, and that there should be felt throughout 'cette tristesse majestueuse qui fait tout le plaisir de la tragédie'.[58] Otway's 'so Noble a pleasure' was no doubt inspired by Racine's words, but more important, the feeling of 'tristesse majestueuse' is precisely what gives the last scene of *Don Carlos* its special character.

In *The Orphan* (1680) there is even more 'tristesse', but it is considerably less 'majestueuse', with important consequences for the effect of the tragedy. Here the principal characters are Castalio and Polydore, the sons of Acasto, 'A Nobleman retired from Court, and living privately in the Country', and Monimia, 'The Orphan', Acasto's ward. There is no 'grand intérêt d'état' as there is in *Don Carlos* and in the other Restoration plays considered so far. The tragedy is purely personal.

Castalio and Polydore are not entirely what literary convention might lead us to expect. Unlike the Polydore and Cadwal of *Cymbeline*, another pair of boys brought up in the country by a refugee from the corruptions of court, they engage at their first appearance in a conversation that is more courtly than pastoral. It seems that both are in love with Monimia, but Castalio, expressing a fashionably libertine abhorrence of marriage, which might cheat him of his freedom, offers to let Polydore try to win her for himself. The situation is even further removed from the pastoral ideal than we are led to suppose; for Castalio, while encouraging his brother to court Monimia and leaving him alone with her for this purpose, is planning to marry her secretly. His libertine sentiments are a mask worn to deceive the brother for whom he professes an ideal friendship. His reason for this strange behaviour is that Polydore is a true libertine, who would not marry Monimia (II, 313–15) and might betray Castalio's plan, but Aline Taylor is right in saying that his 'motive for concealing his marriage from Polydore is the weakest point in the structure of *The Orphan*'.[59] The situation resulting from his behaviour is, in any case, a strange variation of the old theme of love and friendship.

Thanks to a page who manages to overhear and report some crucial conversations, Monimia knows what Castalio has said to Polydore about her, and Polydore knows that after a tempestuous misunderstanding, Castalio and Monimia have been reconciled. Suspecting foul play on his brother's part, he manages on his own to overhear an assignation between Castalio and Monimia, and, unaware that they have already been secretly married, succeeds in substituting himself for his brother on the wedding night. As one situation develops out of another in this triangular relationship, misunderstandings based on partial knowledge keep the emotional tension at a maximum, the climactic instance being Castalio's outrage when he is refused admission to Monimia's apartment by the maid, who believes that the true Castalio is with her mistress. By means of a technique reminiscent of Beaumont and Fletcher, Otway contrives a series of quarrels followed by reconciliations until at last full knowledge of the true situation leads each of the three principal characters to seek and find death.

By his handling of the wedding-night episode, which gives the play its understated alternate title, 'The Unhappy Marriage', Otway makes the most of the emotional potential. First Castalio declaims against all women because of his belief that Monimia has betrayed him with some unknown man; then comes a violent quarrel with Monimia, incomprehensible to her, since she still believes she was with him the previous night; next, other members of the family become enraged by Castalio's treatment of his wife. The first clarification of what has happened comes in a scene in which Polydore, after numerous mysterious hints, tells Monimia that she slept with him, and she informs him that she is his brother's wife. Now Castalio, hearing that Monimia is in despair, goes to her, determined to forgive her, but is kept ignorant of what has happened. She tells him only that she must leave him forever.

He finds out the truth when Polydore, having goaded him into a
fight, runs on Castalio's sword, and as he dies, accuses himself.
The suicides of Monimia and Castalio end the play.

Even so bald an account of the latter half of the play suggests
Otway's overriding concern with the emotions, but with somewhat
different emotions from those most brilliantly depicted by Lee.
Despite the numerous misunderstandings in *The Orphan* there is
far less fury than in *Nero* or *The Rival Queens*, and more pity. One
of Otway's characteristic effects is that of rage melting into forgiveness, as in the page's description of Monimia and Castalio:

> For of a sudden all the Storm was past,
> A gentle calm of Love succeeded in; . . .
>
> (III, 9–10)

Expressions of pity abound: Castalio pities Monimia before he
realizes that she was not to blame, and she pities him without
having the courage to tell him the truth.

To project intense emotion Otway, like most of his contemporaries, has recourse to simile, metaphor and extended description, though his diction is comparatively simple—what was then
thought to be 'natural'. To a twentieth-century sensibility extravagant language that is also transparently clear may seem overdone
in comparison with the more complicated language of Shakespeare
or Chapman, which is rich in suggestion. Thus, when Monimia
imagines herself 'in some Cell distracted',

> these unregarded Locks
> Matted like Furies Tresses; my poor Limbs
> Chain'd to the Ground . . .
>
> (IV, 209–12)

the effect is one of unnecessary and grotesque ornament. Similarly, Castalio's self-description when he is upbraiding Monimia
seems more decorative than deeply felt:

> When I stood waiting underneath the Window,
> Quaking with fierce and violent desires;
> The dropping dews fell cold upon my head,
> Darkness enclos'd, and the Winds whistl'd round me;
> Which with my mournful sighs made such sad Musick,
> As might have mov'd the hardest heart: . . .
>
> (V, 250–5)

Another self-description later in this same scene is more functional in that the figurative language is used as a means to communicate an emotion not easily described. Monimia has just told him they must never see each other again:

> Methinks I stand upon a naked beach,
> Sighing to winds, and to the Seas complaining,
> Whilst afar off the Vessel sailes away,
> Where all the Treasure of my Soul's embarqu'd; . . .
>
> (V, 288–91)

But most successful of all is Monimia's three-word reply to this speech, 'Ah, poor *Castalio*!' If Otway sometimes faltered when he sought for a 'literary' rendition of emotion, he had a sure touch for the brief exclamation which implies a great deal without making anything explicit.

Mrs Barry's rendition of this speech was remembered for many years and contributed to the making of her reputation. Thomas Betterton reported her as saying that she never spoke the line without weeping.[60] Commenting on her versatility in acting roles of different sorts, Colley Cibber testified to the effect she had on her audiences:

> Mrs. *Barry*, in Characters of Greatness, had a presence of elevated Dignity, her Mien and Motion superb, and gracefully majestick; her Voice full, clear, and strong, so that no Violence of Passion could be too much for her: And when Distress, or Tenderness possess'd her, she subsided into the most affecting Melody, and Softness. In the Art of exciting Pity, she had a Power beyond all the Actresses I have yet seen, or what your Imagination can conceive. Of the former of these two great Excellencies, she gave the most delightful Proofs in almost all the Heroick Plays of *Dryden* and *Lee*; and of the latter, in the softer passions of *Otway's Monimia* and *Belvidera*.[61]

The triumph of Mrs Barry's 'Ah, poor *Castalio*!' tells a good deal about the dominant effect of *The Orphan*, which differentiated it from the heroic plays of Dryden and Lee. As Cibber implies, there are no 'Characters of Greatness' here. Emotional intensity is divorced from heroic grandeur, and pity solicited for characters who are the victims of circumstances and of their own limitations, however noble they may be in intent. It is impossible to feel admiration for Castalio or true horror at Polydore. Nothing leads us to believe that either brother is exceptional in the way that Almanzor is, nor that Monimia, for all her compassion, has the strength of Almahide or even Indamora. Here, then, the heroic dream has faded, and something much closer to domestic tragedy has taken its place.

In *Venice Preserved* (1682), where the plot concerns a conspiracy to overthrow the government, the magnitude of the issues is once more what is expected in heroic drama, as is the high-mindedness of the two principal men, Jaffeir and Pierre. Yet the effect is not truly heroic. Jaffeir, who is clearly at the centre of the play, is acted upon more often than he acts, and Pierre, by force of circumstance, accomplishes nothing. It is he who lures Jaffeir into the conspiracy with eloquent speeches about the corruption of the Venetian senate, but both he and Jaffeir also have personal grudges to settle. Jaffeir has been cruelly treated by Priuli, his father-in-law, a senator who considers him unworthy of his daughter Belvidera; Pierre's mistress, Aquilina, has been appropriated by another senator, Antonio. The motives of both men are a thoroughly understandable mixture of the personal and the altruistic—much more humanly understandable than the motives of the greatest heroes. Furthermore, Jaffeir conspicuously lacks heroic constancy. Having made the splendid, if absurd, gesture of leaving Belvidera and his dagger with the conspirators as pledges of his loyalty to the cause, he is, of course, disenchanted when he finds out from her that Renault, one of the leaders, has attempted to rape her. Convinced by Belvidera that the conspirators will do more harm than good, he betrays them to the senate on the assurance that their lives will be spared. But when they are condemned to death after their arrest, Jaffeir is so horrified by what he has done, especially to his friend Pierre, who has called him a traitor and a coward, that he vows never to see his wife again and even threatens to kill her. After a tearful reconciliation of the two friends Jaffeir accompanies Pierre to the scaffold, where he kills him to save him from torture and then kills himself. The tragedy is complete when Belvidera dies after going mad with grief.

When *Venice Preserved* was first mounted, not only did the acting of Betterton as Jaffeir and Mrs Barry as Belvidera contribute to its great success, but also the topical references to the 'Popish

Plot', which had rocked the political scene a few years earlier. Titus Oates had sworn in 1678 that the Pope was supporting a plot to assassinate the king and restore Catholicism to England. Though the evidence for such a conspiracy was soon shown to be highly imaginative, the Whigs under the leadership of the first Earl of Shaftesbury took full advantage of the scare to embarrass the Tory government. By the time that Otway's play was performed, however, the Whigs had been discredited, and audiences could relish the satirical portraits of Shaftesbury as the conspirator, Renault, and also as the perverted senator, Antonio (Shaftesbury's first name was Anthony), who hires Aquilina to abuse and kick him while he fawns on all fours and calls her his Nicky Nacky.[62]

At most, however, the political allusions heighten the effect of a play whose meaning is not essentially political. Though the principle of order is preferred to the chaos of revolution, neither the actual rulers nor the conspirators win any sympathy. The tragedy is finally a personal one, in which the lives of the three chief characters are destroyed by conflicting loyalties. Otway is extraordinarily adroit in the management of Jaffeir's dilemma, balancing Belvidera, a character of his own invention, against Pierre, as the spokesmen for order and revolution, respectively, and the embodiments of love and friendship. An effective detail is Jaffeir's dagger, given to the conspirators with instructions to kill Belvidera if he is false to them. Pierre returns it after his arrest, as he curses Jaffeir and tells him their friendship is over. Jaffeir threatens Belvidera with it when he hears that the conspirators are to be tortured and killed, and uses it to kill both Pierre and himself. Otway's insistence on the device not only reinforces the unity of the dramatic action but provides a symbol for the theme of laceration which dominates the play.

The one feature of *Venice Preserved* which is less acceptable to a modern audience than to the audiences of the seventeenth, eighteenth and nineteenth centuries, which continuously acclaimed the play, is the piling up of sentiment in certain of the speeches. Belvidera's plea to Jaffeir is a truly purple passage:

> Save the poor tender lives
> Of all those little Infants which the Swords
> Of murtherers are whetting for this moment;

Think thou already hearst their dying screams,
Think that thou seest their sad distracted Mothers
Kneeling before thy feet, and begging pity
With torn dishevel'd hair and streaming eyes,
Their naked mangled breasts besmeared with bloud,
And even the Milk with which their fondled Babes
Softly they hush'd, dropping in anguish from 'em.

(IV, 48–57)

The moving description prescribed in the handbooks of Roman rhetoric is here carried to intolerable lengths, with the result that, despite the genuine importance of the issue, what should be gripping seems merely sentimental.

This characteristic of the style is intimately related to the unremitting appeal, especially in the last acts of the play, for pity for Jaffeir and Belvidera. Thus, once again, though the characters of *Venice Preserved* are more elevated than those of *The Orphan*, one is reminded of domestic tragedy. As David R. Hauser says, there is a merging of the heroic and the pathetic, or, as he puts it, of 'the heroic and the humble ways of life'.[63] The heroic is not entirely gone, but pity predominates over the admiration with which it is mingled.

Ten years after Otway's death Dryden wrote in 'A Parallel of Poetry and Painting' (1695):

> Mr. Otway possessed this part [i.e. the gift of expressing the passions] as thoroughly as any of the Ancients or Moderns. I will not defend everything in his *Venice Preserved*; but I must bear this testimony to his memory, that the passions are truly touched in it, though perhaps there is somewhat to be desired, both in the grounds of them, and in the height and elegance of expression; but nature is there, which is the greatest beauty.
>
> (Ker, II, 145)

Almost twenty years earlier he had praised Lee in very similar terms for moving the passions and warming the heart, and in Lee, too, he found nature triumphing over art. When he mentioned the lack of a proper 'height and elegance of expression' in Otway, however, he pointed to a characteristic which differentiates one author from the other. Presumably he referred to the comparative simplicity of Otway's language, which seems to us sometimes an asset and sometimes a liability, but always a factor in that slight lowering of the tone which we feel when we compare Otway with Lee.

4 Dryden's Later Plays

Dryden's comments on nature, the passions and the relative height of style raise issues about which he had been thinking all his life, and which he had discussed in an important dedication to his hybrid play, *The Spanish Friar*, part comedy, part heroic drama, performed in 1680 (the year of *The Orphan*) and published the following year. In the passage most frequently quoted Dryden recalls his disappointment in reading *Bussy D'Ambois*, whose 'glaring colours' had 'amazed' him on the stage:

. . . but when I had taken up what I supposed a fallen star, I found I had been cozened with a jelly; nothing but a cold, dull mass, which glittered no longer than it was shooting; a dwarfish thought, dressed up in gigantic words, repetition in abundance, looseness of expression, and gross hyperboles; the sense of one line expanded pro-digiously into ten; and, to sum up all, uncorrect English, and a hideous mingle of false poetry, and true nonsense; or, at best, a scantling of wit, which lay gasping for life, and groaning beneath a heap of rubbish. A famous modern poet used to sacrifice every year a Statius to Virgil's *Manes*; and I have indignation enough to burn a *D'Amboys* annually, to the memory of Johnson. But now, My Lord, I am sensible, perhaps too late, that I have gone too far: for, I remember some verses of my own *Maximin* and *Almanzor*, which cry vengenace upon me for their extravagance, and which I wish heartily in the same fire with Statius and Chapman. All I can say for those passages, which are, I hope, not many, is, that I knew they were bad enough to please, even when I writ them; but I repent of them amongst my sins; and if any of their fellows intrude by chance into my present writings, I draw a stroke over all those Delilahs of the theatre; and am resolved I will settle myself no reputa-tion by the applause of fools.

(Ker, I, 246)

Dryden's censure here is frequently misunderstood together with the nature of his retraction. He has been discussing well written plays as opposed to those which succeed on the stage, where 'everything contributes to impose upon the judgment; the lights, the scenes, the habits, and, above all, the grace of action...' (Ker, I, 245). Chapman's rhetoric, which seemed to work brilliantly in the theatre, appears overblown and confused when Dryden examines it critically, and it is indeed hard to think of an Elizabethan style which would be less congenial to him than Chapman's. The more important point, however, is his denunciation of Maximin and Almanzor. Does it grow out of a revulsion against heroic drama, or high-flown rhetoric, or the theatre itself? There is no doubt that writing for the theatre was more a financial necessity than Dryden's freely chosen profession. If he could have obtained sufficient financial support, he would have preferred to write an epic poem. In 'A Discourse concerning the Original and Progress of Satire' (1693), after giving his ideas on the epic, he says that he had intended to put them in practice,

> ... and to have left the stage, (to which my genius never much inclined me,) for a work which would have taken up my life in the performance of it.
>
> (Ker, II, 37–8)

For comedy in particular he considered himself unsuited, as he says in 'A Defense of an Essay of Dramatic Poesy' (Ker, I, 116). Yet, having addressed himself to the task of writing plays, he gave a great deal of thought to it, and especially to heroic plays, which were so closely related to the epic which he most wanted to write: 'an heroic play ought to be an imitation, in little, of an heroic poem' (Ker, I, 150). Hence, when he speaks of knowing that his passages of rant were 'bad enough to please', one must not infer that they were carelessly tossed off. Nor does Dryden totally condemn the results of his earlier efforts. It is 'some verses'—certain 'passages', which he hopes were not many—characterized by 'extravagance'. He goes on to say:

> Neither do I discommend the lofty style in Tragedy, which is naturally pompous and magnificent; but nothing is truly sublime that is not just and proper.
>
> (Ker, I, 246)

The main thrust of the argument is contained in this last clause. Chapman's verse is not 'just and proper' by Dryden's standards, and hence fails of sublimity. The 'injudicious poet who aims at loftiness', as he says later, 'runs easily into the swelling puffy style' (Ker, I, 247). Similarly, he sees a lack of proper judgment in some of the speeches he wrote for Maximin and Almanzor, though he knew at the time that they might succeed well enough on the stage. Now, wishing to be read as well as applauded in the theatre, he aims at 'the propriety of thoughts and words, which are the hidden beauties of a play', and 'are but confusedly judged in the vehemence of action' (Ker, I, 248). He lists the qualities which he hopes to achieve but which will be fully appreciated only by the reader:

> The purity of phrase, the clearness of conception and expression, the boldness maintained to majesty, the significancy and sound of words, not strained into bombast, but justly elevated; . . .
>
> (*Ibid.*)

Neither the praise of Otway and Lee for adhering to nature nor the repentance for his earlier extravagance indicates that Dryden was renouncing the heroic enterprise. He revered heroic poetry to the end of his life, opening the dedication of his translation of the *Aeneid* in 1697 with the statement: 'A heroic poem, truly such, is undoubtedly the greatest work which the soul of man is capable to perform' (Ker, II, 154), and, even in his last plays, concerning himself with the problem of achieving sublimity in dramatic poetry. In the Preface to *Don Sebastian* (published in 1690), after lamenting the necessity of writing once more for the stage, he takes pride in the result of his renewed efforts:

> And I dare boldly promise for this Play, that in the roughness of the numbers and cadences, (which I assure was not casual, but so design'd) you will see somewhat more masterly arising to your view, than in most, if not any of my former Tragedies. There is a more noble daring in the Figures and more suitable to the loftiness of the Subject; . . .
>
> (ll. 69–74)[64]

As we have already seen, Dryden's recognition of Lee's and Otway's success in moving the passions of the spectators was accompanied by a shift in his own dramatic writing towards a greater emotional appeal, especially an appeal to pity, which he described in the Preface to *Troilus and Cressida* (1679) as 'the noblest and most god-like of moral virtues' (Ker, I, 210). Both the advocacy of a lofty style freed of extravagance and the emphasis on moving the passions were characteristic of René Rapin, whose *Réflexions sur la poëtique d'Aristote* (1674) were translated by Thomas Rymer and cited with approval by Dryden in the same preface.[65] In speaking of how to create admiration without offending against probability, Rapin says (in Rymer's translation):

> But most part of those that make Verse, by too great a Passion they have to create *Admiration,* take not sufficient *Care* to Temper it with *Probability.* Against this Rock most ordinarily fall the *Poets,* who are too easily carried to say *incredible Things,* that they may be *admirable.*[66]

Later on, after exhorting the poet to read not only Homer and Virgil, but Pindar, Sophocles and Euripides in his search for 'Loftiness of *expression*', he says:

> 'Tis only by the most lively Figures of Eloquence that all the *Emotions* of the Soul become fervent and passionate: Nature must be the only Guide that can be proposed in the Use of these Figures and *Metaphors,* and must therefore be well understood, that it may be trac'd and follow'd without Mistake; . . .
>
> (*Ibid.,* XXIX)

The pleasure of tragedy 'consists in the Agitation of the Soul mov'd by the Passions. . . . The Theatre is dull and languid, when it ceases to produce these Motions in the Soul of those that stand by' ('Reflections . . . in Particular', XVIII).

No doubt this affective theory of the proper operation of tragedy, as propounded by Rapin and adopted by Dryden, helped to produce the shift of emphasis in the heroic play from the hard valour of the warrior to the capacity for more tender feelings, but it did not encourage any lowering of tone or any reduction in the stature of the protagonist. The further shift of attention to more ordinary and more limited heroes, such as Castalio in *The Orphan*, was what led directly to domestic and sentimental tragedy. In this development Dryden played no part.

The long quotation from the dedication of *The Spanish Friar* points the direction in which Dryden was moving in his treatment of the heroic, and a summary of the action of the play shows in what ways it resembled and differed from his earlier heroic plays. The serious plot presents us with a situation typical of heroic romance. Leonora, the Queen of Aragon, daughter of a usurper, falls in love with Torrismond, a noble warrior, who, without knowing it, is the son of the deposed king, now languishing in prison. Bertran, the villain of the piece, does all he can to thwart the affair so that he can marry Leonora and establish himself on the throne. For further assurance he persuades Leonora to order the death of the old king. When Torrismond describes to Leonora his visit to the prison and the lamentable state of 'The good old king, majestic in his bonds' (III, 3, 180),[67] urging her to spare the old man's life, he demonstrates the compassion and largeness of spirit so conspicuously lacking in Bertran. News that the king has been executed induces a conflict of emotions in Torrismond, greatly accentuated soon after, when his foster-father tells him his true identity and urges him to kill the queen. The big scene of the fifth act exploits the emotions of all to the hilt. Leonora, repenting of her cruelty, announces her desire to 'lengthen out the payment' of her tears in 'Some solitary cloister', whereupon Raymond, the stern foster-father, is reduced to tears himself. 'He weeps! now he's vanquish'd,' Torrismond comments (V, 2, 190, 197, 204). Unable to see her leave, he takes the 'fair penitent' in his arms. In a brief concluding episode, however, sorrow is changed to joy by the revelation that the old king still lives. Leonora worries only that he may not sanction her marriage to his son, but Torrismond reassures her that 'pity and he are one' (V, 2, 417). Even Bertran is forgiven and gathered into the new order.

The Spanish Friar contains as amusing a parody of heroic drama as any in *The Rehearsal*: Torrismond asks Lorenzo, the protagonist in the comic plot, to join him in opposing their fathers and saving the queen, against whom the citizens have rebelled. Lorenzo, finding himself in a dilemma, proceeds to debate with himself like a good hero of romance, but also rather like Falstaff:

Let me consider:
Bear arms against my father? He begat me;
That's true; but for whose sake did he beget me?
For his own, sure enough: for me he knew not.
O! but says Conscience: 'Fly in Nature's face?'—
But how, if Nature fly in my face first?

(V, 1, 171–6)

Heroic and anti-heroic exist side by side here as they do in the comedies, *Secret Love* and *Marriage à la Mode*.

In *Don Sebastian* (1689), another serious play with a comic sub-plot, the comedy is less prominent than in *The Spanish Friar*, and the serious plot more heroic. The historical material is the same that inspired Peele to write *The Battle of Alcazar*. The battle has been fought, Mahumet (Peele's Muly Mahamet) is dead, Sebastian is presumed dead, and the tyrannical Muley-Moluch reigns as emperor. But Dryden chose to dramatize the legend that Sebastian was not killed in the battle. Since the legend left his fate in doubt, and thus put him at Dryden's disposal, as he says in the Preface, 'whether to bestow him in *Affrick*, or in any other corner of the World' (ll. 117–18), Dryden chose to place his hero in a group of prisoners brought before the emperor. In the same group is Almeyda, a captive queen with whom Sebastian is in love, but who is eventually revealed to be his sister. The chief complications of the story, stemming from this affair and from Sebastian's relations with Dorax, a renegade Portuguese, are pure invention.

Dorax, the part played by Betterton, is Dryden's final version of the irregular hero, whose 'gloomy outside, like a rusty Chest,/ Contains the shining Treasure of a Soul,/Resolv'd and brave' (I, 1, 47–9). Formerly, as Don Alonzo, a trusted warrior of King Sebastian's, he suffered what he considered the insupportable indignity of seeing the hand of the woman he loved awarded to a rival by the king. To him, his rebellion against Portugal was a 'noble Crime' (II, 1, 317). Superficially he resembles the bluff soldier of many seventeenth-century plays, full of coarse humour and cynical observations, but a further dimension of his character is suggested by that first allusion to hidden light. Later in the play he compares himself briefly with Lucifer, though, as it turns out, his angelic glory is not irredeemably lost.

258

Almeyda, played by Mrs Barry, is a more complex character than most in heroic drama, and again a combination of character types. Supposing herself the sister (she is actually the half-sister) of the dead Mahumet, she has moments of queenly self-assertion that remind one, by their sheer vivacity, of Lyndaraxa or Nourmahal. Muley-Moluch comments, 'What Female Fury have we here!' (I, 1, 439) after her first outburst. But she is also the virtuously loving heroine of romance, an Almahide or Indamora:

> Mine is a flame so holy, and so clear,
> That the white taper leaves no soot behind;
> No smoak of Lust; . . .
>
> (II, 1, 576–8)

Dorax gives the first description of Don Sebastian, where admiration wins out over resentment:

> . . . he was a Man,
> Above man's height, ev'n towring to *Divinity*.
> Brave, pious, generous, great, and liberal: . . .
>
> (I, 1, 101–3)

To these typical attributes of the great hero are added his extraordinary appearance, as described by Benducar, the most villainous character in the play:

> He looks as Man was made, with face erect,
> That scorns his brittle Corps, and seems asham'd
> He's not all spirit. . . .
>
> (I, 1, 317–19)

This admiring appraisal of him as, in Chapman's words, 'Man in his native noblesse', is the more surprising since it is made when Sebastian is brought as an unknown prisoner before the emperor. Like Almanzor, he is at this moment a noble stranger whose innate superiority is revealed by his bearing. Unlike Almanzor, he is at the mercy of the tyrant, but Muley-Moluch spares his life when he sees Don Sebastian weep for the loyal subjects he lost in the battle. Restraining his own tears, the emperor says:

> . . . owe thy Life, not to my gift,
> But to the greatness of thy mind, *Sebastian*: . . .
>
> (I, 1, 409–10)

Pity is once more the sign of magnanimity.

Muley-Moluch is seldom in such a melting mood, however. More often he is the typical power-mad tyrant, who can say, like a Nero or a Maximin, 'What's Royalty but pow'r to please my self?' (II, 1, 46). In the grotesquery of some of his threatening speeches Dryden strikes a nice balance between melodrama and satire, revealing a more firm and easy control of tone than he had when he wrote *Tyrannic Love*.[68] When the tyrant, in one of his grimmer moments, condemns Sebastian to death, the situation is comparable, *mutatis mutandis*, to that of Almanzor when he is condemned to death by Boabdelin. If the speeches of the two heroes are set side by side one can see the change in Dryden's style from *The Conquest of Granada* to *Don Sebastian*. Almanzor's speech is probably the most familiar passage in the play:

> No man has more contempt than I of breath,
> But whence hast thou the right to give me death?
> Obey'd as sovereign by thy subjects be,
> But know that I alone am king of me.
> I am as free as nature first made man,
> Ere the base laws of servitude began,
> When wild in woods the noble savage ran.
>
> (I, 203–9)

Sebastian says:

>   I'll shew thee
> How a Man shou'd, and how a King dare dye:
> So even, that my Soul shall walk with ease
> Out of its flesh, and shut out Life as calmly
> As it does words; without a Sigh, to note
> One struggle in the smooth dissolving frame.
>
> (III, 1, 214–19)

The obvious patterning of rhyme is, of course, missing in the second passage, and also the driving rhythm. Enjambment constantly plays syntactical units off against line divisions, to strengthen further the effect of 'natural' speech. Rhythmic differences may be discerned between individual lines: 'How a Man shou'd, and how a King dare dye' is more emphatically irregular in accentuation than 'I am as free as Nature first made man', which has a similar pattern. Compared with the brilliant but facile phrases, 'I alone am king of me' and 'When wild in woods the noble savage ran', 'One struggle in the smooth dissolving frame' is sombre and less immediately comprehensible, but finally more powerful. 'My Soul shall walk at ease/Out of its flesh' is a less ostentatious brag than 'Know that I alone am king of me', but it is just as great, and is enhanced by its quiet tone and deliberate simplicity. In the passage as a whole—and it is characteristic of the play—the language is flexible and pithy. Dryden had reason to claim that the verse of *Don Sebastian* was 'more masterly' than in his earlier plays.

The two big scenes of the play occur in the fourth and fifth acts respectively. In the fourth act Dorax reveals himself to his former master and complains openly of his bad treatment. Don Sebastian explains why he was obliged to honour Dorax's rival, Enriquez, but Dorax continues with increasing vehemence to vent his hurt feelings until the two men are on the verge of a duel. Then, when a word from Sebastian reveals that Enriquez is dead, Dorax delays the fight to inquire how his rival died. Discovering that Enriquez gave his life to save the life of his king, Dorax begins a painful reappraisal of his own attitudes towards Sebastian, who, however, refuses to blame Dorax for his resentment, weighing good deeds against errors with almost superhuman impartiality. Finally Sebastian even takes part of the blame for provoking Dorax's crime of rebellion. At this point Dorax suddenly returns to his first allegiance:

> O stop this headlong Torrent of your goodness: . . .
>
> (IV, 2, 906)

It is a brilliant scene in a line descending from the quarrel and reconciliation of Cassius and Brutus in *Julius Caesar* through the scene which Dryden admittedly modelled on it—the quarrel and reconciliation of Hector and Troilus in the third act of his *Troilus and Cressida*—and owing something to the reconciliation scenes in *Aureng-Zebe* and *Don Carlos*.

Don Sebastian, in his relations with Dorax, is the almost perfect hero, whose virtue is neither fugitive nor cloistered, but supremely active, as is suggested by the figure of the 'headlong Torrent'. In his relations with Almeyda he is the innocent perpetrator of a crime. Having met her as the sister of the Moorish prince who came to Portugal to ask his assistance, he falls in love with her, and, while they are both prisoners of Muley-Moluch, persuades her to marry him despite some mysterious warnings which he chooses to ignore. Only after the marriage has been consummated does the old counsellor, Don Alvarez, manage to reveal the fact that Almeyda is the illegitimate daughter of Sebastian's father. Following a recognition scene reminiscent of Greek tragedy, Sebastian is dissuaded by Dorax from committing suicide. He then expresses the ironic reversal of his heroic ambitions in three lines:

> The world was once too narrow for my mind,
> But one poor little nook will serve me now;
> To hide me from the rest of humane kinde.
>
> (V, 1, 557-9)

It is as if Dryden could not resist the temptation to add finality by slipping in a rhyme.

Though 'one poor little nook' will serve him now, the final view of the hero in no sense diminishes his stature. Both Sebastian and Almeyda decide to lead solitary lives, and Dorax arranges a safe retreat for each. Almeyda is to be in a convent, but Sebastian in a remote cave 'Under the ledge of *Atlas*' (l. 679). The touching scene of his farewell to Almeyda leaves no doubt of the strength of his feelings and therefore of the greater strength of his resolve. An almost saintly renunciation of the world is the final proof of the hero's superiority.

After *Don Sebastian* Dryden wrote only one more serious play, *Cleomenes, the Spartan Hero* (1692), and because of illness, had to leave the finishing touches to his friend Thomas Southerne. It is not an impressive play, though it moved Theophilus Parsons, 'a young gentleman under twenty years of age', to send Dryden anonymously some highly complimentary verses, which he published with the play. He could not help being pleased by such a couplet as:

> O wond'rous man! where have you learned the art,
> To charm our reason, while you wound the heart?
>
> (*Works*, VIII, 228)[69]

This was, one may suppose, what he always hoped to do.

The play is interesting chiefly as showing the direction in which

Dryden moved after *Don Sebastian*. Another warrior hero is the protagonist, but this time a hero in prison throughout most of the play, unable to act until at last a friend releases him. Then for a moment Cleomenes and his friend try to raise the populace against the oppressor who has kept him in prison, but 'The people will not be dragged out to freedom' (V, 2; VIII, 359), the revolution fails, and the hero and his friend commit suicide. It is a story of virtue oppressed, of Stoic courage, of greatness largely wasted on a hostile world. Dryden chose it because, as he said in the Preface, he thought it 'was capable of moving compassion on the stage', and because Cleomenes, 'as he was the last of the Spartan heroes, so he was, in my opinion, the greatest' (VIII, 219, 226). Cleomenes is more nearly one of the 'patterns of exact virtues', more devoted to the public good, and perforce less active than the Herculean heroes Dryden celebrated earlier in his career. In fact, this Spartan is remarkably similar in some ways to the Roman Cato, the Stoic hero of Chapman's *Caesar and Pompey*, and of the play Addison would write some twenty years later.

In all his heroic plays, much as they differ one from another, Dryden strove for some kind of sublimity, and though in his later plays he made more open appeal to the emotions, he believed from first to last that the passions must be engaged if the requisite response of admiration was to be attained. In 'The Author's Apology for Heroic Poetry and Poetic Licence', prefixed to *The State of Innocence* (1677). the unperformed opera Dryden made from *Paradise Lost*, he discussed the relation of style to sublimity, with frequent references to Longinus. The passions are to be 'raised' by figurative language, especially by catachreses and hyperboles, which Dryden compares to 'heightenings and shadows' in a painting (Ker, I, 184). Somewhat later he says:[70]

> Imaging is, in itself, the very height and life of Poetry.
> It is, as Longinus describes it, a discourse, which, by a
> kind of enthusiasm, or extraordinary emotion of the soul,
> makes it seem to us that we behold those things which the
> poet paints, so as to be pleased with them, and to
> admire them.

(I, 186)

At the end of the essay he gives a famous definition of wit as 'a propriety of thoughts and words; or, in other terms, thoughts and words elegantly adapted to the subject', in order to make the point 'that sublime subjects ought to be adorned with the sublimest, and consequently often with the most figurative expressions' (I, 190).

Dryden's comments on his contribution to two operas which *were* performed, *Albion and Albanius* (1685) and *King Arthur* (1691), reveal the contemporary belief that music might achieve the emotional effect entrusted to figurative language in a heroic play. In the Preface to *Albion and Albanius*, after explaining that opera 'admits of that sort of marvellous and surprising conduct, which is rejected in other plays', he says:

> If the persons represented were to speak upon the stage, it would follow, of necessity, that the expressions should be lofty, figurative, and majestical: but the nature of an opera denies the frequent use of these poetical ornaments; for vocal music, though it often admits a loftiness of sound, yet always exacts a harmonious sweetness; . . .
>
> (Ker, I, 270–1)

The language of songs is intended mainly 'to please hearing rather than to gratify the understanding' (p. 271), but the pleasure given by such music is clearly related to the 'enthusiasm' induced by the 'sublimest' and the 'most figurative' language.

Though *Albion and Albanius* was sung throughout, *King Arthur*, for which Henry Purcell wrote the music, was of that special form of opera which combined spoken and sung sections, most of the climactic moments in the story being set to music. At these moments the contrast between the deliberate flatness of the poetry and the 'loftiness of sound' is striking, and furnishes an unexpected insight into the operation of the very different sort of poetry Dryden wrote for his heroic plays. The music, unassisted by the words, still elicits the desired emotional response; no doubt an age which accepted Dryden's poetic conventions gave a similar response to heroic poetry which leaves most contemporary readers unmoved. But even in a heroic play poetry did not have to achieve its sublime effects without assistance. Music, in greater or lesser quantities, was always present to reinforce the emotional effect.

5   *Lesser Lights*

Of the dramatists affected by the heroic ideal Dryden, Lee and Otway were by far the most gifted and the most individual. There were, of course, many others who wrote heroic plays, but, as James Sutherland says, 'The minor tragic drama of the period is a bourne from which the few travellers who venture at all usually return as quickly as possible'.[71] There will be no attempt to describe this bourne in detail here, but a few of the minor practitioners deserve mention.

Aphra Behn, whose most heroic achievement was to earn her livelihood with her pen when only men were expected to do so, was known mainly for her novels, comedies and tragicomedies. She occasionally wrote in a heroic vein, however, and in her *Abdelazer, or The Moor's Revenge* (1676) she revived the heroics of the Elizabethan period. It is instructive to see how little she altered in the brags of her villain-hero, as she (admittedly) plundered *Lust's Dominion*. Where Eleazar says:

> I rusht amongst the thickest of their crowds,
> And with a countenance Majestical,
> Like the Imperious Sun disperst their clouds; . . .
>
> (III, 4, 16–18)[72]

his Restoration avatar says:

> I rush'd amongst the thickest of their Crouds,
> And with the awful Splendor of my Eyes,
> Like the imperious Sun, dispers'd the Clouds.
>
> (IV, 1)[73]

As she wrote to a friend, she merely 'weeded and improv'd' the garden from whence she 'gather'd' her play (*Works*, I, xxxviii). In some respects fashion had not greatly changed.

John Crowne and Elkanah Settle achieved great theatrical success with heroic drama in the decades of Dryden's major plays and the first plays of Lee and Otway. Settle's *The Empress of Morocco* (1673) is known today by students of Restoration drama because of the cuts of scene designs published with the first edition. It was the only play of the period to be honoured with such illustrations, and they constitute unique evidence of the appearance of the stage at the Dorset Garden theatre. No doubt these elaborate scenes, which vary from the exotic landscape of Africa to a prison scene and a grisly torture chamber with naked bodies impaled on spikes, contributed to the success of the play. They should remind us once more of the great importance of the staging of Restoration heroic drama. The play is innocent of the conflict of ideas found in Dryden's plays and of the forceful presentation Lee or Otway might give of the emotional tensions between characters. Settle provides, instead, an exciting tale of villainous intrigues and true love between comic-strip characters, whose only claim to heroism is the violence of their ambitions and desires.

Crowne is a considerably better playwright, but not original in any way. *The Destruction of Jerusalem* (1677) is like *The Conquest of Granada* in being a two-part play. Though the writing is uniformly competent, the plot filled with incident, and the conflicts related to issues of some importance, very little is memorable or distinctive. The play seems a rather well-done exercise in a popular genre. The first part is dominated by the love of the Parthian king Phraartes for Clarona, the daughter of the high priest of Jerusalem. Since Phraartes is an atheist, though a noble warrior, and Clarona has dedicated herself to a life of religious celibacy, the courtship is characterized by debates in the manner of Dryden. Phraartes' friend Monobazus is in love with Queen Berenice, who, however, is in love with the Roman Titus. To the danger of the approaching Romans is added the scheming of the rebellious Pharisees, who are made to resemble the Puritans, and the first part ends with their discomfiture by Phraartes on behalf of Clarona and her father. To these sufficient complications is added the famous and tragic love of Titus and Berenice, which dominates the second part of the play. Racine had dramatized this story in his *Bérénice*, of which an undistinguished adaptation by Otway had been produced in London a month before *The Destruction of Jerusalem*. To do Crowne justice, he was right in insisting that he had not borrowed from Racine, though to present the same story was to invite a comparison which could not be in Crowne's favour. This part of his play contains a large measure of the fashionable pathos of the day both in the story of Titus' renunciation of love because of his duty to Rome, and in the death of Clarona at the hands of the Pharisees. Phraartes and his friend Monobazus, both disappointed in love, go to seek a glory elsewhere:

> Our Persons, Fames, and Glories we will bear,
> To live and reign, we know not how nor where.
>
> (V, 1)[74]

The Destruction of Jerusalem, as this summary shows, has a little of everything and something for everybody.

John Banks won himself a place in dramatic history by a treatment of English history which differed sharply from the heroic romanticism of Orrery, and contributed to the vogue of pathos. He did not seem to be interested in the heroic as Orrery, Dryden or Lee understood it, but since the English history play was so closely related from the first to the development of the heroic play, Banks's experiments concern us. Two of them will illustrate his way with the historically great. No less a personage than Queen Elizabeth I is the leading lady of *The Unhappy Favourite: or The Earl of Essex* (1681), but it is not she who opens the play. The first words are an angry torrent from a cast mistress of Essex, the Countess of Nottingham:

> Help me to rail Prodigious minded *Burleigh*,
> Prince of bold *English* Councils, teach me how
> This hateful Breast of mine may Dart forth words,
> Keen as thy Wit, Malitious as thy Person; . . .[75]

As the editor, Thomas Blair, says, she and some of Banks's other villainous women 'draw their fury from such memorable ladies as Zempoalla . . . Nourmahal . . . and Roxana' (p. 14). Here the accent of the heroic play is clearly heard, and the smart balance of the fourth line partly conceals its deficiency of sense. This is only one of the styles in the play, however, and perhaps not the most characteristic. Often there is an oddly Elizabethan overtone (no doubt deliberately so), as in these lines of the queen:

> How now my *Rutland*? I did send for you——
> I have observ'd you have been sad of late.
> Why wearest thou black so long? and why that Cloud,
> That mourning Cloud about thy lovely Eyes?
>
> (III, 1; p. 33)

> Unhand the Villain——
> Durst the vile Slave attempt to Murder me!

(III, 1; p. 41)

Banks is at his best in the well-conceived series of interviews which form the bulk of the third act at a point in the story when Essex has been impeached. The queen first speaks to the Countess of Nottingham, whose hostility to Essex infuriates Elizabeth; next the former Countess of Rutland, now secretly married to Essex, comes to plead for him with the queen, and in so doing, reveals her love, which agitates Elizabeth more than Lady Nottingham's malevolence. Immediately after this revelation, Essex himself arrives, and after almost melting the queen's resentment, boasts so audaciously of his former services that she loses her temper and boxes his ear. Steele commented many years later that though 'there is not one good line' in it, 'the incidents in this drama are laid together so happily, that the spectator makes the play for himself, by the force which the circumstance has upon his imagination'.[76] It is true that the emotional tensions of these scenes are conveyed by speeches totally lacking in distinction. The situations, nevertheless, are strong enough to command attention and, according to Steele, to draw tears at every performance. For the most interesting characters, Queen Elizabeth and the Countess of Essex, are both objects of pity. After Essex's death they join in mourning and form a friendship based on mutual compassion.

The next year Banks wrote another play about a famous Englishwoman, *Virtue Betrayed, or Anna Bullen*, where the heroine, far from being the flirtatious and easy-going woman of familiar stories about Henry VIII, is the innocent victim of fiendish political intrigue. The hero, Piercy, is also a helpless victim of the schemers, who destroy the love affair between these two good people and arrange first Anna's marriage to the king and then her disgrace and death. At the end comes a touching scene with little Elizabeth, who is lifted to the condemned queen's arms, so that her 'little Coral-Lips' may be kissed and her 'tender, blooming Soul' blessed.[77] When the baby weeps, the queen says:

> Strive not for Words, my Child; these little drops
> Are far more Eloquent than Speech can be—

(Sig. L)

thus heralding the final triumph of tears over verbal excellence. Though Anna and many other characters in Banks's plays have a nobility both of mind and of social standing which relates them to characters in heroic plays, the emphasis on their helplessness gives the pathos a significance and importance it does not have in *Aureng-Zebe* or *All for Love*. In spite of their elevated rank, these victims are more like the pathetic protagonists of *The Orphan*, with whom they share the distinction of foreshadowing the characters of sentimental drama.

6   Rowe and Addison

Most directly Banks's mournful, injured ladies anticipate what Nicholas Rowe called 'she-tragedies' in a half-joking epilogue to one of them, *Jane Shore* (1713). The term stuck, both to this kind of play and to Rowe. In view of Rowe's reputation for sentimentality, it is surprising to find that his first play, *The Ambitious Stepmother* (1700), is far more conventionally heroic than, for example, Southerne's *The Fatal Marriage* of six years earlier. That resounding success, based on a novella by Aphra Behn and acted by Betterton and Mrs Barry, is the domestic (and melodramatic) tragedy of the return of a husband, supposed dead, to find his wife remarried (the alternate title is *The Innocent Adultery*) and his younger brother plotting to get the inheritance. The husband is murdered by his scheming brother and the heroine shocked into madness and suicide. The didacticism which usually accompanies domestic tragedy is conspicuous here in a valedictory admonition to parents not to push younger brothers towards crime by discriminating against them. The gloom is periodically relieved in the first three acts by a comic plot about the successful deception of a jealous husband by some young rakes. Here too a moral is drawn—in this case, a homily against jealousy.

From this world of homely morality and immorality *The Ambitious Stepmother* is far removed, though the title has a deceptive ring of domesticity. In fact, the story is about one of those royal second wives whose schemes to secure thrones for their sons had been dramatized by Corneille, Davenant, Orrery and Dryden, among others. At her first entrance Artemisa displays her formidable ambitions, which are given a much more adequate expression than the Countess of Nottingham's 'Help me to rail

Prodigious minded *Burleigh* . . .'. Rowe's verse has a vigour which
had recently been heard only in the plays of the aging Dryden:

> Be fixt, my Soul, fixt, on thy own firm basis!
> Be constant to thyself; nor know the weakness,
> The poor Irresolution of my Sex:
> Disdain those shews of danger, that would bar
> My Way to glory. Ye Diviner Pow'rs!
> By whom' tis said we are, from whose bright Beings
> Those active sparks were struck which move our clay;
> I feel, and I Confess the Ethereal energy,
> That busie restless principle, whose appetite
> Is only pleas'd with greatness like your own: . . .
>
> (I, 1)[78]

Nor is Artemisa the only one who carries on in the old heroic
vein. Her assistant, the priest Mirza, proclaims his villainy with a
gusto reminiscent of heroic rant even when his objectives are
ordinary enough. As he considers raping the heroine, Amestris,
he says:

> Love! What is Love? the Passion of a Boy,
> That spends his time in Laziness and Sonnets:
> Lust is the Appetite of Man; and shall
> Be sated, till it loath the cloying Banquet.
>
> (III, 2; sig. G 4ᵛ)

Both the rightful heir to the throne, Artaxerxes, and the queen's
son, Artaban, have great and haughty souls, and appropriate
aspirations to go with them. Artaban challenges his brother to a
duel, saying, 'Like thine,/Immortal Thirst of Empire fires my
soul', to which Artaxerxes replies with the condescending praise:
'O Energy Divine of great Ambition,/That can inform the Souls
of beardless Boys' (II, 2). The two differ mainly in the fact that
Artaban has been misled by his mother, though during the
course of the play he ceases to follow her Machiavellian lead.

The first acts of *The Ambitious Stepmother* seem to be a relatively
successful recreation of the heroic play of the early years of the
Restoration, but by the end of the play another tone has become
dominant. In the third act the rhetoric of ambition gives way
briefly to the quiet lamentation of Cleone, the daughter of Mirza,
who '*is discover'd lying on a bank of Flowers*', telling her confidante of

her hopeless love for Artaxerxes. The scene is by no means gratuitous, for not only does Cleone rescue the hero when he is imprisoned by her father, but also the pathos of her situation prefigures the pitiful dénouement of the tragedy.

Rowe was completely conscious of this shift. He wrote in his Epistle Dedicatory:

> . . . since Terror and Pity are laid down for the Ends of Tragedy, by the great Master and Father of Criticism, I was always inclin'd to fancy, that the last and remaining Impressions, which ought to be left on the minds of an Audience, should proceed from one of these two. They should be struck with Terror in several parts of the Play, but always Conclude and go away with Pity, a sort of regret proceeding from good nature, which, tho an uneasiness, is not always disagreeable, to the person who feels it. It was this passion that the famous Mr. *Otway* succeeded so well in touching, and must and will at all times affect people, who have any tenderness or humanity.
>
> (sig. A 3)

Despite the toughness of the opening, the tragic programme, precisely in line with the increasing regard for tenderness and pity, is carried out in the second half of the play in a striking fashion. First pity is enlisted for Artaxerxes and his wife Amestris when they are the victims of foul play by Artemisa and Mirza, and are seemingly powerless to halt the triumph of wickedness. When Artaban rebels against his mother's methods, he too appears to be thwarted—another victim of the evil plotters. Nor does the turn which ultimately defeats the villains bring any brightening of the picture. When Cleone, disguised as a boy, brings Artaxerxes the key to his cell, she commits suicide to prove that she is not baiting a trap laid by her father. In the mêlée following Artaxerxes' escape his wife is killed by Mirza, whom she has fatally wounded while defending her virtue. Artaxerxes, with power almost in his grasp, then lies down by the body of Amestris and kills himself. It is left for Artaban to take control and to strip Artemisa of all her power. Some justice is done, as Rowe asserted against those who looked for a happier ending, but there is no doubt that pity is likely to be the impression with which the audience leaves the theatre.

Tamerlane (1701), Rowe's next play, makes a striking contrast to Marlowe's play. In Rowe the hero has 'No Lust of Rule' or any aspiration other than 'to redress an Injur'd People's Wrongs' (I, 1; p. 58),[79] and save the weak from oppressors. It is Bajazet who talks like Marlowe's Tamburlaine:

> . . . yet still my Soul,
> Fixt high, and of it self alone dependant,
> Is ever free, and royal, . . .
>
> (II, 2; p. 81)

while Tamerlane says: 'Great Minds (like Heav'n) are pleas'd in doing good' (II, 2; p. 86). Here, then, in a play which ends happily, we have the one kind of hero which the new age could whole-heartedly admire[80]—the completely virtuous public servant—a type not new to heroic drama, but largely avoided by Dryden, Lee and Otway. Villain heroes and the morally more ambiguous Herculean heroes were now out of fashion.

In *The Fair Penitent* (1703), the first of his great successes, Rowe again sought pity, but for a different kind of character from Cleone, Amestris and Artaxerxes. Betterton, speaking the Prologue, said:

> Long has the Fate of Kings and Empires been
> The common Bus'ness of the Tragick Scene,
> As if Misfortune made the Throne her Seat,
> And none cou'd be unhappy but the Great.
>
> * * *
>
> Stories like these with Wonder we may hear,
> But far remote, and in a higher Sphere,
> We ne'er can pity what we ne'er can share: . . .
>
> * * *
>
> Therefore an humbler Theme our Author chose,
> A melancholy Tale of Private Woes: . . .
>
> (p. 61)

He took his plot from Massinger and Field's *The Fatal Dowry*, but shifted the emphasis from a puzzling choice between gratitude and

honour to the simple pathos of betrayal. Altamont marries
Calista, who has already had an affair with Lothario. Though
Altamont's friend Horatio warns him of this relationship, he
refuses to believe it, and breaks with his friend. Then, finding his
wife and her lover together, he kills Lothario. In the older play
the girl's father has rescued the hero from prison, and while
condemning his daughter, also accuses the young husband of
ingratitude. In Rowe's play Altamont, who has no such indebtedness to his father-in-law, has to prevent him from killing his
daughter, whereupon she is overwhelmed by her husband's
generosity:

> Have I not wrong'd his gentle Nature much?
> And yet behold him pleading for my Life.
> Lost as thou art to Virtue, oh *Calista*!
> I think thou canst not bear to be outdone;
> Then haste to die, and be oblig'd no more.

This highly charged scene is followed by one in which Altamont,
coming to ask forgiveness of Horatio, is at first coldly spurned by
his friend. When Altamont swoons at this cruelty, however,
Horatio's hurt feelings are replaced by 'A Flood of Tenderness'
(IV, 1; p. 230); he takes Altamont in his arms, and they are
reconciled. It might seem to be the quarrel-and-reconciliation
scene to end all quarrel-and-reconciliation scenes, but more were
to follow, not only in tragedies but in comedies such as Steele's
The Conscious Lovers. This scene ends with a speech by Altamont's
sister, the wife of Horatio, in which the bitter-sweet tone of
Lear's 'Come, let's away to prison' has become both sweeter and
more self-pitying:

>   Oh, my Brother!
> Think not but we will share in all thy Woes;
> We'll sit all day, and tell sad Tales of Love,
> And when we light upon some faithless Woman,
> Some Beauty, like *Calista*, false and fair,
> We'll fix our Grief, and our Complaining, there;
> We'll curse the Nymph that drew the Ruin on,
> And mourn the Youth that was like thee undone.
>   (IV, 1; pp. 230–1)

This luxuriant grief, characteristic of the play as a whole, is the sole and particular theme of the fifth act, which opens with these stage directions:

> Scene *is a Room hung with Black*; *on one side,* Lothario's *Body on a Bier*; *on the other, a Table with a Skull and other Bones, a Book, and a Lamp on it*
> CALISTA *is discover'd on a Couch in Black, her Hair hanging loose and disordered: After Musick and a Song, she rises and comes forward* (p. 232).

The very rhythm of Calista's famous line, 'Is this that Haughty, Gallant, Gay *Lothario*, . . .' (p. 233) has a dying fall which distinguishes it from a comparable line in Lee's *Sophonisba*: 'This cruel, haughty, happy Hannibal' (III, 2, 145). Calista is so overcome by her offences both to Altamont and to her father that she commits suicide, asking for pity. Altamont is kept from following suit by Horatio, who has the last speech, as Altamont faints once more and is carried off the stage. It begins:

> The Storm of Grief bears hard upon his Youth,
> And bends him like a drooping Flower to Earth.
>
> (V, 1; p. 244)

Though the characters in *The Fair Penitent* are inspired by some of the ideals which informed the heroic play in its prime, it requires no subtlety to see that a drastic change has occurred. The old heroes were not 'drooping flowers'.

Like Banks, Rowe found in English history a rich mine of sad stories, and in another very successful play, made Edward IV's mistress, Jane Shore, into a pathetic heroine. Here, though there are noble and even royal personages, the 'intérêts d'état' are kept in the background, while to pathos is added the unequivocal instruction of domestic tragedy:

> Let those, who view this sad Example, know,
> What Fate attends the broken Marriage Vow;
> And teach their Children in succeeding Times,
> No common Vengeance waits upon these Crimes,
> When such severe Repentance could not save,
> From Want, from Shame, and an Untimely Grave.
>
> (V, 1; p. 333)

The success of the 'she-tragedies' testifies not only to a general shift of sensibility but to the increasing numbers of middle-class spectators in the audience. Elizabethan citizens also applauded the combination of pathos and pat morality in plays like Heywood's *A Woman Killed with Kindness*, and their descendants were now in a position to make their taste prevail.

About a year before *Jane Shore* there was a flicker of the old heroic flame in Joseph Addison's *Cato* (1713). It is an appropriate play with which to end a study of this genre, since it both recalls the past and proclaims a present in which the concept of heroism has greatly altered. Pope made the nature of this change clear in the prologue he wrote, first by his statement of the purpose of tragedy:

> To wake the soul by tender strokes of art,
> To raise the genius and to mend the heart,
> To make mankind in conscious virtue bold,
> Live o'er each scene and be what they behold;—
> For this the tragic muse first trod the stage,
> Commanding tears to stream through every age; . . .
>
> (ll. 1–6)[81]

then, more specifically, by his comment on Addison's play:

> Our author shuns by vulgar springs to move
> The hero's glory or the virgin's love;
> In pitying love, we but our weakness show,
> And wild ambition well deserves its woe.
> Here tears shall flow from a more gen'rous cause,
> Such tears as patriots shed for dying laws.
> He bids your breasts with ancient ardor rise,
> And calls forth Roman drops from British eyes.
>
> (ll. 9–16)

Despite what Pope says here, a considerable portion of the tragedy is devoted to the loves of Marcus and Portius, Cato's sons, for Lucia; and to the love of Juba, Prince of Numidia, for Cato's daughter Marcia. Treated in a highly romantic fashion, these love stories contribute nothing to the development of the main plot. Joseph Spence reported Pope as saying, 'The love-part was flung in after, to comply with the popular taste';[82] though, as Dr Johnson remarked in his life of Addison, '. . . if it were taken away what would be left?'[83] It must have been added to Addison's plan at an early point in the long process of writing the play.[84] The love of Juba for Marcia involves a conflict between love and valour, and the rivalry of the two brothers a conflict between love and friendship, but both are resolved by changes in the situation which remove the necessity of choice. Portius' brother is killed in battle, and the hopelessness of Cato's position frees Juba from his obligations as a warrior. During a section of the play, however, it must be admitted that these stories provide dramatic complication for the otherwise simple story of Cato's last hours.

The story of Juba serves another function by furnishing a perspective on the heroic character of Cato. Syphax, a Numidian general, tries to lure Juba into a plot to desert Cato and go over to Caesar. He begins by praising the Numidians as at least the equals of the Romans in valour and their superiors in leading the good, simple life, far from the corruption of civilization, but Juba rejects this primitivistic ideal in favour of the 'higher views' of Rome, which he describes in a paraphrase of Virgil:

> To civilize the rude, unpolished world,
> And lay it under the restraint of laws;
> To make man mild and sociable to man;
> To cultivate the wild, licentious savage
> With wisdom, discipline, and lib'ral arts—
> Th'embellishments of life . . .

(I, 4, 31–6)

And as to Cato himself, Juba accuses Syphax of not seeing 'how the hero differs from the brute' (l. 74). He admires Cato's humanity, as revealed by the way he bears affliction—'Great and majestic in his griefs'—and with a steady mind, 'triumphs in the midst of all his sufferings!' (ll. 77–80). In the eyes of his disciple Cato is half a god.

On stage, Cato appears as the advocate of those unspectacular and undramatic virtues, reason and moderation, but the source of his strength is his total, unyielding integrity. Decius cannot persuade him to save his life by making terms with Caesar, and the more inevitable Caesar's victory becomes, the more heroic Cato's refusal appears. The first major demonstration of his Stoic fortitude comes in the fourth act when he hears that Marcus has been killed in the rebellion led by Syphax. To Portius' des-

cription, '. . . obstinately brave, and bent on death,/Oppressed
with multitudes, he greatly fell' (IV, 4, 64–5) he replies simply
'I'm satisfied', but after viewing the corpse and expatiating on the
Roman theme that death for one's country is beautiful, he turns
to the topic of Rome's loss of freedom under Caesar, and begins
to weep. Juba says:

> Behold that upright man! Rome fills his eyes
> With tears, that flowed not o'er his own dead son.

> (ll. 96–7)

The greatness of this spirit is shown both by iron control over
personal feeling and by the ability to weep for Rome.

Cato's suicide in the last act is carefully prepared for by the
tableau with which the act opens: 'CATO *solus, sitting in a thought-
ful posture: in his hand Plato's book on the immortality of the soul. A
drawn sword on the table by him.*' The rebellion has failed, its leaders
are dead, but Caesar has not yet arrived in Utica. In this moment
of calm the only action is Cato's departure and his suicide off
stage. Borne on stage again in his chair, dying but triumphant, he
dominates the scene as at the opening of the act with an image
of transcendence.

Tamburlaine in his chariot, drawn by the pampered jades of
Asia, and Cato in his chair, reading philosophy, are emblems of
two opposed conceptions of heroism. One is energetic self-
affirmation, 'alwaies moouing as the restles Spheares'; the other,
calm self-denial, almost motionless. While one is unpredictable,
emotional, impetuous, the other is reliable, reasonable, superbly
controlled. Both are admirable, both courageous, but in ways that
differ as much as the active and the contemplative life. Neither
can accept the condescension of pure pity as 'poor Castalio' can,
though in both of their lives there are moments of pathos:
'*Tamburlaine*, the Scourge of God must die', and virtuous Cato
must end his own life.

Though Addison's tragedy was a legitimate extension of one
conception of heroism, it was not possible to go further in this
direction without basically modifying the genre by surrendering
to the sort of pathos cultivated by Rowe. After *Cato* English play-

wrights wrote very little that can be called heroic drama, though certain examples of the genre continued to be performed. The closest approximation to the plays we have been considering was the drama of Lord Byron, directly influenced by Dryden and Otway. Here a noble, suffering hero dies denouncing the world more bitterly than Cato, and asserting himself more vigorously, as he confronts his executioners:

> Thou den of drunkards with the blood of princes!
> Gehenna of the waters! thou sea Sodom!
> Thus I devote thee to the infernal gods!
> Thee and thy serpent seed! Slave, do thine office!
> Strike as I struck the foe! Strike as I would
> Have struck those tyrants! Strike deep as my curse!
> Strike—and but once![85]

But Byron's plays were never meant for the stage; for, as he said in the Preface to this play, 'in its present state it is, perhaps, not a very exalted object of ambition; besides, I have been too much behind the scenes to have thought it so at any time. And I cannot conceive any man of irritable feeling putting himself at the mercies of an audience.' The depiction of 'heroic heroes' was left to poetry and fiction.

In the twentieth century Eugene O'Neill, obscurely motivated, perhaps, by a form of the American dream, put on the stage a series of dreamers who were also, in their way, men of noble aspirations, elevated by their imagination above the level of ordinary humanity. Their heroism, however (if it can be so called), was never translated into heroic acts. They represent at most a longing for heroic drama in an unheroic or anti-heroic age.

Notes

1 *Love and Honour and The Siege of Rhodes*, ed. Tupper, 187-8; all quotations from *The Siege of Rhodes* are from this edition.
2 'Of Heroic Plays', Ker, I, 149.
3 *The Dramatic Works of Sir William D'Avenant*, ed. James Maidment and W. H. Logan (Edinburgh, 1872-4), III, 199, 202.
4 Davenant, *Dramatic Works*, III, 204.
5 A revised version of *The Siege of Rhodes*, which opened the theatre in Lincoln's Inn Fields in June 1661, brought painted scenery to the public

theatre in England for the first time unless, as has been mentioned in the previous chapter, an occasional court play in the Caroline period was publicly repeated with some of its scenery.

6 See William S. Clark, 'Historical Preface', in *The Dramatic Works of Roger Boyle, Earl of Orrery*, 2 vols. (Cambridge, Mass., 1937), 24; all quotations from Orrery are taken from this edition. As Harbage points out (*Cavalier Drama*, 61-9), rhyming couplets were used in several Caroline plays. See also California Dryden, VIII, 264 n. 2.

7 See esp. 50-2, 251-2. See also California Dryden, VIII, 292.

8 Helen McAfee, *Pepys on the Restoration Stage* (New Haven, 1916), 175-6. See Arthur Kirsch's discussion of this example in *Dryden's Heroic Drama* (Princeton, N.J., 1965), 77-8.

9 *The Adventures of Five Hours*, ed. A. E. H. Swaen (Amsterdam, 1927), 56.

10 See California Dryden, VIII, 264.

11 See Kirsch's discussion of the play, 72-9, and California Dryden, VIII, 267-9.

12 *The Dramatic Works of Sir George Etherege*, ed. H. F. B. Brett-Smith, 2 vols. (Oxford, 1927), I, 18.

13 See Kirsch, 77.

14 Pepys was understandably unhappy that in the last act the king did rather less for his friend than he promised to do; see *Pepys on the Restoration Stage*, 178.

15 Sir Robert Howard published the play in his *Four New Plays* (1668), and though Dryden said in the 'Connexion of the *Indian Emperour*, to the *Indian Queen*' (printed with *The Indian Emperor* in 1668) that he wrote 'part' of the earlier play, it was not published with his works until 1717, long after his death. Harold J. Oliver argues strongly for Howard as the one mainly responsible for the play, and the external evidence supports this view (*Sir Robert Howard* [Durham, N.C., 1963], 61-79). Nevertheless, the dissimilarity of Howard's other heroic plays to *The Indian Queen*, and its striking resemblance to Dryden's plays lead me to conclude with the editors of the California Dryden (VIII, 283, 298) that the final form of the play was due mainly to Dryden.

16 All quotations from *The Indian Queen* are taken from the Calfornia Dryden, VIII; those from *The Indian Emperor* from vol. IX.

17 On the romance sources see California Dryden, VIII, 289-92.

18 Spingarn, II, 14.

19 *The London Stage 1660-1800, Part I: 1660-1700*, ed. W. Van Lennep (Carbondale, Ill., 1965), 75.

20 In the introductory pages of her tale, *Oroonoko* (1668), Mrs Behn wrote: 'Then we trade for Feathers, which they order into all Shapes, make themselves little short Habits of 'em, and glorious Wreaths for their Heads, Necks, Arms and Legs, whose Tinctures are unconceivable. I had a Set of these presented to me, and I gave 'em to the *King's Theatre*; it was the Dress of the *Indian Queen*, infinitely admir'd by Persons of Quality; and was inimitable' (*The Works of Aphra Behn*, ed. Montague Summers, 6 vols. [New York, 1967; orig 1915], V. 130). See the California Dryden, VIII, 282, 314-16, where the staging of the play is discussed in detail.

21 John Webb's sets for *Mustapha* may not have been seen till the following season. See Boyle, *Dramatic Works*, I, 227.

22 *Pepys on the Restoration Stage*, 149-50.

23 Compare Peter Dronke's comments on what he calls 'the courtly experience'—'something which cuts across the notions of popular and courtly poetry'. He describes it as a 'sensibility' which is not restricted to the aristocracy (*Medieval Latin*, I, 3).

24 'The Voice of Mr. Bayes', *Studies in English Literature*, III (1963), 336-43.

25 'Connexion of the *Indian Emperour*, to the *Indian Queen*', California Dryden, IX, 27.

26 *Dryden's Heroic Drama*, 90. The discussion of the play is typical of the excellence of the book as a whole.

27 He was probably following an account in Montaigne's essay 'Of Coaches' (California Dryden, IX, 311).

28 22 August and 11 November 1667; *Pepys on the Restoration Stage*, 149.

29 See Charles E. Ward, 'Massinger and Dryden', *Journal of English Literary History*, II (1935), 263-6.

30 *Pepys on the Restoration Stage*, 118.

31 Quotations from *Tyrannic Love* are taken from *The Works of John Dryden*, ed. Sir Walter Scott, rev. George Saintsbury, 18 vols. (Edinburgh, 1882-3); since the lines are unnumbered, volume and page are indicated following act and scene.

32 *Dryden's Major Plays* (New York, 1966), 50-8.

33 *An Apology for the Life of Colley Cibber*, ed. B. R. S. Fone (Ann Arbor, Mich., 1968), 72.

34 *Dryden's Poetry* (Bloomington and London, 1967), 104. Other critics, such as Bruce King (*Dryden's Major Plays*), have gone so far as to suppose that the heroic plays should be taken as satirical in their entirety. One indication that this interpretation is mistaken is Dryden's conviction, repeated up to the end of his life that 'A heroic poem, truly such, is undoubtedly the the greatest work which the soul of man is capable to perform' (Dedication of the *Aeneid*, 1697; Ker, II, 154). He related heroic drama to heroic poetry both early and late in his career.

35 *John Dryden: Four Tragedies*, ed. L. A. Beaurline and Fredson Bowers (Chicago and London, 1967), 4.

36 I discuss this play, *Aureng-Zebe*, and *All for Love* in some detail in *The Herculean Hero*, 152-200. Here, while inevitably repeating some points, I shall restrict myself to those aspects of these plays which are most closely related to the theme of this book.

37 Quoted in *London Stage*, I, 177, as is Evelyn's entry, 180.

38 See Bernard Weinberg, *Literary Criticism*, II, 954-1073; also John C. Sherwood, 'Dryden and the Critical Theories of Tasso'. *Comparative Literature*, XVIII (1966), 351-9.

39 Quotations from *The Conquest of Granada* are taken from *Selected Dramas of John Dryden*, ed. George R. Noyes (Chicago and New York, 1910); references are to Part I unless otherwise noted.

40 *Leviathan*, I, 13.

41 *To the Palace of Wisdom* (New York, 1964), 38, 41.

42 *Four Tragedies*, ed. Beaurline and Bowers, 107. All quotations from *Aureng-Zebe* and *All for Love* are taken from this collection.
43 See *The Herculean Hero*, 164, for a further discussion of this point.
44 *Restoration Drama* (Madison, Wis., 1967), 3-23.
45 The phrase is Arthur Kirsch's (p. 126). Though much of what he says about the play is true, I believe he exaggerates the differences between it and its predecessors. I also disagree with Eric Rothstein that an 'attack upon heroics' at this time brought about a sudden 'public *volte-face*' (*Restoration Drama*, 26).
46 Meaning by 'imitate', as L. A. Beaurline reminds us (p. 190), not a return to Elizabethan technique or language, but an 'imaginative transposition'.
47 Arthur Kirsch finds that 'the heroism of *All for Love* is subverted at every turn by sentimental effects' (p. 128). This assessment, like the comparable one of *Aureng-Zebe*, seems to me extreme.
48 Montague Summers prints relevant passages from Daniel in *Dryden: The Dramatic Works*, 6 vols. (London, 1932), IV, 529-30.
49 All quotations from Lee are taken from *The Works of Nathaniel Lee*, ed. Thomas B. Stroup and Arthur L. Cooke, 2 vols. (New Brunswick, N.J., 1954).
50 *Restoration Tragedy* (Oxford, 1929), 118. The entire chapter is one of the best pieces of criticism on Lee. I am also indebted to Roswell Ham's *Otway and Lee* (New Haven, 1931).
51 *Apology*, ed. Fone, 63.
52 Gerard Langbaine, *An Account of the English Dramatick Poets* (Oxford, 1691), 320-1.
53 See Aline M. Taylor's chapter on his reputation in *Next to Shakespeare* (Durham, N.C., 1950), esp. 251.
54 All quotations from Otway are taken from *The Works of Thomas Otway*, ed. J. C. Ghosh (Oxford, 1932).
55 *Next to Shakespeare*, 5-7, 69, 73 and *passim*.
56 His use of the term 'Heroick Play' in the preface to an edition which describes it as 'A Tragedy' on the title page is one indication of how these categories overlapped.
57 *Morales du grand siècle*, 240.
58 *Œuvres complètes de Racine*, ed. Raymond Picard, 2 vols. (Paris 1964), I, 465.
59 *Next to Shakespeare*, 24.
60 [Charles Gildon], *The Life of Mr. Thomas Betterton, The late Eminent Tragedian* (London, 1710), 40.
61 *Apology*, ed. Fone, 92. Though Mrs Barry did not appear in the early productions of these plays, Cibber saw her in them later.
62 See Aline Taylor's discussion of the political allusions in *Next to Shakespeare*, 54-9.
63 'Otway Preserved: Theme and Form in *Venice Preserv'd*', *Restoration Dramatists*, ed. Earl Miner (Englewood Cliffs, N.J., 1966), 148.
64 All quotations from *Don Sebastian* are taken from *Four Tragedies*, ed. Beaurline and Bowers.
65 On the importance of Rapin's commentary in England, see Rothstein, *Restoration Tragedy*, 10-23.

66 *Monsieur Rapin's Reflections on Aristotle's Treatise of Poesie*, tr. Thomas Rymer (1674). 'Reflections . . . in General', XXIII.
67 All quotations from *The Spanish Friar* are taken from *Selected Dramas*, ed. Noyes.
68 See Bruce King's comments on these speeches in *Dryden's Major Plays*, 185-7. The entire chapter is a perceptive appreciation of the play.
69 All quotations from *Cleomenes* are taken from the Scott-Saintsbury edition of the *Works*; volume and page are indicated following act and scene.
70 See Robert Moore's discussion of the opera in *Henry Purcell and the Restoration Theatre* (Cambridge, Mass., 1961), 70-99.
71 *English Literature of the Seventeenth Century*, The Oxford History of English Literature (Oxford, 1969), 81.
72 *The Dramatic Works of Thomas Dekker*, ed. Bowers, IV.
73 *The Works of Aphra Behn*, ed. Montague Summers (New York, 1967; orig. 1915), II, 57.
74 *Five Heroic Plays*, ed. Bonamy Dobrée (London, 1960), 237.
75 All quotations from *The Unhappy Favourite* are taken from the edition by T. M. H. Blair (New York, 1939); since the lines are unnumbered, the page number follows the indication of act and scene.
76 *The Tatler*, No. 14, 12 May 1709; quoted by Blair, Introduction, 33.
77 *Virtue Betrayed* (1682).
78 *The Ambitious Stepmother* (1701), sig. B 4.
79 *Three Plays by Nicholas Rowe*, ed. J. R. Sutherland (London, 1929). All quotations from *Tamerlane*, *The Fair Penitent* and *Jane Shore* are taken from this collection. Since lines are unnumbered, the page number follows the indication of act and scene.
80 He was apparently intended as an idealized portrait of William III, while Bajazet represented Louis XIV.
81 *British Dramatists from Dryden to Sheridan*, ed. George H. Nettleton and Arthur Case (Cambridge, Mass., 1939); all quotations from *Cato* are taken from this anthology.
82 *Observations, Anecdotes, and Characters of Books and Men*, ed. James M. Osborn, 2 vols. (Oxford, 1966), I, No. 154.
83 *Lives of the English Poets*, ed. G. Birkbeck Hill (Oxford, 1905), II, 103.
84 He seems to have begun work in 1694; see Osborn's note to Spence, No.154.
85 *Marino Faliero, Doge of Venice*, V, 3, 794-800 in *The Complete Poetical Works of Lord Byron*, ed. Paul Elmer More (Cambridge, Mass., 1905).

Select Bibliography

This bibliography consists mainly of general works on the topics covered by each chapter. In the sections relating to Chapters 2, 3 and 4 books on individual authors have not been included because of the very large number of playwrights treated; references to such books will be found in the notes. An invaluable reference book for all three of these chapters is:

HARBAGE, ALFRED, *Annals of English Drama 975-1700*, rev. S. Schoenbaum (London, 1964).

1. The Ideals of Chivalry

BEZZOLA, RETO S., *Le sens de l'aventure et de l'amour* (Paris, 1947). Imaginative criticism of romance.

FERGUSON, ARTHUR B., *The Indian Summer of English Chivalry: Studies in the Decline and Transformation of Chivalric Idealism* (Durham, N.C., 1960).

FRAPPIER, JEAN, *Chrétien de Troyes: l'homme et l'oeuvre*, revised ed. (Paris, 1957).

HARDISON, O. B., *The Enduring Moment: A study of the Idea of Praise in Renaissance Literary Theory and Practice* (Chapel Hill, N.C., 1960).

KER, W. P., *Epic and Romance* (London, 1926). A standard, but somewhat outdated, account of the two genres, in which romance comes off second best.

PAINTER, SIDNEY, *French Chivalry: Chivalric Ideas and Practices in Medieval France* (Ithaca, N.Y., 1965; orig. 1940).

VORETZSCH, KARL, *Introduction to the Study of Old French Literature*, tr. F. M. DuMont (New York, 1931). A standard source of information about the origins and development of the *chanson de geste* and the romance; see Chaps. III and VI–IX.

WEINBERG, BERNARD, *A History of Literary Criticism in the Italian Renaissance*, 2 vols. (Chicago, 1961). An account of the controversy over epic and romance will be found in Chaps. XIX and XX in Vol. II.

2. Emergence

BEVINGTON, DAVID M., *From Mankind to Marlowe: Growth of Structure in the Popular Drama of Tudor England* (Cambridge, Mass., 1962).

CHAMBERS, E. K., *The Elizabethan Stage*, 4 vols. (Oxford, 1923). The standard reference work for the period ending in 1616.

CLEMEN, WOLFGANG, *English Tragedy Before Shakespeare: The Development of Dramatic Speech*, tr. T. S. Dorsch (London, 1961).

COLE, DOUGLAS, *Suffering and Evil in the Plays of Christopher Marlowe* (Princeton, N.J., 1962). Though focusing on Marlowe, Cole discusses many other plays treated in this chapter.

ELIZABETHAN THEATRE, ed. J. R. Brown and B. Harris, Stratford-upon-Avon Studies IX (London, 1966). A collection of essays.

ELLISON, LEE M., *The Early Romantic Drama at the English Court* (Menasha, Wis., 1917).

HARBAGE, ALFRED, *Shakespeare and the Rival Traditions* (New York, 1952). On the difference between the repertories of the public theatres and the private houses.

LEWIS, C. S., *English Literature in the Sixteenth Century*, The Oxford History of English Literature, III (Oxford, 1954).

MOCKLER, R. J., *The Heroical Romance in Elizabethan Drama* (unpublished dissertation, Columbia University, 1961).

RIBNER, IRVING, *The English History Play in the Age of Shakespeare* (Princeton, N.J., 1957).

WILSON, F. P., *The English Drama 1485-1585*, ed, G. K. Hunter, The Oxford History of English Literature, IV, 1 (Oxford, 1969).

3. The Early Seventeenth Century

BENTLEY, G. E., *The Jacobean and Caroline Stage*, 7 vols. (Oxford, 1941-68). The standard reference work for the years 1616-42.

ELLIS-FERMOR, UNA, *The Jacobean Drama*, revised ed. (London, 1947).

HARBAGE, ALFRED, *Cavalier Drama: An Historical and Critical Supplement to the Study of the Elizabethan and Restoration Stage* (New York, 1964; orig. 1936).

JACOBEAN THEATRE, ed. J. R. Brown and B. Harris, Stratford-upon-Avon Studies I (London, 1960). A collection of essays.

Select Bibliography

ORNSTEIN, ROBERT, *The Moral Vision of Jacobean Tragedy* (Madison, Wis., 1960).

RIBNER, IRVING, *Jacobean Tragedy* (London, 1962).

Interchapter: Corneille

BÉNICHOU, PAUL, *Morales du grand siècle* (Paris, 1967; orig. 1948). Relates the growth and decline of the heroic to the social, intellectual and religious movements of seventeenth-century France.

DOUBROVSKY, SERGE, *Corneille et la dialectique du héros* (Paris, 1963).

HERLAND, LOUIS, *Corneille par lui-même* (Paris, 1968; orig. 1956). A convenient source of information.

NELSON, ROBERT J., *Corneille: His Heroes and their Worlds* (Philadelphia, 1963).

MAY, GEORGES, *Tragédie Cornélienne, tragédie Racinienne*, Illinois Studies in Language and Literature XXXII (Urbana, Ill., 1948).

4. The Restoration

DEANE, C. V., *Dramatic Theory and the Rhymed Heroic Play* (New York, 1968; orig. 1931).

DOBRÉE, BONAMY, *Restoration Tragedy 1660-1720* (Oxford, 1929).

THE LONDON STAGE 1660-1800, PART I: 1660-1700, ed. William Van Lennep, Emmett L. Avery and Arthur Scouten (Carbondale, Ill., 1965). Day-to-day records of the London theatre and valuable introduction.

NICOLL, ALLARDYCE, *A History of English Drama 1660-1900*, I, *Restoration Drama 1660-1700*, 4th ed. (Cambridge, 1952). The standard history, containing a useful hand list of Restoration plays.

PRICE, MARTIN, *To the Palace of Wisdom: Studies in Energy and Order from Dryden to Blake* (New York, 1964). Sets a major concern of heroic drama in a broad literary and philosophical context.

PRIOR, MOODY E., *The Language of Tragedy* (Bloomington, Ind., and London, 1966; orig. 1947). Contains an excellent chapter on 'Tragedy and the Heroic Play'.

ROTHSTEIN, ERIC, *Restoration Tragedy: Form and the Process of Change* (Madison, Wis., Milwaukee, Wis. and London, 1967).

SORELIUS, GUNNAR, *'The Giant Race Before the Flood': Pre-Restoration Drama on the Stage and in the Criticism of the Restoration*, Studia Anglistica Upsaliensia IV (Uppsala, 1966).

SUMMERS, MONTAGUE, *The Playhouse of Pepys* (New York, 1964; orig. 1935).

—— *The Restoration Theatre* (New York, 1964; orig. 1934).

WILSON, JOHN HAROLD, *A Preface to Restoration Drama* (Boston, 1965). An excellent brief introduction.

Index